Leader and Vanguard in Mass Society

M.I.T. STUDIES IN
COMPARATIVE POLITICS

Under the general editorship of Harold D. Lasswell, Daniel Lerner, and Ithiel de Sola Pool.

The Emerging Elite: A Study of Political Leadership in Ceylon, Marshall R. Singer, 1964.

The Turkish Political Elite, Frederick W. Frey, 1965.

World Revolutionary Elites: Studies in Coercive Ideological Movements, Harold D. Lasswell and Daniel Lerner, editors, 1965.

Language of Politics: Studies in Quantitative Semantics, Harold D. Lasswell, Nathan Leites, and Associates, 1965 (reissue).

The General Inquirer: A Computer Approach to Content Analysis, Philip J. Stone, Dexter C. Dunphy, Marshall S. Smith, and Daniel M. Ogilvie, 1966.

Political Elites: A Select Computerized Bibliography, Carl Beck and J. Thomas McKechnie, 1968.

Force and Folly: Essays on Foreign Affairs and the History of Ideas, Hans Speier, 1969.

Quantitative Ecological Analysis in the Social Sciences, Mattei Dogan and Stein Rokkan, editors, 1969.

Euratlantica: Changing Perspectives of the European Elites, Daniel Lerner and Morton Gorden, 1969.

Revolution and Political Leadership: Algeria, 1954–1968, William B. Quandt, 1969.

The Prestige Press: A Comparative Study of Political Symbols, Ithiel de Sola Pool, 1970.

The Vanishing Peasant: Innovation and Change in French Agriculture, Henri Mendras, 1971.

Psychological Warfare against Nazi Germany: The Sykewar Campaign, D-Day to VE-Day, Daniel Lerner, 1971 (reissue).

Propaganda Technique in World War I, Harold D. Lasswell, 1971 (reissue).

Leader and Vanguard in Mass Society: A Study of Peronist Argentina, Jeane Kirkpatrick, 1971.

Leader and Vanguard in Mass Society:
A Study of Peronist Argentina

JEANE KIRKPATRICK

The M.I.T. Press
Cambridge, Massachusetts, and London, England

Copyright © 1971 by
The Massachusetts Institute of Technology

Set in Linotype Baskerville by Port City Press, Inc.
Printed by Port City Press, Inc.
and bound in the United States of America by
The Colonial Press Inc.

ISBN 0 262 110415 (hardcover)

Library of Congress catalog card number: 72-161849

TO MY MOTHER AND FATHER

Contents

Figures

Tables

Foreword

I propose to underline some points that indicate why this book is of interest to a circle of readers that extends well beyond specialists on Latin American affairs.

It has been suggested that the modern study of government has attained a remarkable level of vitality because it relies on new tools to reappraise old ideas. Professor Kirkpatrick's use of a stratified national sample to explore the Peronist movement lends support to this interpretation. New facts are made available that were beyond the reach of traditional approaches. The author expressly relates them to the great questions and prestigeful answers concerning political power that have been handed down from Graeco-Roman times.

It is no novelty to ask whether a movement, such as the Peronist, is lower, middle, or upper class. The innovation is to be able to describe the degree to which its ideology is class-bound, or in fact is shared with other classes or groups. There is no novelty in asking whether a movement is revolutionary or reformist. It is new to be able to demonstrate the degree of distinctiveness in the perspectives of Peronists when compared with other participants in the political process.

When survey data are skillfully integrated with other sources of information, it is possible to classify political phenomena in ways that corroborate the relevance of traditional distinctions and introduce a degree of refinement equivalent to supplementing the hand lens with a two-hundred-inch telescope. While the older categories retain their significance as first approximations, they give way to a far richer contextual map in which the macro- and microstructure of events gains visibility. Professor Kirkpatrick's discussion of "polycracies" is a case in point. In polycratic systems a multiplicity of actors and arenas is essential to political power.

A by-product of the analysis is the pinpointing of structural characteristics that Argentine politics have in common with the public and civic order of some other countries. The Peronists share a political culture in which limited violence is institutionalized. It is an established method of introducing changes in the personnel and, to some extent, in the policies adopted and put into effect by official elites. To institutionalize a practice is to stabilize certain expectations among those whose acts are necessary to initiate and complete the practice. In appropriate circumstances they must expect to be relatively better off by conforming than by deviating from the practice. As a result of institutionalization the component elements of the power elite in Argentina—such as officers, officials, and party leaders —are prepared to press their disagreements to a point that calls for a show of force, or even a limited use of force, instead of relying on mutual consent that is achieved after peaceful persuasion. The data show how widely the pertinent perspectives are distributed through all levels of Argentine society. Violence is not only expected. There is evidence of a disposition to approve a resort to coercive acts as a means of breaking out of a frustrating situation. Self-respect is perceived as restored by the deed itself. As Professor Kirkpatrick indicates, more tools than the survey instrument are needed to go behind the disposition and to explain how the routines of socialization bring violent conduct to the focus of attention as a desirable model to be incorporated into the self-system.

Another set of institutional practices can be identified that, taken together with the acceptance of limited coercion, constitute a political system that is found in a number of countries. The reference is to "vanguardism" or reliance on an imposing leader and his band of heroes to take the initiatives necessary to mobilize the mass support required for decisive action on behalf of social justice.

If a political act culminates in a simple palace revolution, it lacks the popular visibility and the support that are essential to vanguardism. If a movement does no more than appeal to the relatively comfortable classes, it may be popular, though it cannot qualify as a mass movement. In the perceptions of the contemporary world, the principal "masses" are the urban masses, whose vanguard organs are labor unions and "the movement." Vanguardists are capable of gaining enough involvement by the masses to project a self-confirming image that they provide a secular savior for the underprivileged components of the body politic. The message is spoken in the name of all, which covers the sacred-secular body politic of the national whole. Salvation depends on social justice for all, especially for the many who have been too long neglected by the stalemated politics of the dominating few.

In the world revolutionary symbolisms of our epoch, the conception of vanguardism was given currency to justify the dictatorship of a party that spoke, not in the name of the whole body politic of the world community, but on behalf of the imperialism of the "proletariat." The effective domain of world revolutionary governments and parties was restricted by the counterassertion of parochial (national) identities, coupled with the partial incorporation of socialist measures put forward in the language of social justice.

Vanguardists, it appears, have emerged where two principal conditions occur. First, it is assumed that limited coercion will periodically supersede persuasion as the strategy necessary to achieve workable outcomes in the decision process. Second, a common stock of predispositions (of value priorities and interpretations) sets limits to the value deprivations that are permissible to impose on rivals in the national arena. Vanguardism is the latest in a cyclical series of popularly led movements that make it possible to operate a body politic composed of nucleated centers of power.

The dynamics of change are more likely to be disclosed by studying the future than by exploring a past that is largely closed to the use of the most rewarding methods of observation. As events unfold, the feedback of data confirms or disconfirms an explanatory model. It is by no means out of the question for a scientist-adviser to introduce future-oriented research. The present study of Argentine politics can prove to be particularly fruitful if it is taken as a point of departure for continuing seminars conducted by Argentine and other political scientists who concern themselves with the dynamics of national and comparative politics. For instance, the Peronists stayed within the confines of a system of limited coercion and succeeded in obtaining modest value-indulgences for the benefit of the groups to whom their appeal was most distinctive. A question for the future to answer is whether they introduced a sufficiently new intensity of demand to provoke a counterstrategy that employs more unrestricted coercion. If so, will this in turn change the composition of the leadership and alter the strategy of future egalitarian movements?

Until the invention of modern tools, the study of the symbol component of politics lagged behind other dimensions of the field. Professor Kirkpatrick gives full weight to the contributions of her predecessors and contemporaries—Almond and Verba, Lipset, Lerner, Pye, Silvert, and many more—and thereby emphasizes the cumulative sophistication of contemporary political science.

Harold D. Lasswell

Preface

This study grew out of an interest in nondemocratic politics stimulated originally by the late Franz Neumann while I was still a Barnard undergraduate. Political systems that are neither democratic nor totalitarian have only recently begun to receive systematic attention from political scientists. Even today traditional and semi-traditional autocracies are generally neglected, a neglect reflected, for example, in the paucity of research and writing on the political systems of Spain and Portugal. Despite their antiquity and ubiquity, traditional and other autocracies tend even now to be treated as "transitional" systems, political incidents on the way to becoming democratic regimes. One consequence of the "developmental" approach is an emphasis on elements of change, which often, though not necessarily, tends to obscure enduring factors in nondemocratic systems.

For the student of nondemocratic regimes Latin America is an especially fruitful scene for research. The continent and the related Caribbean nations provide an intriguing range of nondemocratic systems. There are "new" and "old" military dictatorships, modernizing and traditional autocracies, left and right nationalist movements and regimes. There are *Fidelismo* in Cuba and the total terror of Duvalier in Haiti. There are democratic systems balanced precariously on the foundations of authoritarian political traditions and dictatorships that have incorporated elements of democratic style and selected democratic practices. Cultural and ethnic similarities make Latin systems relatively accessible to analysis with the conceptual tools developed out of the study of European and North American institutions; and almost all our analytic tools fall in this category.

Argentina with its wealth, largely European population, near-universal literacy, advanced industrial technology, and Latin political tradition that mixes democratic and autocratic elements is an especially interesting example of the complex relations among social, economic, and political factors. The Peronist movement is interesting for the same reasons, providing, as it does, a clear-cut example of a contemporary Caesarist movement in a technologically advanced society. While we have grown accustomed to the idea that a revolutionary military officer in a "new" nation may attract a mass following, the nonrevolutionary military leader with a tenacious lower-class mass base is somehow less expected. Perón has been such a leader with such a mass base. The Peronist movement, therefore, seemed to me to provide an excellent opportunity to examine a type of nondemocratic politics that may well become more common as technological advances are achieved in societies with autocratic political traditions.

In addition, the Peronist movement provided an excellent field for the study of another subject of long-standing interest for me—namely, the political ideologies of mass publics. I am convinced that it is crucially important for political science that survey research based on scientific sampling has made it possible to study and test the many hypotheses about the wants, goals, and beliefs of masses that fill the classics of political philosophy, the polemics of reformers, and the halls of government.

The study of the Peronist movement proved as engrossing and, I think, rewarding as anticipated.

There are a few specific aspects of the study on which I should like to comment briefly.

First, with reluctance and some sense of apology I must admit that this is a book about a number of things. I greatly admire small, tight studies that commence with a hypothesis (or two or three) and limit themselves to presenting only those data and conclusions directly involved in testing it (or them). I fully intended this to be such a study, and it was with some sense of loss that I began the process of inclusion that resulted finally in the present book. In fact, very tight studies are quite rare in political science. I wonder if the reason is that other investigators succumb to the same felt exigencies of interconnection that led me to abandon the clean, simple design that I admire and to expand this study by bits from some four hypotheses, all of which concern the perspectives of rank-and-file Peronists. The final study includes a description of the Argentine political system, some analysis of Argentine political development, and, finally, an epilogue that attempts to project into the future this analysis of mass perspectives and the Argentine political system. The existential relevance of these to the mass base of the Peronist movement ultimately seemed to me more compelling than their formal irrelevance to my hypotheses. The result is a volume lacking the economy and symmetry that I find so admirable. I hope that readers will find that the additional chapters enhance the book's ability to explain the political phenomena with which I am principally concerned.

Second, Chapters 2 and 3 obviously make no original contribution to the study of Argentine political institutions. Their inclusion here reflects my strong conviction that political attitudes cannot be profitably analyzed outside the institutional context that conditions their formation and determines their behavioral consequences. Although a general knowledge of the Argentine system might have been assumed, there are several main lines of interpretation of that system and tradition. Clarity, therefore, seemed to me to require a brief explication of my reading of Argentina's political life.

Third, it will be clear that my approach to the study of the Peronist movement is basically comparative; I have tried throughout to relate findings to broadly relevant theory.

Fourth, naturally, I have been retrospectively dissatisfied with the questionnaire. Some issues that seemed important to Peronist orientations then have long since declined in salience. (The Dominican intervention is an example.) Some then current questions and assumptions about the Peronist movement have since disappeared over the horizon of expanding knowledge. Some omissions became painfully clear in the light of findings of this and other studies and of later political developments. I was in a far better position to design the study after I had completed it than when I undertook it. But the decisions seemed rational enough as I drafted and redrafted the questionnaire. And they still seemed rational when the late "Budd" Wilson and I huddled over a table in Provence, cutting and revising the questionnaire to take account of the pretest. I should like to do a second study of Argentine politics; it would be much better.

Finally, unless otherwise indicated, all translations from Spanish sources are my own.

A grant from the Andreas Foundation and assistance from my parents financed the costs of the fieldwork: I have also enjoyed support from Georgetown University and the National Humanities Foundation. Naturally, I should like to express my gratitude for the financial assistance that made the study possible. I want also to express my gratitude to my friends Helen Dinnerman and the late Elmo ("Budd") Wilson, and various of their colleagues at International Research Associates, for their assistance at various stages of planning and conducting the survey, and to George Demetriou and the Institute for the Comparative Study of Political Systems for access to their electoral and demographic data collection and for some administrative services. Thanks are also due a number of friends, colleagues, and advisers who read the manuscript and offered criticisms, suggestions, and encouragement, especially Harold Lasswell, Karl Cerny, Austin Ranney, Warren Miller, Howard Penniman, Dankwart Rustow, James Rowe, Charles Anderson, David Truman, Juan Linz, Douglas Chalmers, and José Luis de Imaz. In addition, José Sorzano, then a Georgetown graduate student and now a colleague, provided useful bibliographic assistance, and John Hebert prepared a chronology on Peronist organizational matters. Various persons have assisted in manuscript typing, but I owe special thanks to Jeannette Patrick and Winifred Wuterich, who have seen this manuscript through several versions. Finally, I am pleased to acknowledge my greatest debt—to my husband whose criticism and encouragement were of inestimable value. I alone am responsible for the analysis and interpretation of the data. All faults of omission and commission are mine.

Georgetown University   Jeane Kirkpatrick
January 1970

Postscript

Unfortunately, Argentine politics did not stop for the publication of this book. Between the time the manuscript was delivered to the publisher and the receipt of the galleys, Argentina experienced two new military coups, each of which brought to power a new president from the military sector. Neither the coups nor the governments they brought to power have altered the pattern of politics described in Chapter 3. To the contrary, these developments constitute new evidence of the continuation of politics as usual.

Leader and Vanguard in Mass Society

1

Purposes, Methods, Assumptions, and Data

This is a book about Argentine politics. It includes some discussion of the Argentine past and some consideration of the present and future, but mainly it deals with that interlude between the regimes of Juan Perón and Juan Onganía when at least some of the chiefs of state were chosen by popular election and at least some decisions were made by popularly chosen officials. During that period of relatively open politics the pattern of political competition and the identity of the competitors were revealed with special clarity, illuminating the mix of traditional and modern democratic and autocratic elements that make Argentina a fascinating example of contemporary Latin politics.

In Argentina we are confronted with a society that has passed through most of what are generally conceived to be the stages of economic, social, and political development. Highly urban, overwhelmingly literate, industrially advanced, technologically sophisticated, Argentina has developed a participatory pattern of politics that is neither democratic nor totalitarian. The fact that masses can and do participate in political decisions (now through elections, now through strikes and demonstrations) means that this polity does not fit neatly into the category of premodern politics, if, indeed, it ever makes sense to so describe the politics of a highly modern society. And the fact that all the major elements of Argentine politics have existed for half a century suggests that this pattern of politics does not fit neatly into the category of transitional regimes, except in the sense that change is a characteristic of all but the most purely traditional societies.

The central purposes of this study are to describe the interactions among those who bid for political power in the first post-Perón decade (1955–1965), to explore the underlying political culture, and to delineate those aspects of Argentina's earlier experience that seem to have been decisive in producing the contemporary pattern of politics. This pattern is perhaps less unusual than we tend to believe, more persistent than we tend to expect. It is a pattern that mixes political elements that our taxonomies have generally separated.

The Argentine political system can be conceived as a continuation of traditional Latin politics under conditions of mass society. But what does that mean? Obviously, it emphasizes the affinities between Argentine politics and the politics of its Latin neighbors. It calls to mind regime instability, oligarchy, democratic interludes, military coups, a tradition of direct action, and *personalismo*.[1] These have been the chief characteristics of Latin politics through most of the last century—found in such otherwise disparate societies as Guatemala, Peru, Brazil, Venezuela, Bolivia, and Argentina. But in a modern society where traditional patterns of life have been broken by urbanization, industrialization, and mass communication, traditional Latin politics undergoes several, now familiar, changes.

Almost from the moment of their arrival in cities, the urban masses constitute a potential power base. It is not surprising, therefore, that there should appear on the political scene persons ready to represent the claims of these masses and to profit by their support. The rhetoric of politics soon comes to reflect awareness of the new power of the poor. Competition develops for the support of this urban poor. A champion emerges at the head of a new, loosely organized movement. Welfare programs are given unprecedented attention. Strikes and demonstrations become significant modes of political action, and union leaders are likely to be taken into account by decision makers. All these changes reflect the new political importance of the masses. None of them necessarily implies, entails, or leads to democratic politics. Masses may be politically active without having political influence, as in totalitarian states. And they may have influence in systems where decisions are not made by majorities, as in most of the Latin systems today.

It now seems clear that mass participation in politics is as compatible with the Latin political tradition as it is with democratic or totalitarian politics, despite the fact that our analytic categories

---

[1] The resemblances between Latin American politics and the politics characterizing Mediterranean nations are obscured by the conventions of area specialization in political science. It is after all barely a decade since French officers (1) preferred their own Algerian policy to that made in Paris, and (2) ended a long period of ministerial instability by securing—through the threat of force—the installation of General Charles de Gaulle, whom they mistook for "their" man. France, too, has a tradition of regime instability, direct action, mass participation, and military participation in politics. (Note that there have been repeated instances of direct military participation in French politics since Napoleon.) The politics of Spain, Portugal, and Greece have an even more obvious resemblance to those of the Latin tradition.

have conditioned us to think otherwise. We are no more accustomed to thinking of masses of citizens having limited but real power in a political system than we are accustomed to thinking of popular sovereignty as one among several competing principles of legitimacy. The habit of associating authentic mass participation with democratic politics is so strong that we tend to gloss over the phenomenon of the popular dictator whose mass support is crucial to his power, despite the rather frequent recurrence of such regimes in the political history of the West, and to misinterpret (or ignore) the many political systems in which masses constitute one kind of power in a system that includes various types of competitors.

Argentina is, and for a number of decades has been, an example of this unfamiliar mix—a traditional Latin system under conditions of mass society. The Peronist movement is, and for a number of decades has been, a particularly clear-cut manifestation and carrier of this pattern of politics, a Caesarist movement in a technologically advanced society. Perón, the Peronist elite, and the masses that rallied round him embody many of the unfamiliar combinations and complexities that characterize Argentine politics. They also constitute an especially interesting and illuminating perspective from which to view Argentine politics. In this study I shall be particularly concerned with the Peronist movement, with the analysis of its vanguard and mass base.

The Peronist movement merits attention not only because of its importance to Argentine politics but also because of its relevance to a number of broadly influential hypotheses concerning political movements. The relatively unexpected combination of political groups, goals, and behavior—of personalism, class conflict, nationalism, and selected traditional values—doubtless explains the various and often mutually incompatible interpretations of the movement. Peronism has been cited as a prime example of "working-class authoritarianism" [2] and as a "spurious ideological movement" of the type common to Latin America.[3] It has been identified as an inci-

---

[2] See especially Seymour Martin Lipset, *Political Man: The Social Bases of Politics* (New York: Doubleday & Company, 1960), chaps. 4 and 5, pp. 97–179, and Gino Germani, *Política y sociedad en una época de transición: de la sociedad tradicional a la sociedad de masas* (Buenos Aires: Editorial Paidos, 1962), especially chaps. 4 and 8.

[3] George I. Blanksten, "Latin America," in Gabriel A. Almond and James S. Coleman, eds., *The Politics of the Developing Areas* (Princeton: Princeton University Press, 1966), p. 492. Blanksten is using here the conception of ideology that restricts it to a comprehensive rational system of ideas about the organization of social and political life.

dent on the road to development, a political by-product of the transition to an urban society.[4] It has been described as a triumph of indigenous Argentine politics [5] and as a European import—made in fascist Italy. It is said to have been a conservative authoritarian movement,[6] a revolutionary movement,[7] an authentic working-class movement,[8] a movement dominated by the traditional "oligarchy" in modern dress, and so forth.[9] The variety of interpretations of the movement's past and present reveals its ambiguity, its importance, and the range of still-open questions about its character and its consequences. In the course of this volume, I shall explore some of these questions, not to determine which of the extant characteristics is correct but to illuminate, with new data, the significance of the movement within the Argentine political system.

I shall also be especially, but never exclusively, concerned with the subjective dimension of the Argentine political system. Since there have been few empirical studies of the political cultures of polities such as Argentina, it seemed to me desirable to explore the psychocultural aspects of the mass base of Argentine society. Since there have been few studies of the followers of popular dictators, it seemed to me desirable to undertake a detailed investigation of the identifications, expectations, and demands of Peronists.

The focus of the study shifts repeatedly between the whole society and the Peronist movement, between the objective and subjective aspects of Argentina's political life.

The questions to which the study is addressed involve all these dimensions. The structure of the study reflects the shifting focus. Chapter 2 deals with objective aspects of the system, with past events

[4] See Robert J. Alexander, *The Perón Era* (New York: Columbia University Press, 1951).

[5] See Rafael Funes, *Reflexiones políticas para militares: hacia una política nacional* (Buenos Aires: Ediciones Relevo, 1963).

[6] See Blanksten, "Latin America"; also his *Perón's Argentina* (Chicago: University of Chicago Press, 1953).

[7] George Pendle insists that Perón's aim was social and economic revolution and emphasizes Perón's hostility to traditional ruling groups. See his *Argentina* (London: Oxford University Press, 1963); also, most Peronist writers take this position.

[8] Alberto Belloni, *Peronismo y socialismo nacional* (Buenos Aires: Ediciones Coyoacán, 1962), and Mario Amadeo, *Ayer, hoy, mañana* (Buenos Aires: Ediciones Gure, 1956).

[9] Irving Horowitz, "The Military Elites," in Seymour Martin Lipset and Aldo Solari, eds., *Elites in Latin America* (New York: Oxford University Press, 1967), pp. 146–189. Horowitz does not deny the working-class base but believes that the leadership represented a continuation of the "oligarchy."

that determined the identity and character of the political actors and past interactions that eventually defined the political system. The rise and fall of Perón, his political style and political bases, and the institutional practices associated with his presidency are emphasized. Chapter 3 identifies the actors, arenas, and patterns of interaction that characterized the democratic interlude from 1955 to 1965. An attempt is made to delineate the pattern of politics characteristic of contemporary Argentina, the pattern that I have described as one of traditional Latin politics under conditions of mass society. Chapters 4 and 5 examine the size and socioeconomic composition of the Peronist movement as compared to other major political blocs, and they explore the nature and significance of party identification in this type of political system. An effort is made to test the "two cultures" by hypothesis, according to which Argentine culture, and political culture, comprises one urban, democratic, and internationalist, European culture and one autocratic, materialist, "interior" culture. Chapter 6 examines aspects of interpersonal and intergroup relations, with special attention to patterns of group identification and hostility. Chapters 7 and 8 explore orientations of Peronists and of other Argentines to government. The focus is on the individual's relations to government—on his perceptions, expectations, and demands. The last chapter is addressed to some rather broad and basic questions concerning the psychocultural bases of Argentine society, the Peronist movement, and the relations between them. More specifically, the chapter attempts to assess the extent to which the Peronist movement constitutes a durable subculture with goals, values, and beliefs that isolate the Peronist rank and file within Argentine society. The Epilogue relates the regime of General Onganía to the pattern of politics analyzed in the study, notes some findings, and makes some hesitant suggestions about future research.

The survey data reported and analyzed in this study were collected in October, November, and December 1965. The interviewing was done by International Research Associates. Two thousand and fourteen Argentines, selected by probability sampling methods from among all Argentines living in towns of 2,000 or more, were interviewed by native Argentine interviewers.[10] The survey provides evidence on (1) the distribution within the general population of persons with reliable Peronist sympathies and identifications, (2) the distribution of persons with real but less comprehensive pro-Peronist

[10] See Appendix A for a discussion of how the sample was drawn and for some implications of the sample's structure.

orientations, and (3) the distribution of relevant demands and expectations among Peronist sympathizers and among other Argentines.

The questionnaire used in the survey was designed to elicit information on those orientations believed most relevant for assessing the character of the mass base of the Peronist movement. Naturally, it reflects my views and assumptions about the nature of political aggregates, about learning, and about political culture. Most of these views are rather widely shared among contemporary social scientists. It is perhaps nonetheless worthwhile to describe briefly those with the most pervasive influence on the study.

First, the study assumes that adaptive processes are learned and that they differ among cultures. It also assumes that culturally distinctive constellations of assumptions and expectations exist, which are relatively stable and integrative and which orient the individual vis-à-vis diverse phenomena in the present and the future.[11]

Second, it assumes that an individual's location in society affects the content and style of these learned expectations, demands, and identifications, and that these effects may be significant whether or not they are recognized as such by the individuals. Sharing important experiences—joblessness, a move from country to city, life in the same region, or low education—may result in the development of distinctive responses among persons who shared the experience.[12]

[11] This is of course the assumption on which the literature of national cultures is based. See, among others, Margaret Mead, "The Study of National Character," in Daniel Lerner and Harold D. Lasswell, eds., The Policy Sciences: Recent Developments in Scope and Method (Stanford: Stanford University Press, 1951); Edward Sapir, Selected Writings of Edward Sapir in Language, Culture, and Personality (Berkeley: University of California Press, 1948); and Alex Inkeles and Daniel J. Levinson, "National Character: The Study of Model Personality and Sociocultural Systems," in Gardner Lindzey, ed., Handbook of Social Psychology, 2 vols. (Cambridge, Mass.: Addison-Wesley Publishing Co., 1954), pp. 977–1020. Essays on Argentine national character describing purportedly broadly shared conceptions of reality include Tomás Roberto Fillol, Social Factors in Economic Development: The Argentine Case (Cambridge, Mass.: The M.I.T. Press, 1961); Torcuato S. di Tella, El sistema político argentino y la clase obrera (Buenos Aires: Editorial Universitaria de Buenos Aires, 1964); James Bruce, Those Perplexing Argentines (New York: Longmans, Green and Co., 1958); Arturo López Peña, Teoría del Argentina (Buenos Aires: Librería Huemul, 1965); and many others. Spanish men of letters since the "Generation of '98" have been particularly concerned with national character. See, for example, Ortega y Gasset's Invertebrate Spain (New York: W. W. Norton, 1937) and his essay on Argentine national character, "Intimidades," in Obras completas, 3rd ed., 2 vols. (Madrid: Espasa-Calpe, 1943), pp. 654–681.

[12] This is another way of saying that "the positions occupied by the individual in his society limit the effects upon him of society as a whole. . . ." See David Truman, The Governmental Process (New York: Alfred A. Knopf, 1958), p. 16.

Thus distinctive patterns of behavior may develop among aggregates in the absence of mutual identification. These distinctive perceptions and behavior patterns may have social and political significance independent of mutual identification. There is good reason to believe that shared experiences may also have significant, independent effects on the durability and cohesion of political aggregates whether or not these effects are cognized.

All political movements comprise individuals who share *some* characteristics, the minimum being some shared demands concerning the movement itself. Shared demands are the raison d'être of political groups, which is why political movements may be most appropriately conceived as demand aggregates.[13] The stability of the demands (and therefore of the demand aggregate) depends on the events to which they are linked. Demands may be anchored in such enduring events as social class, profession, or kinship or in such fleeting circumstances as attack by a hostile "other" or by a natural disaster of limited duration such as a drought or flood. The most durable movements are those whose followers share psychological characteristics that are linked to continuing or repeated events, for example, those experienced by persons of similar race, social status, economic role, and minority linguistic habits. Knowledge of these factors is therefore indispensable in assessing a political movement and requires investigating respondents' objective social characteristics and analyzing relations between social roles and perspectives.

Third, it is assumed that the portions of respondents' subjective lives that are relevant to this study include the following:

1. Expectations, that is, views about the nature of political reality, including beliefs concerning the goals, arenas, actors, processes, and strategies constituting the system and beliefs about the position of

---

[13] The concept of demands and demand aggregates employed here has been explicated by Harold Lasswell. Lasswell and Kaplan define a demand aggregate as "persons making the same demand." They add: "The members of a demand aggregate need be engaged in no interactions with one another, . . ." and "The probability that an aggregate of persons will identify with one another varies with the number and intensity of shared demands." See Harold D. Lasswell and Abraham Kaplan, *Power and Society: A Framework for Political Inquiry* (New Haven: Yale University Press, 1950), pp. 18–19. Persons familiar with Lasswell's work will recognize his pervasive influence in this study. See especially his *World Politics and Personal Insecurity* (New York: Whittlesey House, 1935); Lasswell and Kaplan, *Power and Society;* and Lasswell's introduction to Lasswell and Daniel Lerner, eds., *World Revolutionary Elites: Studies in Coercive Ideological Movements* (Cambridge, Mass.: The M.I.T. Press, 1965).

the self in this system. These views about reality make up the cognitive map on which the individual orients himself and acts.[14]

2. Identifications that relate individuals to social and political groups, including goals, arenas, and strategies. Identifications include all extensions of the self, as well as views about the characteristics of the self that define (and limit) social space and available strategies.

3. Demands on the system, including their content, quantity, urgency, flexibility, style, and so forth. *Distinctive* Peronist demands identify the boundaries of the movement and distinguish it from other demand aggregates.[15]

Fourth, for reasons of both economy and theory, no effort was made to explore basic personality and adaptive mechanisms characteristic of Argentines and of relevant subgroups. While it would have been interesting and perhaps rewarding to investigate these basic integrative mechanisms, my purposes did not require, nor did my methods permit, investigation of basic personality. Although basic personality has undoubted relevance to political systems, I believe it is demonstrable that cognitive and affective factors that integrate political experience can be investigated independently of basic personality, and that knowledge of the relatively superficial cognitive constellations dealing specifically with political and social events is more useful to understanding political behavior (especially mass behavior) than are the data of basic personality formation. To understand why Russians react in a given fashion in the international arena, it is more useful to know how they perceive the rules, stakes, and power positions than to know which decision makers are the products of swaddling.

[14] Abram Kardiner (with the collaboration of Ralph Linton, Cora DuBois, and James West), *The Psychological Frontiers of Society* (New York: Columbia University Press, 1945), p. 5.

[15] The distinctions among these aspects of subjectivity are analytical. They were developed by Lasswell and are most fully explicated in Lasswell and Kaplan, *Power and Society*, pp. 10–28 passim. These categories seem to me to possess marked advantages over the more frequently utilized Parsonian categories, which view consciousness as comprising cognitive, affective, and evaluative orientations. The Lasswell categories more accurately depict psychological reality and therefore constitute a sharper cutting tool for relating subjective reality to behavior. Furthermore, Lasswell's categories bypass the various sticky and perhaps insoluble problems associated with distinguishing between preferences and values. Finally, they focus more directly and centrally on those aspects of perspectives most directly relevant to political life.

I am *not* suggesting that studies of basic personality are without interest or utility to political science, but emphasizing the validity and utility of exploring subjective realms nearer to the psychological surface.[16] I would have welcomed psychoanalytic data on early patterns of interpersonal adaptations. I do not really doubt that "The differences in solidarity, cohesiveness, the presence or absence of great amounts of anxiety, will influence the stability or instability of any culture." [17] But psychoanalytic data were not available. Furthermore, in complex societies, requirements for intermediate integrative constellations relating basic assumptions and expectations to more complex, more impersonal, more remote events are many; the number of possible adaptive patterns is multiplied by distance, by decreasing similitude, and by increasing abstraction from early experience. The predictive utility of basic personality is therefore limited to establishing parameters. To explain political behavior, the most pressing need is for knowledge about the more superficial, more sophisticated intermediate integrative constellations that link basic expectations and demands to a specific arena, for example, politics. For some purposes, including mine in this study, knowing the content and targets of projections and displacements may be more useful than knowledge about the organization of basic drives.

Fifth, I have been very much aware of several salient pitfalls surrounding cross-cultural survey research on politics. I have been especially concerned with the danger of imposing or projecting onto respondents through the questionnaire or the analysis my own structure of reality and mistaking it for theirs. Social scientists are particularly prone to building and projecting hyperrational perception and behavior models. The problem of distorting respondents' attention frames is compounded by the fact that political relations have a less direct, obvious, and crucial impact on most individuals than, for example, taxes and the availability of food, housing, and jobs. The shoe that pinches is most often of an economic last. Experiencing political dissatisfactions requires a more elaborate cognitive map that explains concrete felt discomforts in terms of the distribution of power. Explaining economic problems in political

---

[16] For a recent exploration of the relevance of biographical data to political behavior, see Lewis J. Edinger and Donald D. Searing, "Social Backgrounds in Elite Analysis: A Methodological Inquiry," *American Political Science Review,* vol. 61, no. 2 (June 1967), pp. 428–446.

[17] Kardiner, *Psychological Frontiers of Society,* p. 417.

terms requires (1) adopting a manipulative perspective on the problems, believing someone or some policy has caused them and could remedy them, and (2) identifying rulers as persons capable of influencing them. Political orientations are relatively abstract, at least one level removed from concrete experience.[18] Collecting and analyzing information on the political orientations of mass publics therefore involves a heightened danger of confusing researchers' and respondents' priorities. Certain limited safeguards can be and were built into the interview instrument.[19] Hopefully, awareness of the problem throughout the process of data analysis can also help to mitigate its adverse consequences.

A number of questions used in the survey were borrowed from the questionnaire developed by Almond and Verba for their comparative study of the political cultures associated with democratic institutions.[20] Using questions from *The Civic Culture* study had the obvious advantage of providing data on Argentina comparable to data already available on Mexico, Italy, the United States, Germany,

[18] Survey research has already made us aware of the fact most people are not much concerned with issues; it is now making us aware of the low level of concern with politics. We do not really know the consequences for democratic institutions of various levels of citizen attention and participation. We know almost nothing about the level of attention to political questions among the citizens of different polities, and little about the levels of concern with political questions within a single polity. Neither do we know much about which levels of attention to politics are characteristic of which kinds of movements. Michigan Survey Research Center studies have revealed American voters' very low levels of attention to politics and explored some of the implications of this finding. See Angus Campbell, Philip E. Converse, Warren E. Miller, and Donald E. Stokes, *The American Voter* (New York: John Wiley & Sons, 1960), pp. 60–63.

[19] The surest way to avoid distorting the structure of the respondents' perceptions is to conduct relatively unstructured, permissive, "depth" interviews comprised of flexibly ordered, open-ended questions, but it is very unlikely that any researcher can conduct large enough numbers of such interviews to permit statistically warranted generalization. Riesman's recent study of Japanese national character is an example of studies based on interview data, the generalization of which is not statistically warranted. See David Riesman and Evelyn Thompson Riesman, *Conversations in Japan* (New York: Basic Books, 1967). Robert Lane's *Political Ideology* (Glencoe, Ill.: Free Press, 1962) is another example. Such studies may be valuable and brilliant, just as comparable anthropological studies have been, but, when generalized, their evidential base is no stronger than nineteenth-century studies of national character, and like them depend for their worth on the insight and discipline of the author.

[20] The questionnaire is published in Gabriel A. Almond and Sidney Verba, *The Civic Culture: Political Attitudes and Democracy in Five Nations* (Princeton: Princeton University Press, 1963); hereafter cited as Almond and Verba, *The Civic Culture*. Questions from *The Civic Culture* are identified as such where they are first discussed in this study.

and the United Kingdom. While comparison of Argentines with respondents in these countries was not a principal purpose of this study, selected comparisons illuminate the meaning of Argentine and Peronist political orientations.

The Civic Culture study, however, "stresses orientation to political structure and process, not orientation to the substance of political demands and outputs." [21] This study is concerned with a demand aggregate; it therefore emphasizes substantive demands on the system and expectations concerning policy outcomes as well as orientations to the system as a whole.

The problem of timeliness must also be considered. Since the interviews were conducted in the last months of 1965, they reflect perspectives that were current at that time. Of course, the intervening years have been marked by important political changes in Argentina, and it is possible that major shifts have occurred in the politically relevant perspectives of Argentines. In technologically advanced nations, opinion is rarely static and is sometimes quite volatile. Still, though magnitudes of distributions change, many aspects of perspectives appear to be quite stable, and it is with those relatively more stable aspects that I am concerned.

History and recent studies of political socialization alike suggest that identifications are relatively enduring and that shifts in the objects of identification are consistent with already existing patterns of identification. This is another way of saying that the self-systems of individuals normally derive from early experience and are not readily susceptible to change. Expectations are similarly stable. The cognitive map on which an individual orients himself and acts reflects the patterned behavior of the society experienced by the individual through a lifetime of interactions. Neither expectations nor identifications are subject to rapid change. Demands are more closely tied to changing events, more likely therefore to shift with changes in economic or political conditions. But even demands have stable dimensions. A demand for higher wages may disappear when a raise is secured, but the demand that government act to secure the desired raise reflects more enduring views about the appropriate functions of government.

The concepts of culture and of national character alike assume the durability of perspectives. Both assume the existence of culturally distinctive constellations of expectations and identifications that are

[21] Ibid., p. 29.

relatively stable and integrative and that orient individuals vis-à-vis diverse phenomena in the present and the future. Obviously, perspectives change, culture changes, behavior changes. But all are notable as much for their resistance as for their susceptibility to change. In assessing the probable stability of Argentine perspectives, it is important to note, too, that no sharp breaks with the past have occurred in Argentina since 1965. General Onganía replaced President Illía; republican institutions were suspended. But this interruption of the democratic process hardly marked a departure from Argentina's political tradition. To the contrary, the evidence suggests persistence of all basic aspects of the political system described in this book. If all this is true, then the information collected at the end of 1965 remains useful in delineating the fundamentals of Argentine political perspectives.

Finally, I have attempted throughout to define concepts operationally and then to write in terms of these definitions. I have also attempted to make explicit the theoretical assumptions influencing the interpretation of the data. The effort has complicated my syntax, Latinized my vocabulary, and generally weighted down my prose. Hopefully, the gain in conceptual clarity justifies the aesthetic loss.

2

The Argentine Political System before 1955

> . . . history is concerned not with "events" but with "processes";
> . . . "processes" are things which do not begin and end but turn into
> one another. . . .
>
> R. G. Collingwood [1]

Today in political science it is more fashionable to speak of political culture than of political history. I share this bias of my times and propose to begin this essay with some comments on recent Argentine political history, not because of regressive historicist or determinist predilections but as an aid to understanding that nation's political culture, which is the context in which were formed the political orientations that are my chief concern. The socialization process, expectations, needs, and role system are all products of past experience linking the past to the present and future. The political culture of a given era is formed through the interaction of material with nonmaterial environments, of personality with events, of past time with the present. A good deal of the past is always encapsulated in the present of both man and nations. Obviously, past events are as relevant to political culture as personal history is relevant to personality.

Psychiatry, survey research, and cross-cultural experience demonstrate the pitfalls of inferring subjective from objective events, meaning from appearance. They also teach the relevance of past to present, of objective to subjective universes. Although no amount of analysis of past political events can provide the kind of information about the subjective lives of actors obtainable through skillful survey research, psychoanalysis, or autobiography, it can delineate the arena in which subjectivities were formed and interacted, and

---

[1] *An Autobiography* (New York: Penguin Books, 1944), p. 67. For a fuller discussion of this point, see R. G. Collingwood, *Idea of History*, ed. T. M. Knox (New York: Oxford University Press, 1946).

it can indicate the range of culturally available adaptations.[2] Past experience is particularly useful as a guide to possible and, more especially, to impossible patterns of expectation in a given social context. Personality can never deviate too far from relevant models and experiences without being defined as madness.

Further, just as meaning cannot be inferred in the absence of data reporting on subjective experience, neither can meaning be inferred exclusively from these data. Situational data and "objective" behavioral data on who did what to whom, when, where are always required as referents for subjective opinions, attitudes, and perceptions. Knowledge about a given culture and personality cannot be usefully interpreted in the absence of contextual information that enables us to estimate what meaning is revealed by any set of subjective perceptions. The point would appear to be obvious enough, and is elaborated only because of the current views that "history" is irrelevant, that perceptions may be explored independently of social context.

I do not propose to cover the entire history of Argentina nor to deal in detail with any part of it. I will comment on only a few aspects of Argentine history, the remainders of which are vital factors in present politics. Specifically, I shall deal briefly with three aspects of Argentine political history: the limited experience with democratic institutions since gaining independence in 1810; the distinctive characteristics of the political parties, especially their susceptibility to factionalism, intransigence, and intolerance; and the ambiguous character and residue of the Peronist period, which strengthened both egalitarian and autocratic trends in Argentine society.

Argentina's Limited Democratic Experience

Since independence, Argentina has enjoyed only about twenty years of government by rulers chosen through universal manhood

[2] For a discussion of history as an explanation of social events, see Radcliffe-Brown: "one 'explanation' of a social system will be its history, . . . the detailed account of how it came to be what it is and where it is. Another 'explanation' of the same system is obtained by showing . . . that it is a special exemplification of laws of social psychology or social functioning. The two kinds of explanations do not conflict but supplement one another." (A. R. Radcliffe-Brown, "On the Concept of Function in Social Science," *American Anthropologist*, n.s. 37 [1935], p. 401. Two other social scientists with a high regard for the utility of history were Max Weber and Karl Marx. Harold Lasswell has also stressed the importance of a contextual approach that examines events in the context of the past, present, and future.

suffrage. Most of this experience occurred between 1916 and 1930, when the country was ruled by Radical governments elected in reasonably free and honest elections by an electorate that included all adult male citizens.[3]

To put this democratic experience in perspective, it is useful to look briefly at the pattern of Argentine political development. For decades after achieving independence in 1810, Argentina was plagued by the problems we now think of as characteristic of new nations.[4] Boundaries had to be established, the influence of the former colonial ruler broken, a type of political organization agreed upon, and a government established.

The problem of boundaries proved vexing for more than a decade. The jurisdiction of the old Spanish viceroyalty of the Río de la Plata —of which Argentina was a part—included, in addition to what is now Argentina, modern Paraguay, Uruguay, and part of Bolivia. With the central colonial administration removed, no political institution remained to unite all this territory. Localism was strong; common interests were few. Uruguay, claimed by Brazil as well as Argentina, broke away. So did Paraguay. Bolivia claimed what is now its southern territory. Spain threatened; Brazil attempted political as well as territorial encroachments that culminated in the Argentine-Brazilian war.

Internal problems were, if anything, more difficult; certainly, they were more persistent. Operationally, for more than two decades Argentina was an abstraction, the name given to a "system of interprovincial pacts." [5] Effective political power was held by *caudillos* who warred with one another and with all efforts to establish a central government. There was a continuing debate about the nature

[3] Two other administrations were chosen by universal adult suffrage in free elections: those of former President Arturo Frondizi (1958–1962) and former President Arturo Illía (1963–1966). Since there is some dispute about freedom and intimidation in the 1946 presidential election, I have not included Perón's first term (1946–1951) in this estimate. If it is included, the total number of years of government by rulers elected by majorities comes to approximately twenty-five. In fact, almost all commentators agree that the election was honest and free. See, for example, Arthur P. Whitaker, *The United States and Argentina* (Cambridge, Mass.: Harvard University Press, 1954), p. 172.

[4] Karl Deutsch, working from a definition of Carl J. Friedrich, has identified five criteria for nationhood: independence, cohesiveness, political organization, autonomy, and internal legitimacy. Argentina lacked all these characteristics for several decades after independence. See Karl W. Deutsch and William J. Foltz, eds., *Nation-Building* (New York: Atherton Press, 1963), pp. 11–12, 31.

[5] Arthur P. Whitaker, *Argentina* (Englewood Cliffs, N. J.: Prentice-Hall, 1964), p. 27.

of union, which was somewhat similar to that among the North American colonies in the years following the Revolutionary War and the adoption of the Constitution.

Unitarios, favoring a highly centralized government, vied with *federales,* who advocated a loose confederation. Rivalry and conflict of interest separated Buenos Aires from the interior. Economic and political rivalries reinforced one another and before long were complicated by controversy over Church-state relations. Efforts to establish a government based on a liberal democratic model providing representative institutions, to end Indian serfdom and Negro slavery, and to create a secular state found little support and proved less effective political tools for nation-building than the personal rule of strongman Juan Manuel de Rosas, a powerful *estanciero.*[6]

In his years in office (1827–1852), Rosas was able to establish order, unify the provinces, and secure recognition of central authority. Rosas was the first, but by no means the last, Argentine dictator to combine personal rule with elements of a democratic style; an appeal to tradition with appeals to nationalism; and an egalitarian style with autocratic institutions. With his appeal for "one faith, one language, one ceremonial, one style," Rosas would, in contemporary terminology, be termed a modernizing tyrant and nation-builder. Like many a contemporary example of this type, Rosas was himself a *caudillo,* a member of the established elite to whose opposition he eventually fell victim. Rosas's appeals to liberty, democracy, and constitutional government had symbolic, if not institutional, significance. His appeal to the *gauchos* and the *gaucho* tradition, to the men of the interior as opposed to the urban Europe-oriented *porteños* of the capital city, signaled the inception in Argentina of a new nationalist political style.[7] George Blanksten has said, "Rosas was the 'interior,' the second Argentina, personified."[8] He was the first man of the interior to rule Argentina and the last to do so until 1943.

[6] Scobie asserts that Rosas "symbolized the rise to power of the coastal cattle interests" and describes him as a leading proponent of the "cattle civilization." See James R. Scobie, *Argentina: A City and a Nation* (New York: Oxford University Press, 1965), pp. 77–78.

[7] Scobie quotes Rosas as saying, "You well know the attitude of the have nots against the wealthy and powerful. I have always considered it very important to acquire an influence over the poor in order to control and direct them; and at great cost in effort, comfort, and money, I have made myself into a gaucho like them, to speak as they do, to protect them, to become their advocate, and to support their interests." See ibid., p. 78.

[8] George I. Blanksten, *Perón's Argentina* (Chicago: University of Chicago Press, 1953), p. 26.

The year after Rosas's fall, Argentina adopted a new democratic constitution resembling that of the United States. It established a federal system and provided for separation of powers. Achieving a democratic government proved to be much more difficult than writing a democratic constitution. Nonetheless, the years from 1853 to 1880 were productive ones for Argentina. A strong central government was established, as were territorial integrity and stable boundaries. Buenos Aires was integrated into the union in 1860; the "conquest of the desert" and the end of Indian resistance were completed in 1870. During this period two presidents, Bartolomé Mitre and Domingo Sarmiento, provided Argentina with the best system of public education in Latin America, developed a modern army, and encouraged economic progress—largely financed by private and foreign capital.

Throughout this period national politics was the province of the landowning class, the *estancieros*, mainly Creoles who constituted an elite that blended traditional Spanish and European values with those of the indigenous *gaucho* culture. Land was the principal source of wealth, agriculture the principal occupation. Very large estates worked by landless cowboys and peasants, largely Indian, were the rule.

Argentina's first national census showed that, as of 1869, the population was approximately one-fifth white, three-fourths Indian and Mestizo, with the small remainder being Negro and mulatto. Ruling and ruled classes were separated by race, economic roles, and culture. The vast majority of the population were in no sense participants in politics at the level of the nation-state. Instead, they were integrated into political units headed by a landowner who, as a *caudillo*, combined economic and political power. As late as 1860, portions of Argentine territory were still ruled by Indians with essentially autonomous political organizations. Some commentators believe that the defeat of Rosas signaled the end of Creole landowner domination and Spanish *gaucho* culture—a culture memorialized as well as romanticized in the famous epic *Martín Fierro* (published in 1872).[9] Although for several decades presidents continued to be drawn from among the owners of large estates, Argentine society was clearly in transition. The urban sector was growing (the population of Buenos Aires had grown from 90,000 in 1855 to

[9] Barrington Moore, Jr., in his suggestive and provocative study *Social Origins of Dictatorship and Democracy*, notes that "where commercial relationships have begun to undermine a peasant economy, the conservative elements in society are likely to generate a rhetoric of extolling the peasant as the backbone of society" (Boston, Mass.: Beacon Press, 1966), p. 491.

300,000 in 1880); the population of the agricultural interior was not keeping pace with that of the littoral; the commercial and industrial sectors, though small, were increasing and were already becoming the special province of immigrants.

The landowning oligarchy made the transition to commercial agriculture, but while they were quick to exploit developing and expanding export markets for their crops, they are usually described as disdaining commerce and industry,[10] or at least as not being attracted to them.[11] Gino Germani notes that despite the *estanciero*'s marked preference for living in cities (and thus being absentee landowners), few entered the new economic sectors, though many functioned as urban professionals. He further comments: "Industrialization was produced outside this group; already during the first phase of industrialization . . . virtually all the *non*agricultural activity was in the hands of immigrants." [12]

Intellectually as well as economically, the *estanciero* class looked beyond the borders of Argentina. Many of them were culturally oriented toward Europe and were carriers of rationalist and liberal ideals. This cosmopolitanism of the traditional land-based aristocracy and the rejection of *gaucho* culture led one commentator to describe Argentina, at the time of independence, as "philosophically French, institutionally North American, and economically British." [13] A deliberate national policy of encouraging immigration led to the entrance of some 300,000 immigrants during Sarmiento's presidency. This was but the beginning of the immigrant flood that transformed Argentina's ethnic and racial composition, changed her politics,[14] and provided the manpower to manage and staff commercial and industrial sectors of her economy. "By the early 1900s, 80 percent of the owners of commercial and industrial establishments were immigrants or naturalized citizens." [15] (See Table 2.1.)

[10] Thomas F. McGann, *Argentina: The Divided Land* (Princeton, N.J.: D. Van Nostrand Company, 1966), pp. 31–34 passim.

[11] For a discussion of the Spanish source of Latin American values, see Lipset, "Values, Education and Entrepreneurship," in Seymour Martin Lipset and Aldo Solari, eds., *Elites in Latin America* (New York: Oxford University Press, 1967), p. 8.

[12] Gino Germani, *Política y sociedad en una época de transición: de la sociedad tradicional a la sociedad de masas* (Buenos Aires: Editorial Paidos, 1962), p. 172.

[13] Rafael Funes, *Reflexiones políticas para militares: hacia una política nacional* (Buenos Aires: Ediciones Relevo, 1963), p. 34.

[14] Germani, *Política y sociedad*, pp. 179–216 passim.

[15] Tomás Roberto Fillol, *Social Factors in Economic Development: The Argentine Case* (Cambridge, Mass.: The M.I.T. Press, 1961), p. 28.

New vs Old Oligarchy (1880 – 1916)

TABLE 2.1   POPULATION CLASSIFIED BY ORIGIN

Census of	Total	Native-Born Argentines	Foreign Born	Percentage of Foreign Born
1869	1,737,076	1,526,746	210,330	12.1
1895	3,954,911	2,948,073	1,006,838	25.5
1914	7,885,237	5,494,066	2,391,171	30.3
1947	15,893,827	13,457,900	2,435,927	15.3
1960	20,005,691	17,440,424	2,565,267	12.8

Source: *Censó Nacional, 1960: Población, resultados provisionales* (Buenos Aires, 1961), p. 23.

Some historians point to the team of Julio A. Roca and Carlos Pellegrini as embodying the "new oligarchy" that replaced the "old oligarchy" and ruled Argentina from 1880–1916. The "new oligarchy" combined *criollo* landowners (Roca) and the descendants of successful urban immigrants (Pellegrini). The new ruling class rejected traditional policies in the Church-state area, demanded a secular public school system, and vigorously pursued policies aimed at increasing their own opportunities. It is said to have been guided by "a spirit open to the powerful, evolutionary forces of this century, with faith in science and in human progress." [16] The governments they headed can perhaps most accurately be described as limited democracy. Participation in the choice of rulers was limted to a small land-based upper class, but competition was vigorous even though elections were often fixed.

During these years political parties emerged, trade unions developed, and the groundwork was laid and the transition made to universal manhood suffrage. This period has been widely interpreted as one of development toward democracy, an interpretation made superficially reasonable by the fact that it was followed by a decade and a half of democratic rule. (The "following after, therefore developing toward" argument is treacherous. Was the Argentine system developing toward dictatorship during the fourteen years of Radical rule that ended with a military coup?)

The government of Radical leader Hipólito Irigoyen was the first to be chosen on the basis of universal manhood suffrage, exercised in a reasonably free and honest election. It was made possible by the sweeping electoral reforms of 1911 and 1912 carried out by President Roque Sáenz Peña, which provided for a secret ballot, suffrage for

[16] The words are those of Miguel Cané. They are quoted by José Luis Romero, *A History of Argentine Political Thought*, intro. and trans. by Thomas F. McGann (Stanford: Stanford University Press, 1963), p. 197.

TABLE 2.2 PERCENTAGE OF POPULATION VOTING IN SE-
LECTED PRESIDENTIAL ELECTIONS, 1910–1958

Year	Percentage of Total Adult Population	Percentage of Native-Born Adult Argentines
1910	9	20
1916	30	64
1928	41	77
1936	48	73
1946	56	83
1958	78	94

Source: Gino Germani, *Política y sociedad en una época de transición* (Buenos Aires: Editorial Paidos, 1962), p. 225.

ᵃ 1910–1946, only men; 1958, women, too.

all male citizens, permanent registration, and the incomplete list.[17]
The Sáenz Peña law substantially increased Argentina's voting population, transforming the system from one that permitted only the
small, land-based upper class (about 9 percent of the total adult male
population) to participate in the decision process to one that shared
power with all male citizens. (See Table 2.2.)

The popular vote in 1916, gave Irigoyen and the Radicals almost
as many votes as the other candidates combined (see Table 2.3).
Alone among parties, the Unión Cívica Radical (UCR) showed
strength in all provinces. The electoral reform had done its job.
Irigoyen became president, and the era of Radical rule began.

TABLE 2.3 POPULAR VOTE, 1916

Party	Number
Unión Cívica Radical	340,802
Socialista Argentino	66,397
Demócrata Progresista	98,876
Conservador	96,103
Autonomista	30,968
Unión Cívica Radical Disidente	28,116
Unión Democrática	13,912
Concentración	17,965
Popular	16,141

Source: Darío Canton, *Materiales para el estudio de la Argentina*, vol. 1 (Buenos Aires: Editorial del Instituto, 1968), p. 85. This invaluable compilation corrects and refines the election statistics previously available. Unfortunately, a copy became available to me only as the manuscript was en route to the publisher. Time did not permit me to utilize it throughout this study.

[17] Because of a large immigrant population, many of whom were very slow to seek naturalization, there continued to be a large number of voteless males.

From 1916 to 1930, Radical leaders Irigoyen and Alvear ruled the country. This period remains Argentina's longest experience with constitutional, democratic government. Three popularly elected administrations succeeded one another in office; each had won more than two-thirds of the popular votes in honest elections. These Radicals instituted no sharp breaks with the past. Their welfare and educational policies were reasonably successful, their economic policies conventional and inflationary. Outside the political system, two events were taking place that were to change the shape of future politics: one, the great crash and subsequent international depression; the other, the beginnings of a massive internal migration from countryside to city, from province to province. Outside the democratic system another set of events—plots and plans—was also taking place, which in 1930 erupted into a military coup that replaced the almost senile Hipólito Irigoyen with a revolutionary government headed by General Uriburu. Uriburu claimed power not in the name of popular sovereignty but in the name of the higher duty of the armed forces to guard the nation's honor and oversee her destiny.

Some Characteristics of Parties and the Party System

To identify the date at which political parties emerge is always problematic. Until quite recent times parties developed almost imperceptibly from informal alliances of individuals. In democratic countries the transition from cabal to party was typically slow and ambiguous and coincided with the evolution of other democratic institutional practices. This pattern may be contrasted with that characteristic of some of the new nations, where organizations called parties, and performing some of the functions of parties, have been developed by nondemocratic and antidemocratic regimes interested in mobilizing masses.

Parties that develop alongside other democratic institutions usually have early acquired democratic values, organizations, and patterns of conduct, their rationale and prospects being intertwined with democratic practices. Parties that develop independently of the struggle for democratic rule may be less attached to and identified with democratic norms. Many political systems, especially those whose development has been uneven and conflicted, contain both types of parties.

The goals and practices of political parties are also obviously influenced by their total context. A context in which violence is endemic and interclass civility low will surely produce different parties than a context of social peace and high mutual respect. Argentine parties reflect the influence of traditional practices and value patterns; they also reflect the idiosyncratic development of Argentine society.

In Argentina the first "parties" comprised small, select groups of major landowners who competed with one another for office and influence. These "pure followings of notables" represented no one but themselves, but they were far less politically than socially homogeneous. Rivalries within the *estanciero* class were many. In the interior the *estancieros* ruled virtually autonomous fiefdoms and resisted the formation of strong central government: "To the political leaders of many of the provinces federalism meant only provincial autonomy, the right of the *caudillo* to exploit his province." [18] However, they fought with one another as well as against the establishment of a central power. Though they eventually lost the formal struggle against a central government, they remained important loci of political as well as economic power.

These landowning oligarchs disagreed about a number of subjects, including the fact and nature of an Argentine union, the place of Buenos Aires in such a union, and the role of the Church in the political sphere. Most persistently, they disagreed about *who* should rule. Cliques and claques developed, divided, disappeared, and reappeared. "Parties" in this sense existed in Argentina from the time of the war of independence, when groups calling themselves the *Conservadores* and the *Demócratas* formed around rival would-be leaders. Most observers, however, date the history of Argentine parties from the overthrow of Rosas in 1852, at which time a new Liberal party was formed around Bartolomé Mitre. Argentine parties proved notably fissiparous from their inception. Like cells, they multiplied through division. Liberals split into Nationalists and Autonomists and, later, mutated again, joining in the PAN unity party that split the Republican party in the wake of the so-called Conciliation of Parties, which was in turn opposed by a new Partido Modernista and the Unión Cívica Radical.

The multiplication, division, addition, and subtraction of parties at this early stage foretold problems to come. So did the repeated refusal of defeated candidates to accept the outcome of elections. The tenure of elected officials was repeatedly punctuated by revolutions,

[18] Peter G. Snow, *Argentine Radicalism: The History and Doctrine of the Radical Civic Union* (Iowa City: University of Iowa Press, 1965), p. 3.

usually of very short duration, involving little violence and conforming to the stylized Latin American variant of the palace revolution called a *pronunciamento*. Students of Argentina agree that many of the elections bore little more relation to democratic choice than did the *pronunciamentos*.[19] Not only was the suffrage restricted to a small upper class but, more important, election results were often rigged and, when convenient, falsified, thus beginning the falsification of the electoral process that is a common cause as well as an effect of disrespect for popular institutions.

In functioning democracies, elections and political parties are the institutional mechanisms permitting the participation of large numbers in the choice of rulers. By the turn of the century, elections in Argentina had been used to provide a facade of support as well as to choose rulers. Parties had been used as instruments of revolution as well as of peaceful political organization and choice.

By the end of the nineteenth century two new parties had emerged, each embodying new demands for power from new segments of the population: the Socialist party, small, sectarian, supported by immigrant industrial workers in the cities; and the Radical Civic Union (UCR), an urban party that "was from the start the party of the middle sectors, particularly those in Buenos Aires." [20]

Most students of Argentine politics emphasize the political importance of the development of a middle class. Gino Germani, whose extensive work on Argentine social development has influenced much

[19] See ibid., p. 14, on the refusal of the Radicals to participate in the elections before 1916; McGann, *Argentina*, p. 34; Blanksten, *Perón's Argentina*, p. 32; and John J. Johnson, *Political Change in Latin America: The Emergence of the Middle Sectors* (Stanford: Stanford University Press, 1958), p. 98. Mitre said of the elections of April 1890, "Since the lists of registered voters are falsified and the polling places are closed by fraud as the result of this plot by administration officials against popular sovereignty, the people are divorced from their government, excluded from public life, and expelled from the protection of the constitution." Quoted in Romero, *History of Argentine Political Thought*, p. 191. One clear statement on the ubiquity of electoral fraud was made by Carlos Pellegrini, who stated in the Senate in 1902 that electoral fraud was "permitted and acknowledged as a normal fact" of political life. Quoted in Darío Canton, *El Parlamento Argentino en épocas de cambio: 1890, 1916 y 1946* (Buenos Aires: Editorial del Instituto, 1966), p. 23. Most observers describe the 1916 elections as the first elections sufficiently free of fraud and broad in participation to be considered as permitting authentic democratic choice.

[20] Johnson, *Political Change*, p. 98. See also Joseph R. Barager, "Argentina," in Martin C. Needler, ed., *Political Systems of Latin America* (Princeton, N.J.: D. Van Nostrand Company, 1964), p. 413, and Pan American Union, *Materiales para el estudio de la clase media en América Latina*, 6 vols. (Washington, D.C., 1950–1951).

of the literature, traces the development of an urban or middle class through three phases: first, the development of a largely immigrant urban middle class engaged principally in commerce and small industry; second, the development of a small but noticeable rural middle class comprising peasants who developed some economic resources through the turn-of-the-century prosperity; and, third, the emergence some decades later of new sectors of the middle class, consisting of white-collar workers, employees, bureaucrats, technicians, and other functionaries. Germani, like other commentators, sees the Radical party as the political expression of the new middle class, and the new middle class as carriers of political democracy.[21]

In fact, the political behavior of middle-class parties in Argentina in the period following their emergence does not provide prima facie support for the assumption that they were the carriers of moderation, compromise, and a greater respect for legality and constituted the necessary socioeconomic infrastructure of a stronger democracy. To the contrary, a good case can be made for the proposition that in Argentina the emergence of the middle sector was accompanied by an increase in political violence.[22]

The emergence of a new predominantly urban middle class in Argentina at the turn of the century is clear even though its political

---

[21] Germani, *Politica y sociedad*, pp. 223–224.

[22] Despite his general tendency to assume an identification between the middle classes and the politics of moderation, John Johnson also points out that "The military gave evidence of entering more fully into the political calculation of the middle sectors, not so much because of any greater readiness to interfere in civilian matters as because of its increasing middle sector social background and economic orientation." (See Johnson, *Political Change*, p. 43.) Luis Ratinoff, "The New Urban Groups: The Middle Classes," in Lipset and Solari, *Elites in Latin America*, pp. 61–93 passim, takes a similar position. In fact, the relationship of the middle classes to democracy has never been definitely demonstrated. There is, however, a large literature on the subject. See, for example, Seymour Martin Lipset, *Political Man: The Social Bases of Politics* (New York: Doubleday & Company, 1960), chap. 2, for a notable effort to demonstrate such a relationship; also C. Issawi, "Economic and Social Foundations of Democracy in the Middle East," *International Affairs*, no. 32 (1956), pp. 27–42; James S. Coleman, "Conclusion: The Political Systems of the Developing Areas," in Gabriel A. Almond and James S. Coleman, eds., *The Politics of the Developing Areas* (Princeton: Princeton University Press, 1960); and Phillips Cutright, "National Political Development: Measurement and Analysis," *American Sociological Review*, vol. 28, no. 2 (April 1963), pp. 253–264. See Harry Eckstein, *Division and Cohesion in Democracy* (Princeton: Princeton University Press, 1966), Appendix B, for one criticism of Lipset's effort as well as for a general discussion of efforts to relate stable democracies to economic development; also, Robert M. Marsh, *Comparative Sociology* (New York: Harcourt, Brace & World, 1967), pp. 123–141.

TABLE 2.4   MIDDLE (AND UPPER) STRATA IN ARGENTINA,
1870–1950

Approximate Year	Percentage in Middle (and Upper) Occupations
1870	11
1895	26
1920	32
1950	36

Source: Gino Germani, *Política y sociedad en una época de transición* (Buenos Aires: Editorial Paidos, 1962), p. 170. Estimates of the exact size and growth rate of the middle sector vary. Roberto Tomás Fillol, *Social Factors in Economic Development* (Cambridge, Mass.: The M.I.T. Press, 1961), p. 29, estimates that they constituted 32 percent of the total economically active population in 1895, 43 percent in 1936, and 54 percent in 1947. All agree that the growth was rapid and resulted in a large middle class.

significance is not. The size and rate of development of this new middle class are reflected in Table 2.4.

The Argentine middle class had several distinctive characteristics that doubtless influenced its political behavior. Whitaker has stressed its heterogeneity, asserting that it comprised "an aggregation of disparate groups and individuals who have little in common beyond the fact that they occupy a middle position between the oligarchy above and [workers] beneath." [23] One of the most important characteristics of this middle sector was that it largely consisted of immigrants. Its members, therefore, did not share common ethnic backgrounds, traditions, or experience (except the experience of being successful in a foreign environment). Its growth did not indicate social and economic mobility among indigenous Argentines but rather the addition of a new stratum of new inhabitants. Approximately three-fourths of the early immigrants had rural backgrounds but settled in cities and quickly found their way into commercial, technical, and industrial roles. The persons making up the new middle sector were upward mobile, but their status and role mobility were functions of their prior geographic mobility.

The population of Buenos Aires alone increased ten times between 1869 and 1914, growing from somewhat over 200,000 to more than 2,000,000. Like the growth of a middle class, the processes of urbanization, industrialization, and secularization did not result from the internal social mobility normally associated with these developments. Growing cities did not until several decades later reflect the depopu-

[23] Whitaker, *United States and Argentina*, p. 13.

TABLE 2.5 THE PROCESS OF URBANIZATION IN ARGENTINA,
1869–1957

Year	Percentage of Argentines in Towns of 2,000 or More
1869	27
1895	37
1914	53
1947	62
1957	65

Source: Gino Germani, *Política y sociedad en una época de transición* (Buenos Aires: Editorial Paidos, 1962), p. 220.

lation of the countryside. The growth of the industrial sector did not involve the transformation of an indigenous peasant class into industrial workers. The growth of middle-income groups did not reflect increasing social mobility of indigenous Argentines nor the growth among indigenes of role distributions based on achievement. Instead, it meant the superimposition on a basically traditional society of an economic and social sector that more often has appeared as a consequence of internal social change (see Table 2.6). To be sure, the massive immigration, concomitant rapid urbanization, and industrialization did indeed change Argentine society, but it was a different type of change than that which is typically associated with these develop-

TABLE 2.6 POPULATION OF THE METROPOLITAN AREA OF BUENOS AIRES, INCLUDING THE PERCENTAGE OF INTERNAL AND EXTERNAL IMMIGRANTS, 1869–1957

Year	Total Population (Thousands)	Immigrants from Other Nations: Percentage of Total Population	Immigrants from the Interior: Percentage of Total Population	Annual Rate of Immigration from Interior
1869	230	47	3	—
1895	783	50	8	8,000
1914	2,035	49	11	—
1936	3,430	36	12	83,000
1947	4,720	26	29	—
1957	6,370	22	36	96,000

Source: Gino Germani, *Política y sociedad en una época de transición* (Buenos Aires: Editorial Paidos, 1962), p. 230 (quoted from his *El proceso de urbanización;* cited in *Política y sociedad,* p. 186, as "Buenos Aires: Instituto de Sociologia [en publ.]").

ments.[24] *There were important economic, social, and political con-*
sequences of this pattern of modernization through immigration:
Argentina had not become a typical transitional society in which tra-
ditional patterns were weakened. To the contrary, the modern
sector—urban, industrial, mobile, and achievement-oriented—was
grafted onto the traditional society, whose organization and style of
life and politics remained largely unchanged.[25] For example, patterns of landownership were only marginally affected by changes.
Estates of more than 10,000 acres accounted for more than half the
occupied land; some 500 owners held more than 53,000,000 acres.[26]

An apparently analogous situation existed in politics. The Radicals, who clearly represented the new middle sector, entered politics
from the outside. They represented the demands of a new group for
direct participation in the decision-making process and integration
into the political system. Their strength appears not to have been
a consequence of the weakened condition of previous rulers, nor
did it represent the demands of former subordinates for equality;
rather it embodied the demand of outsiders who had never been integrated into the traditional land-based authority structure. Therefore, the new Radical party confronted at its inception traditional
oligarchs in relatively full possession of their traditional strength.

At the level of platform the early Radicals sounded like the
stereotypical middle-class party: they demanded an expanded electorate, honest elections, and decentralization of authority. In style
and rhetoric they were messianic, making extravagant claims to
moral superiority, unique social virtue, and mystical leadership
qualifications. In method they mixed democratic and military modes.

The Radical leaders assumed from the beginning that these moderate political reforms could not be achieved through existing politi-

[24] See, among others, Daniel Lerner, *The Passing of Traditional Society: Modernizing the Middle East* (Glencoe, Ill.: Free Press, 1958); A. F. K. Organski, *The
Stages of Political Development* (New York: Alfred A. Knopf, 1965); and David
E. Apter, *The Politics of Modernization* (Chicago: University of Chicago Press,
1966).

[25] Canton, whose works I did not see until this manuscript had been completed,
emphasizes that "successive generations of immigrants remained on the margins
of Argentine political life." See his *El Parlamento,* p. 120.

[26] It was pointed out in 1946 that "1,800 Argentine families still own an area
greater than England, Belgium, and the Netherlands together. One clan, the
Unzués, holds 1,000,000 acres in the single, fertile Province of Buenos Aires"
(*Time,* August 12, 1946, p. 36); quoted in Blanksten, *Perón's Argentina,* p. 250.
See also Needler, *Political Systems,* p. 415, and Germani, *Política y sociedad,* for a
discussion of the immigrants' role in the countryside.

cal channels and institutions. It cannot be said that they based this conclusion on evidence, or that they arrived at it only after testing the system and finding it closed. Instead, Radical leaders quickly demonstrated that the middle sector shared with the "conservative oligarchs" a capacity for pursuing their ends through other than electoral means. In cooperation with General Manuel Campos and his followers, the principal Radical founders, led by Leandro N. Alem, attempted an abortive revolution in December 1889 with the help of dissatisfied military officers while the party was still in its prenatal stage.[27]

This was the first but by no means the last armed revolt sponsored by the new middle sector.[28] Their "Revolutionary Manifesto" provided what was to be the UCR's classic justification of violence: "The directors of the Civic Union, convinced of the absolute impossibility of obtaining by peaceful means political reparation that the honor and welfare of the nation demanded, solemnly resolved supreme and very sad sacrifice: revolution." [29]

Failure of the coup did not constitute sufficient evidence to satisfy the Radical leaders that the road to power through violence was also blocked. In subsequent years they repeatedly conspired with military groups to overthrow existing governments. The rationale was always the same: the electoral system was rigged against them, precluding the possibility of achieving power by peaceful means. Most commentators accept their estimate as accurate. The "new oligarchy," like the old, appears to have been skilled in electoral manipulation. However, three facts should at least be taken into account in considering the meaning of the Radicals' early predilections for extraconstitutional action. One has already been alluded to, namely, that the Radicals *assumed* the closed nature of the political system, they did *not* first test it. Second, they demonstrated from the beginning an in-

[27] These revolutions were limited in goal but less so than previous *pronunciamentos*. While the latter aimed at changing only the personnel, the founders of the Radicals had as a goal the overhauling of the structure of government (but *not* of society). For an interesting discussion of types and typologies of revolution, see Chalmers Johnson, *Revolutionary Change* (Boston: Little, Brown and Company, 1966), pp. 133–149 passim.

[28] See José Nun, "A Latin American Phenomenon: The Middle Class Military Coup," in University of California, Institute of International Studies, *Trends in Social Science Research in Latin American Studies* (Berkeley, March 1965), for an interesting argument concerning the military coup as a distinctive form of middle-class political action.

[29] Quoted in Snow, *Argentine Radicalism*, p. 11.

transigence and an abhorrence of compromise that are not hospitable to the formation of electoral majori.ies and are common attributes of leaders willing to seek power through undemocratic means. Their boycotting of elections reflects the same tendency. Third, and most important, electoral reforms actually did take place through the existing system, providing incontrovertible evidence that the system was not, in fact, completely closed and incapable of reform from within.

The Radicals won the first election they ever contested.[30] In 1916, after the electoral reforms already referred to, they were swept into office with a large majority of the popular vote. Once in power, they proved themselves capable of providing democratic and reasonably effective government. But in power as well as out, personal and political rivalries split the leadership, which also seemed ready to sacrifice party unity to any principle. Radical leaders seemed to equate compromise with sellout and disdained it within and outside the party; they would neither compromise differences nor enter coalitions and declined to participate in governments they could not control and elections they were not assured of winning. Despite repeated splits they continued to command a large popular following.

Literally dozens of other parties competed in elections in the years before 1943. Most were not national parties; most were not long-lived; some were corrupt; and none had any chance of winning a free election. All were notably susceptible to factionalism, intransigence, and intolerance.

Before the advent of Perón and his new mass party, organized from a position of power, the Radicals were the only Argentine party with a reliable mass following, a national organization, and experience in governing. During the pre-Peronist period Argentina had a multiparty system with one clearly dominant party; an electoral system that more often than not deprived its major party of victory; and a style of party competition that encouraged factions, fraud, and force.

The Peronist Period

The Peronist period had its beginning in 1943, when Juan Perón participated in a coup d'etat that overthrew a conservative, minority government characteristic of those that had ruled Argentina be-

---

[30] The UCR's first presidential candidate, Bernardo de Irigoyen, withdrew from the campaign of 1892 and thus began a period of electoral abstention that continued until 1916.

tween 1930 and 1943. Writing of the revolution of 1943, George
Pendle comments:

> Basically, . . . the coup d'état of 1943 was the result of the revolution of
> 1930, because that event had restored the monopoly of government to the
> old landed aristocracy, who refused to acknowledge that a change had oc-
> curred in the country's sources of wealth. Of the one hundred persons pay-
> ing the highest income tax in 1941, only ten were *estancieros*. . . . More
> people were now employed in industry than in cattle-raising and farming.[31]

The group of officers (Grupo de Oficiales Unidos—GOU) that
came to power in 1943 conceived themselves as progressive, nationalist revolutionists. Most had Nazi or fascist sympathies and hoped to
bring to Argentina the unity, strength, discipline, and progress they
thought characterized Italy and Germany. In fact, the *Grupo* itself
lacked the unity it hoped to bring to the whole nation. Generals
Rawson, Ramírez, and Farrell succeeded one another in rapid succession. The principal importance of the group derives from its relationship to Perón. With them he made the transition from the military to the political arena. Through them he found his way to
supreme power, with support and a platform they neither fully
understood nor approved.

An old Latin American joke asserts that the end of a successful
military career is a tour of duty as president. Even by this standard
Juan Perón was more than a successful military officer. Whether
demagogue, revolutionary, fascist, front man for Evita, or all four,
Juan Perón is also the man who presided over the participatory revolution in Argentine politics. It was he who perceived the masses of
barely literate but recently uprooted poor on the doorstep of the
political system and invited them in. If he did not exactly prepare
a place for them, he nonetheless made them feel welcome. And if he
did not enter with them, his wife Evita did, and his own entrance
was made more dramatic, more triumphal, and more definitive and
his tenure in office extended by their accompaniment. Arthur
Whitaker has called Argentina a "haunted house." [32] It is Perón
and Eva who haunt it. On polling days their exclusion mocked the
electoral process; in the streets their portraits and their voices still
inspire and intimidate lesser leaders.

Their personal stories are well known. Eva Perón, an impressively

[31] George Pendle, *Argentina* (London: Oxford University Press, 1963), p. 88.
[32] Whitaker, *Argentina*.

dynamic, ambitious, beautiful, and talented woman, made her way through a class-bound society from ig~ominy and poverty to the top political leadership of a powerful Latin nation. She was illegitimate in a society that protected the sanctity of marriage by imposing penalties on children born out of wedlock. Her father, Juan Duarte, was a small landowner in Buenos Aires province; her mother was Juana Ibaguren, the woman for whom Duarte left his wife and with whom he lived and fathered five children. Eva Perón was poor in a society dominated by wealth, and outcast in a society where civility was a function of status. With the death of Juan Duarte, her mother moved the five children to Junín. At sixteen Eva moved on to Buenos Aires to seek fame and fortune through the judicious use of her beauty, wits, and ambition. In October 1943 she met Colonel Juan Domingo Perón; soon afterward she became his mistress, ally, and political partner, and eventually his wife. Her role in returning Perón to power on October 17, 1945, may well have been crucial. Her relationship with those other internal immigrants—the impoverished, despised, impotent, and often unemployed *descamisados*—was based more on mutual identification than on rhetoric. Her precise role in the political structure of Peronist Argentina will never be known, but it is frequently observed that problems multiplied after her death.[33]

The career of Juan Perón was less spectacular, more conventional, but nonetheless well outside the established Argentine political patterns. The son of a small landowner, Juan Perón distinguished himself at school and later at the National Military Academy. His interest in military strategy, politics, and history developed when he was very young. So did his nationalism. From an early age Juan Perón was attractive, articulate, and very handsome. His considerable personal charm and force were widely commented upon, and his rise in the military establishment was steady though not spectacular. Assignments in Chile, Italy, and at the army and then the naval war colleges broadened his perspectives and sharpened his skills. Perón entered politics through the *Grupo* that toppled the conservative and ineffectual government of President Castillo in 1943.

Perón's nationalism and his frank admiration for Mussolini were shared by his GOU colleagues. But his early interest in and concentration on Buenos Aires' urban workers distinguished him from their

[33] Blanksten, *Perón's Argentina*, pp. 87–110, provides an especially colorful description of Eva Perón's career.

more conventional ruling-class orientations. At his own request, Perón was appointed head of the Department of Labor in October 1943. His special relationship with workers, unions, and union leaders began at that time. Ramón Prieto and others—Peronists and non-Peronists alike—assert that Perón's early power rested on a united front of many interests and that only later, in defeat, was this base restricted to the workers.[34] It is true that at his height Perón enjoyed the support of the dominant portion of the military establishment, the Church, indigenous industrialists, and much of the middle class, but it is also true that at various critical junctures it was Argentina's workers who provided Perón the transfusion of strength necessary to save his political life. The symbiotic relation between Perón and Argentina's workers was based on reciprocal needs and reciprocal services. Argentina's workers needed a friend in power who could articulate their interests and secure their welfare. They needed stronger unions and increased power to bargain collectively. Perón needed a mass following and an organizational base. He increased the bargaining powers of friendly unions, encouraged recruitment of new members, decreed compulsory paid holidays, sponsored new housing projects, and raised wages. For their part, unions and workers restored Perón to power when his fellow officers had him arrested in August 1945, and staunchly supported his electoral campaign for the presidency in 1946. Today Argentina's political problems are exacerbated because her workers continue to support the man who championed their cause two decades earlier.

Several histories, brief and otherwise, of the Peronist regime are available. No attempt will be made to duplicate them here. However, several aspects of the regime relevant to the contemporary Peronist movement will be commented on.

The first, the class orientation of the regime, has already been mentioned. In this regard, two aspects of Perón's class politics deserve special attention because of what they reveal about modern Argentine politics and about the Peronist movement: the character of his working-class support, and the nature of his relations to the "oligarchy."

In discussing Perón's working-class support, various commentators have asserted that Perón's support came not from the older, mature,

[34] Ramón Prieto, *El pacto: 8 años de política argentina* (Buenos Aires: Editorial en Marcha, 1963), pp. 12–13.

largely European industrial working class [35] but from the then recently urbanized internal immigrants, whose transfer from countryside to city left them rootless, alienated, unprotected by intermediate associations, and available for mobilization and manipulation.[36] ✓ The authoritarian characters and preferences attributed to rural Argentines are said to have heightened their susceptibility to Perón.[37] Not all analysts agree about the psychology of Peronists and rural Argentines. Most, however, agree that Perón's mass following was drawn disproportionately from among indigenous Argentines who comprised the lowest portions of the lower classes. After World War I, foreign immigration into Argentina declined drastically, but urbanization continued apace, swelling not only the city of Buenos Aires and the Federal Capital but also the provincial cities.[38] These persons are said to have been of "low cultural and economic level, lacking the technical and social requirements of urban life." [39] A consequence was that the burdens of depression and economic hardship fell especially heavily on these migrants from the rural interior. Although they constituted less than a third of the total population of Buenos Aires, more than two-thirds of all unemployed were found in their ranks. (See Table 2.7.)

It was to these miserable, undereducated, often unemployed Indian and mestizo "barbarians" that Eva and Juan Perón turned for

[35] Among others, Alberto Belloni emphasizes that the traditional workers' parties—socialist and communist—attracted only the foreign-born immigrants of Buenos Aires and were without popular appeal among the newly urbanized native Argentines. See Belloni, *Peronismo y socialismo nacional* (Buenos Aires: Ediciones Coyoacán, 1962), pp. 12–13.

[36] See Germani, *Política y sociedad*, pp. 229–252 passim. Germani's interpretation of mass society has a good deal in common with that of Ortega y Gasset in *Invertebrate Spain* (New York: W. W. Norton, 1937) and *The Revolt of the Masses* (New York: W. W. Norton, 1932), with an added emphasis on the importance of intermediate associations—an emphasis that is also found in, among others, Hannah Arendt, *The Origins of Totalitarianism* (New York: Harcourt, Brace & Company, 1951), and Emil Lederer, *The State of the Masses* (New York: W. W. Norton, 1940), and was tested by William Kornhauser in *The Politics of Mass Society* (New York: Free Press, 1965).

[37] See Torcuato S. di Tella, *El sistema político argentino y la clase obrera* (Buenos Aires: Editorial Universitaria de Buenos Aires, 1964), especially chap. 2, "El tipo de vida rural," pp. 13–16. A. M. Hurtado de Mendoza also relates the characteristic rural mentality to Peronism in Silvio Frondizi et al., *Las izquierdas en el proceso político argentino* (Buenos Aires: Palestra, 1959), p. 78.

[38] Di Tella, *El sistema político argentino*, p. 10.

[39] Ibid.

TABLE 2.7 PERCENTAGE OF UNEMPLOYED IN 1932 BY NATIONAL ORIGIN

	Number	Percentage
Argentina	225,262	67.41
Germany	1,702	0.51
Bolivia	551	0.17
Brazil	1,068	0.32
Czechoslovakia	2,528	0.76
Chile	1,131	0.34
Spain	28,763	8.60
France	915	0.27
Britain	99	0.03
Italy	41,423	12.43
Lithuania	1,133	0.34
Paraguay	1,200	0.36
Peru	62	0.02
Poland	9,514	2.85
Portugal	1,648	0.49
Russia	2,949	0.88
Uruguay	2,961	0.89
Yugoslavia	2,425	0.73
Other	8,663	2.60
	333,997	100.00

Source: Departamento Nacional del Trabajo, *La desocupación en la Argentina, 1932* (Buenos Aires: Talleres Gráficos Compañía Impresora Argentina, 1933), p. 147.

support in their quest for political power. Some believe Perón tricked these indigenous masses with an empty rhetoric of revolution that left them as deprived as he found them. But few deny that Perón led these traditionalist rural workers into the twentieth century, integrating them into Argentine political life as Hipólito Irigoyen had the middle classes. The class base of Perón's mass following lent special interest to his relations with Argentina's traditional ruling class.

According to conventional interpretations of Argentine politics, before and after Irigoyen, domination by the "oligarchy" was complete. "Oligarchy" is a word with both political and economic content, and it is both politically and economically ambiguous. Generally, it is used to refer to a ruling class whose power is ultimately based on the ownership of land. In Argentina the "oligarchy" typically also refers to persons whose fortunes were based on activities related to agriculture and cattle raising, and to the upper levels of the Catholic hierarchy, the upper ranks of the military establishment, and the richest merchants. The "oligarchy" presumably enjoyed the highest social status, the greatest political power, the greatest influence in all sectors of Argentine life.[40] They were, in short, those who got "the most of what there [was] to get."[41] The "oligarchy" was the natural enemy of Eva Perón and her poor, uneducated *descamisados*.[42] It became the symbolic enemy of Juan Perón. In Perón's symbolic universe the "oligarchs" were the "bad guys." It was they who betrayed the nation to foreign economic interests; they who prevented the development of domestic industry; they who ran a government of the few, by the few, for the few. It was they, in short, who stood between Argentina and the realization of her three (Peronist) goals: economic independence, popular sovereignty, and social justice. It is no reflection on Perón's sincerity to note that his enemies were well chosen. They were, and he understood them to be, enemies who won him friends: "All that is needed is to furnish several meters of cord to each *descamisado*," he commented on August 14, 1946, before his election, "and then, we shall see who will hang."[43]

Many commentators on Perón's Argentina have suggested that Perón's opposition to the owners of large estates was more vigorous at the symbolic than at the policy level.[44] Some have suggested that a modus vivendi was worked out between Perón and the landowners, with Perón limiting his attack on them to verbal assaults and buying thereby their acquiescence in his rule. This interpretation implies at least a tacit conspiracy between an individual (Perón) and a class (*estancieros*) to hoodwink another class (workers). It has the weaknesses of all theories that define unorganized collectivities as actors in the political process. It also implies that Perón's opposition to the "oligarchy" was more apparent than real. This relationship to the "oligarchy" is clarified by distinguishing between social, political,

[40] For a satisfying attack on the ambiguities of this term and the philosophies of Latin American history built around it, see James L. Payne, "The Oligarchy Muddle," *World Politics*, vol. 20, no. 3 (April 1968), pp. 439–453.

[41] Harold D. Lasswell, *Politics: Who Gets What, When, How*, 1st ed. (New York: Whittlesey House, 1936), p. 3.

[42] José Luis de Imaz's study, *La clase alta de Buenos Aires* (Buenos Aires: Editorial Universidad de Buenos Aires, 1962), pp. 52–55, reveals that even today the "oligarchs" do not believe that Perón's *cabecitas negras* could make it to the upper ranks of the Argentine social ladder. But they do conceive that the contemporary middle class could rise to these social heights.

[43] Quoted in Pierre Lux-Wurm, *Le Péronisme* (Paris: R. Pichon et R. Durand-Auzias, 1965), p. 114.

[44] Blanksten comments, "Perón has declared himself to be no friend of the 'Oligarchy,' but he has not been willing to call for an immediate and thoroughgoing expropriation of rural landed holdings," in *Perón's Argentina*, p. 251.

and economic influence. Perón attacked the position of the "oligarchy" in the social and political spheres. Their status and their influence over national policy were not only attacked but substantially reduced during the Peronist period; their landholdings were left largely intact. Their portion of the nation's wealth was reduced relatively but not absolutely.

Perón did not reform the structure of landholding. He did diminish the prestige and political influence of landholders. Recent studies demonstrate the awareness of this traditional upper class that they were politically if not economically debilitated.[45] In fact the economic bases of their political ascendancy had already been eroded by the industrialization, urbanization, and commercialization of Argentina.[46] Perón attacked an "oligarchy" whose status and influence exceeded its economic power. He perhaps brought these three into a more realistic relationship.

The notion that Perón's hostility to the landowners was not real because it did not lead to comprehensive land reform and the economic destruction of the landowning class rests on the assumption that the only real class antagonisms are those culminating in total war, an assumption comparable to the view that reform is real only when it is revolutionary; that is, this conception makes reality a function of political preference. Peron's attacks on the *"vendepatria* oligarchy,*"* the rich who would sell out their country's national interests, began with his political career and still are not finished. For him it remained—and remains—the fount of evil; his enemies abroad were friends of the "oligarchy"; his enemies in the Church had "compromised with the oligarchy"; [47] political opposition to him, whatever its motives, "objectively" supported the return of the "oligarchs." Most observers agree that Perón exacerbated class antagonisms, leaving Argentines more divided than he found them.

The second, and related, aspect of the regime that deserves comment concerns the degree and kinds of economic and social changes wrought by Perón. Some observers, such as George Pendle, believe that Perón's aim "was to organize a social and economic revolution that would convert Argentina into a powerful and self-sufficient modern state." [48] Others accuse him of being a "pseudoleftist" agent of

[45] De Imaz, *La clase alta,* p. 55–56.

[46] Pendle, *Argentina,* p. 88.

[47] Prieto, *El pacto,* quotes several of Perón's speeches linking his enemies in the Church with the "ladies of the oligarchy," p. 12.

[48] Pendle, *Argentina,* pp. 103–104.

the status quo, unwilling to make basic, structural changes. It is clear that (1) he repeatedly called for changes in the social, economic, and political aspects of Argentine life; (2) he did not attempt radical overhaul of social, economic, and political structures; and (3) he did inaugurate policies aimed at altering the distribution of wealth and other values. Inflation did not consume all the wage increases granted to the lower-income groups or prevent the expansion of domestic industries. Blanksten estimated that the 1950 wages of the average industrial worker were five times those of 1943 and that the cost of living was three and a half to four times higher. "Thus, Argentine workers probably can buy more with their money now than they could in 1943, but not as much more as the sums in their pockets lead many of them to believe." [49]

Summarizing the impact of Perón's economic policies, Fillol asserts: "Proprietors of industry and commerce obtained the proportionately greatest share of benefits; at least until 1948, real industrial wages also showed a steady upward trend; on the other hand, the agricultural, professional, and real estate groups as well as the bureaucracy saw their real incomes shrink alarmingly." [50]

A large number of Peronist welfare measures eased the hardship and insecurity of workers' lives. A comprehensive system of social security guaranteed old-age income, disability pay, and other benefits. Perón's "new deal" for Argentine workers included paid vacations, sick leave, holidays, minimum wage and maximum hour legislation, child labor laws, and separation pay. Price controls inaugurated in 1944 reinforced wage benefits. Collective bargaining, the right to strike, public housing projects, and slum clearance contributed to the urban workers' status, power, and comfort. A greatly expanded system of free public education through the university level democratized the distribution of skill and enlightenment.

Perón's justicialist philosophy articulated the general principles of a social and economic system that was neither capitalist nor communist but blended limited individualism with limited collectivism. Although justicialism is a jerry-built ideology often said to have been improvised from whole cloth, Perón's system of welfare state, benefits, economic planning, and broad controls were consistent with this "third position" (neither capitalist nor communist) in economic affairs. Revolution was not. Perón did not aim at the radical revolu-

[49] Blanksten, *Perón's Argentina,* pp. 269–270.

[50] Fillol, *Social Factors in Economic Development,* p. 29.

tion of Argentine society and culture; it is not surprising that he did not accomplish it. Between the disjunction of revolution and reaction lies a broad excluded middle ground of limited social change. The changes fathered by Perón fell into this spectrum. His regime was reformist; it left standing, but altered, the pre-Perón economic and social structure.

Third, on the assumption that "any fundamental change in the characteristics and methods of elites" [51] signalizes significant change in the distribution of social power and how it is translated into political power, I shall comment briefly on the social characteristics of the Peronist elite. It is here that some clue may be found as to whether the regime constituted a continuation of the "oligarchy" in demagogic dress or whether it embodied the arrival of new social groups to power. De Imaz's recent and indispensable study of Argentina's ruling class makes clear that Perón's principal aides differed in several significant respects from previous rulers. The new political class that assumed power after the Peronist electoral triumph (1946) "modified the criteria of legitimacy, invoked a new political formula, . . . and established new patterns of recruitment. . . . It did not recognize ascriptive values. . . . Ascent was based exclusively on personal success." [52] De Imaz summarizes the distinctive characteristics of the Peronist elite as follows:

(1) The plutocracy was a relatively new ladder for ascending to power. Individuals of this background had served previous regimes. The novelty this time was that the wealthy group [grupo plutócrata] consisted of industrialists, not exporters or importers.
This group comprised first-generation Argentines, the sons of Spaniards. . . . All had served previously in important industries. . . .

[51] Harold D. Lasswell, *World Politics and Personal Insecurity* (New York: Whittlesey House, 1935), p. 3. In this book and elsewhere Lasswell emphasizes the importance of comparing elites "in terms of social origins, special skills, personal traits, subjective attitudes, and sustaining assets such as symbols, goods, and violence." See, among others, his *Politics: Who* and his "Introduction" in Lasswell and Daniel Lerner, eds., *World Revolutionary Elites: Studies in Coercive Ideological Movements* (Cambridge, Mass.: The M.I.T. Press, 1965), pp. 3–28. A comparable emphasis on the importance of the social and psychological composition of elites is found in, among others, Plato, *Republic*, bks. 8 and 9.

[52] José Luis de Imaz, *Los que mandan*, 5th ed. (Buenos Aires: Editorial Universitaria de Buenos Aires, 1966), pp. 12–13. Kalman H. Silvert's much less detailed analysis of Peronist elite backgrounds is reported in *The Conflict Society: Reaction and Revolution in Latin America*, rev. ed. (New York: American Universities Field Staff, 1966), pp. 95–101. He concludes that Peronist elite composition was not *significantly* different from that of previous elites, but his data are much less detailed and comprehensive than those of de Imaz.

(2) To ascend to political power from a trade union background was something unprecedented. Never before had trade union leaders exercised political functions.

(3) In the previous government the "política de comité" had served to give recognition to some experts. But this time there were party leaders elevated to the highest ranks. . . . These party leaders . . . were all of Radical origin. Quijano, Auschter, Bavio, etc. . . . were ex-Radicals separated from their parties and definitively incorporated into Peronism. But in the Radical movement they had not had positions of first-rate importance but, to the contrary, had operated at the second level of influence and importance.

Thus their political triumph owed less to their personal achievement than to their opportune perception that by joining a new movement they could attain influence. They brought with them traditional techniques and methods of political proselitizing.

(4) The fourth sector consisted of officers recently retired from the armed forces.

This channel of recruitment was not new. . . .

The novelty this time lay in the rank of the officers incorporated into political affairs . . . and, above all, in the fact that the two highest figures —the President of the Republic and the Governor of Buenos Aires—had not achieved the highest levels of a military career.[53]

De Imaz points out several other deviant characteristics of the Peronist elite, including the large number of sons of immigrants, the fact that all but two representatives of the "traditional families" were drawn from the Creole families of the interior, the inclusion of a Jew at the ministerial level, and the presence of persons who had started life as workers.[54]

The Peronist regime expressed and reflected the cumulative social changes of the preceding decades of horizontal and vertical mobility. The movement of semiemployed rural workers into the cities, the rise of industrialists to economic prominence, and the displacement of the Buenos Aires aristocracy as the principal claimants to political power were all reflected in the identity and policies of Peronism.

The fourth aspect of the Peronist regime of particular interest in assessing the future of Peronism and Argentine politics concerns Perón's cultural and economic policies. Perón saw freedom, like private property, as limited by comprehensive social goals. Free speech was good only insofar as it served truth; a free press was good only insofar as it disseminated truth. Specifically, newspapers were prohibited from publishing items held "to (1) be contrary to the general

---

[53] De Imaz, *Los que mandan*, pp. 13–14.

[54] Ibid., pp. 14–15.

interest of the nation or disturbing to public order; (2) undermine
Christian morals or good customs; (3) upset Argentina's relations
with other states; (4) injure government officials; or (5) be untrue." [55]
The problem with such policies is that they require some one or some
institution who will decide what is truth. In Perón's Argentina the
decision makers were Peronists. Thus journalism was "purified" by
the harassment and ultimate closing of most, but not all, opposition
newspapers. A famous Peronist statute made it a crime to bring into
"disrespect" any official of the regime.[56] Enforcement of these and
similar Peronist laws was secured by a selective purge of the judi-
ciary. George Blanksten reports that the number of political prisoners stood at 14,500 in August 1945.[57]

Still, it is necessary to make it clear that Perón did not prohibit or
destroy all opposition. Anti-Peronist newspapers, harassed by news-
print shortages, threats, and occasional arrests, published anti-
Peronist editorials. Radical politicians, harassed by threats and arrests, did continue to criticize the government. In the elections of
1946 and 1951 Perón was opposed. In 1946, before he had consoli-
dated his power, the opposition polled more than a million votes
(1,527,231 for Perón and Quijano; 1,207,155 for the Radical slate).
Arthur Whitaker describes this election as "according to the best
evidence, free and honest." [58] By 1951 the opposition parties were
weaker, debilitated by five years of restrictive legislation. But they
had not been destroyed. Perón hamstrung and limited his opponents
but did not silence all opposition. He did not attempt to achieve full
control of the symbolic environment, but he dominated it through a
combination of censorship, intimidation, and harassment. His treatment of opposition parties was never as repressive as General
Aramburu's treatment of Peronist leaders and organizations less than
a decade later.

There has been continuing discussion of whether Perón's Argentina was or attempted to be totalitarian. It seems to me clear that it

---

[55] Blanksten, *Perón's Argentina*, p. 204.

[56] Disrespect was defined as "anything which offends the dignity of any public
official, whether the statement refers directly to the person or by allusion to him
or the governmental organization of which he forms a part" (Pendle, *Argentina*,
p. 113). Blanksten has an excellent discussion of Perón's policies in this field in
Perón's Argentina, pp. 161–219 passim. See also Lux-Wurm, *Le Péronisme*, especially pp. 126–134.

[57] Blanksten, *Perón's Argentina*, p. 179.

[58] Whitaker, *Argentina*, p. 120.

lacked most of the distinguishing characteristics of totalitarian systems. (1) There was no official ideology that defined man's place and ends in the universe and prescribed a plan for reordering society, culture, and personality. (2) There was no effort to establish total control of the political process, including (a) full control of political socialization and the destruction or "coördination" of all associations, for example, family, church, schools, that influence it; (b) full control of interest groups in the society; (c) full *positive* control of the mass media, including the press, the educational system, and entertainment (not merely to eliminate oppositional material but to communicate the official ideology). (3) There was no single mass party hierarchically organized with a monopoly of political functions in the society. (4) There was not ubiquitous terror.[59]

In addition to lacking these basic characteristics of totalitarian regimes, Peronism lacked certain other qualities sometimes associated with totalitarianism and especially with its fascist variant. It did not attribute mystical values to the nation nor define human ends in relation to them. No charismatic relation existed between follower and leader (though perhaps Eva Perón had charismatic appeal to the *descamisados*).[60] Finally, Germani argues persuasively that the relationship between Perón and his followers was basically rational as opposed to the relationship of European fascist leaders to their followers, which he describes as irrational.[61]

The dominant trends of Perón's Argentina can be illuminated by a brief look at institutional practices in selected areas.[62]

Power   Perón definitely attempted to alter the distribution of political power in Argentina. He undertook to do this in two ways: by increasing the influence of some groups, for example, workers and

[59] Points 1, 3, and 4 are three of five criteria developed by Friedrich to distinguish totalitarian from other societies. See his essay, "The Unique Character of Totalitarian Society," in Carl J. Friedrich, ed., *Totalitarianism* (New York: Grosset & Dunlap, 1964).

[60] Silvert argues that Peronism was not "effectively totalitarian" and specifically denies that a charismatic relation existed between leader and followers in "The Costs of Anti-Nationalism: Argentina" in Kalman H. Silvert, ed., *Expectant Peoples: Nationalism and Development* (New York: Vintage Books, 1967), pp. 362–366 passim.

[61] Germani, *Política y sociedad*, pp. 245–252 passim.

[62] The categories utilized are those of Lasswell's value-institutional analysis, which are discussed by him in a number of his works and recently explicated in Lasswell and Lerner, *World Revolutionary Elites*, pp. 3–28. There, Lasswell suggests eight valued outcomes and institutions, two of which I have not utilized.

women, who previously had had no voice in the political process, and by decreasing the influence of some groups who had previously exercised political influence based on a traditional relationship of their social or economic role to political power. His revision of institutional practices relevant to the distribution of power had the effect of distributing political power somewhat more evenly throughout the society.

All constitutions, no matter how centralized, require intermediate offices whose incumbents enjoy limited power over middle- and lower-range decisions. In traditional systems, incumbents of these middle- and lower-level roles are determined by ascription. Cautiously and gingerly, Perón attempted to prevent the translation of traditional social and economic power into political power. For traditional requirements for office he sought to substitute new ideological and personal requirements, that is, he attempted to alter the criteria by which incumbents for political roles were chosen as well as the incumbents themselves. The new criteria emphasized personal and political services to the Peronist regime. Political loyalty became a factor that influenced the general distribution of power in society.

Both these changes, the increased number permitted to share power and the changed criteria for occupying political roles, had the effect of reducing the relative power of traditional ruling groups. At no time, however, did Perón attain a monopoly of power in Argentina. There is ample evidence to demonstrate that persons outside the government retained influence in decision processes. The withdrawal of Eva Perón's candidacy for the vice-presidency is a famous datum concerning the autonomous power of some military leaders, their active participation in decision making, and the continuing importance of the military establishment as a source rather than an instrument of political power.

Ecclesiastical opposition to Perón's legislation on sex, marriage, and family similarly identified the Church as a power base independent of the government, and priests as contenders for influence on the decisions of the government. In the elections of 1946 and 1951 the Radicals polled 43 and 32 percent, respectively, of the total vote. In short, while various limited efforts were made to stifle vocal opponents during the Perón rule, these efforts by no means eliminated competition for power. There remained plural claimants of power and plural bases for such claims. Perón did not eliminate other contenders for power; he manipulated them. And when anger, pride, and error undermined his manipulative skills, he fell. Perón's most

TABLE 2.8   EDUCATION AND AGE: PERCENTAGE OF ALL RE-
SPONDENTS WITH AT LEAST A PRIMARY EDUCATION

Age	Percentage
18–24	67
25–29	56
30–39	36
40–49	26
50 or more	24

important influence on the sources of power was his role in the
emergence of organized labor as a major factor in Argentine political
life.

· *Enlightenment*   The egalitarian tendencies of the regime were especially clear in regard to enlightenment outcomes. Perón launched
a massive effort to build schools and get Argentine children into
them; 401 new primary schools were opened in 1951 alone.[63] Public
schools at all levels were declared free and open to every qualified
Argentine. The effect of abolishing all tuition at institutions of
higher education was reflected in university enrollment figures. At
the University of Buenos Aires, enrollment increased from 16,631
in 1940 to 64,425 in 1953.[64] Perón boasted in 1951, "The Argentine
republic at the present time has no illiterate children." [65] The democ-
ratization of enlightenment during the Peronist period is reflected
in the sharply different educational experiences of different age
groups in the sample (see Table 2.8). These make clear that the trend
toward wider education began before Perón but was sharply acceler-
ated after Perón took power. At the same time enlightenment outcomes were affected by regulations submitting schools and universities to new political controls. Government approval of textbooks was
required, and expression of oppositionist statements was prohibited.

In sum, opportunities for acquiring enlightenment were more
evenly distributed throughout the society. Political factors became
relevant to the content of available information. The freedom of
teachers and upper-level students was diminished but not destroyed.

Wealth   The effort to alter the distribution of wealth in society
has already been discussed. Perón aimed at increasing aggregate income through industrial development and at redistributing available

[63] Blanksten, *Perón's Argentina*, p. 198.

[64] Pendle, *Argentina*, p. 117.

[65] Blanksten, *Perón's Argentina*, p. 198.

wealth. He increased the relative share of the national wealth available to low-income groups through legislation directly granting increased financial benefits, through strengthening the organization and legal position of trade unions, and through broadening access to skilled trades and professions. Less effort was made to redistribute income through punitive measures. All observers agree that some redistribution of wealth did take place during the Peronist era.

The economic chaos that ultimately resulted from mismanagement and the end of Argentina's World War II boom ultimately resulted in a reduction of the total national wealth.

Well-being   The well-being of lower-income groups was clearly increased during the Peronist period. Legislation prohibiting child labor and regulating the conditions of employment of women and youth obviously enhanced the physical safety and welfare of these groups. The establishment, principally through the María Eva Duarte de Perón Foundation, of new public clinics and hospitals made modern medical care available to lower-income groups who had not before enjoyed it. Increased leisure available to workers—paid vacations and holidays—constituted an increment to their physical well-being as well as general enjoyment of life.

Only political opponents, actual and suspected, suffered diminished well-being during the Peronist regime. It cannot be doubted that the health and safety of several thousand political prisoners in the jails of Perón's Argentina were reduced.[66] Political behavior also became one of the determinants of well-being in Perón's Argentina.

Respect   We have already commented on the status revolution attempted by the Peróns. The traditional social leaders were excoriated repeatedly and publicly. Contempt was directed to the gentlemen of the "oligarchy" (the *vendepatria*) who had repeatedly sold out the national interest for quick profit from foreigners; obloquy was heaped on the ladies of the "oligarchy" for parasitic snobbery. Professions associated with the "oligarchy"—landowning and exporting—suffered unaccustomed disrespect. Conversely, industrialists and workers received unprecedented attention and deference from spokesmen for the new regime. Representatives of both groups were included among the highest elite.

The greatest prestige was programmed for the president and his

---

[66] See Blanksten, *Perón's Argentina*, pp. 179–185, for a description of prisoner treatment.

wife, who were guaranteed against disrespectful treatment by law. Politics became a factor relevant to the distribution of deference.

Rectitude   From the outset, Perón was prepared to reinforce the influence of ecclesiastical institutions in the society. His early promise of religious instruction in public schools won him important support in the Church.

Perón never attempted to define ultimate values for the society. To the contrary, he repeatedly asserted the commitment of the regime to Christian and specifically to Catholic norms. Nonetheless, problems with the Church did eventually arise through a jurisdictional dispute. When Perón attempted to revise the legal status of illegitimate children (and equalize their legal rights), key Church officials believed he was encroaching on their sphere and attempting to undermine canons of rectitude. The quarrel between Perón and the Church grew from mutual frustration of their mutual demands: the Church's demand to have the government enforce its ethical and religious positions and the government's desire to have the Church sanctify its policies. The conflict first occurred when the egalitarian principles of the regime conflicted with the Church's interest in having the political hierarchy enforce its prescriptions.

Summary   The clear tendency of the redistribution of values carried out in Perón's Argentina was to diminish the number and importance of ascriptive roles and to increase the number and importance of roles to be filled on the basis of individual achievement. If the transition from traditional to modern society includes the transition from ascriptive to achievement-based role systems, then significant strides toward a more modern social system were taken during the Peronist period.

All adults were admitted as formal participants in the decision-making process, but the opportunities for mass participation were decreased, compared to the earlier democratic interval. The portion of society formally eligible to participate in the political system was increased at the same time that the effective influence of the system over society was also increased. Perhaps more important, labor unions emerged as a power base of first-rate importance, and union leaders took their place alongside leaders of the military establishment, Church, and political parties as influential counters in power calculations. A traditional oligarchy was reduced in privilege and power; a new oligarchy arose, whose power derived more from its skills than from inherited status and whose principles, if more egalitarian, were assuredly less libertarian.

Comment   Argentine political experience before 1955 does not seem to support the hypothesis that between 1810 and 1955 Argentina was necessarily on the road to the development of democratic institutions. The tendency to regard political development as a march of progress toward democracy is still strong in the literature of political science,[67] as is the related tendency to prefer unilinear models of development.[68] It is easier to assume progress toward democracy than to produce the evidence. By 1955 the Argentine political system had evolved toward (1) more complete integration of territorially based subsystems into a single system; (2) greater role specificity, including the development of political structures not dependent on prior structures; and (3) political styles and institutions providing for greater direct participation of more persons in the political system. But participation, we have learned, is compatible with totalitarian as well as with democratic systems.[69] It is not participation in the political system but participation in the decision process through which rulers are chosen and held responsible that defines democratic systems.[70]

Still, there is substantial evidence of the continuing existence of strong pressures in Argentine society for popular government. Military coups then as now were often followed by announcements that elections would be forthcoming. Participation in political life was

[67] Apter, *Politics of Modernization,* is an example.

[68] There is a general tendency to regard any amelioration of the human condition as progress toward democracy. An example of this tendency in its purest form is found in Russell H. Fitzgibbon, "Measuring Democratic Change in Latin America," where he comments: "It seemed desirable, at any rate, to select as large a number of indices as could be found which presumptively contributed to improvement of the human situation in Latin America, on the assumption that that in turn would be conducive to democratic development." He adds: "The relationship here is indirect and tenuous, but perhaps as good as can be devised, granted the reliance on objective data only." See *Journal of Politics,* vol. 29, no. 1 (February 1967), p. 160.

[69] See Germani, *Política y sociedad,* for an interesting, expanded discussion of mass systems, with special application to Argentina.

[70] There is not yet adequate evidence to support an assumption, or even a presumption, that participatory systems eventually evolve into democratic systems. It is not impossible that some may eventually do so, but until now not one single nondemocratic participatory system has so evolved—without the intervention of war and occupation. Conversely, no existing democratic government has developed out of a system that provided mass integration and participation without political power.

continually broadened, and popular sovereignty was established as one principle of legitimacy. A democratic regime was toppled, but multiple democratic institutional practices and symbols remained. Egalitarian values were institutionalized. Libertarian values were never fully lost, never fully embodied in institutional practices.

Alongside the growth of the institutional practices prerequisite to modern democratic government, incompatible practices also flourished. Military participation in politics became increasingly frequent after 1900,[71] a date that coincided not only with the emergence of new demands from the middle sector but also with the weakening of the traditional authority structure and the establishment of a professional national army.[72] Repetition made military intervention a tradition. And it is a tradition that, whatever its consequence for policy, is clearly incompatible with constitutional democracy.

The overthrow of Perón not only signified an end to the rule of a popular tyrant but also constituted one more military intervention in national political life. So also the rise of Perón did not simply signify the elevation of one more modern Caesar to the presidency but the continuation of a tradition of hybrid government combining democratic and autocratic elements. To be sure, the Peronist mix differed from that of the pre-1916 "oligarchs." But it shared with them democratic forms and a range of democratic and autocratic practices. By 1955 Argentina had experienced several decades of near anarchy, more than half a century of modified autocracy or oligarchy, and less than two decades of constitutional democratic rule.

Given Argentine experience, it would have been extraordinary in 1955 if Argentine poltical culture had been characterized by attitudes, opinions, and, especially, expectations typical of developed democracies. It would have been most surprising if, just after the downfall of Perón, broadly aggregative democratic parties had emerged capable of organizing and channeling opinion, recruiting leaders, competing in elections, and accepting the results. It would

[71] For a recent discussion of the politization of the military, see Liisa North, *Civil-Military Relations in Argentina, Chile, and Peru* (Berkeley: University of California, Institute of International Studies, 1966). See also Davis B. Bobrow, "Soldiers and the Nation-State," *Annals of the American Academy of Social and Political Science*, vol. 358 (March 1965), pp. 65–76.

[72] There can be no national army until a nation has passed the earliest stages of development; however, an army is characteristically an early translation of nationhood from an idea to an institutional structure. It is one of the very first national institutions and for this reason alone is, in new nations, one of the few competitors for power at the level of the nation-state.

have been very surprising if Argentines had expected that political decisions should, could, and would be made by majorities whose preferences would be peaceably expressed through honest institutions and implemented by officials responsive as well as responsible to the people. It would have been very surprising if military officers, politicized by several decades of participation in the distribution of values in the society, should have promptly eliminated themselves from the political arena. It would have been surprising indeed if, after 150 years of experience with a different tradition, Argentina should have emerged after the fall of Perón a full-blown, Anglo-Saxon democracy.

3

The Competition for Political Power, 1955-1965

The most general way to think of social process is as "people" who are "interacting" with one another and with their "resource environment." The people may be classified as "individuals" or "collectivities"; and the collectivities are "organized" and "unorganized." To interact is to affect others and, in turn, to be affected.

Lasswell and Lerner, *World Revolutionary Elites*

This chapter deals with some aspects of the Argentine political system from 1955 to 1966, from the fall of Perón to the ascent of Onganía. During these years the legal context of the competition for power in Argentina differed from that of the preceding and succeeding regimes. The equilibrium on which Perón's power depended was destroyed when his opponents in the armed services combined with those in the Church and the opposition parties and presented themselves as the standard-bearers of tradition, democracy, and Christianity. It is customary to say that after Perón fell Argentina enjoyed a return to democratic politics. This is formally true, but it is also a characterization that distorts the realities of Argentine political life both before and after Perón.

During this decade (1955–1965) Argentina had six chief executives, not one of whom succeeded another constitutionally. Describing the system of interactions in Argentina that determined who ruled and to what ends taxes intellectual and semantic habits. The particular and persistent combination of democratic and autocratic characteristics that comprised the system lies well outside conventional taxonomies. It was not simply an unstable democratic system in which democratic processes worked erratically and were punctuated by periodic incursions from antidemocratic forces; neither was it simply an autocracy. It was and is a system in which are blended characteristics associated with modern and premodern, democratic and oligarchic, constitutional and arbitrary regimes. Fortunately, the habit of

discussing Argentina and other Latin systems simply as feeble, beleaguered versions of European or North American democracies is
giving way to more accurate descriptions that take account of the
durable elements of the systems.[1]

A functional description of the Argentine system from 1955–1965
must take account of the following enduring characteristics (which
were also found in the years preceding and following this democratic
interval):

1. *The system was competitive.* No man or party held power for
as long as four years.[2] A clear implication of this continuing competition is that no one group possessed sufficient power to preempt control of the machinery and policies of government.[3]

2. *The competitors for power over the personnel and policies of
government comprised diverse types of actors with diverse goals,
structures, clienteles, and modes of behavior.*[4] Almond and Coleman
have described as a defining characteristic of modern political systems the requirement that governmental and political functions be
performed by specifically political structures, adding that, in such

[1] Merle Kling's characterization of political instability in Latin America applies
well to Argentina during the period: "(1) it is chronic; (2) it frequently is accompanied by limited violence; (3) it produces no basic shifts in economic, social, or
political policies"; see his essay, "Toward a Theory of Power and Political Instability in Latin America," in John D. Martz, ed., *The Dynamics of Change in
Latin American Politics* (Englewood Cliffs, N.J.: Prentice-Hall, 1965), p. 130.
Kalman H. Silvert, in *The Conflict Society: Reaction and Revolution in Latin
America*, rev. ed. (New York: American Universities Field Staff, 1966), also empha-
sizes the persistent, predictable, durable character of political instability in Latin
America. So do Charles W. Anderson, *Politics and Economic Change in Latin
America* (Princeton, N.J.: D. Van Nostrand Company, 1967), and James Payne,
Labor and Conflict in Peru (New Haven: Yale University Press, 1965) and *Pat-
terns of Conflict in Colombia* (New Haven: Yale University Press, 1968).

[2] See Anderson, *Politics and Economic Change*, especially pp. 87–138 passim,
for a suggestive and realistic account of Latin American political systems that has
much in common with the interpretation advanced here.

[3] And in the twentieth century no man or party has held power consecutively
for as long as either the Democratic party in the United States or the Conservative
party in the United Kingdom.

[4] In a recent discussion of the propinquity for utilizing direct action to determine policy in Argentina, it was pointed out that "In the United States one can
exert *influence* [emphasis added] through wealth, prestige, 'connections,' riots,
etc., but to *determine* policy one must be able to determine who the policy-makers
shall be, and here only one currency serves: votes. . . . In Argentina, however,
military action . . . or mass demonstrations and strikes . . . can determine
policy as effectively as votes." See Eldon Kenworthy, "Argentina: The Politics of
Late Industrialization," *Foreign Affairs*, vol. 45, no. 3 (April 1967), p. 474.

systems "armies and religious organizations are nonparticipant in the performance of governmental and political functions." [5] By this criterion the Argentine system was and is definitely not modern.

3. *Competition took place in a variety of arenas.* Despite legal arrangements, competition was not limited to the arenas typical of constitutional democracies. The principal effect of the legal arrangements on the arenas of struggle was to add an electoral arena, not to eliminate those previously existing.

4. *Competition among all actors continued despite formal restrictions.* All competitors continued to exist and to be directly involved in the effort to influence the policies and personnel of government despite the formal restrictions on classes of actors and modes of competition.

5. *The involvement of multiple classes of actors in the competition for political power affected the character of competition in all arenas.* Party leaders behave differently in the legislature or an election campaign if they anticipate possible military intervention; military leaders behave differently if they anticipate the possibility of a general strike; and so forth.

6. *The style of politics was broadly affected by the variety of actors, arenas, instrumentalities, and modes of behavior.* Party behavior in legislatures was sometimes characterized by intransigent direct action more typical of street clashes or military ultimatums. Military interventions sometimes involved prior consultation and efforts at conciliation of other functional groups more characteristic of democratic politics.

Competitors

In Argentina the competitors for political power (that is, for influence over the personnel and policies of government) in the 1955–1965 period comprised various types of actors, each with distinctive goals, structures, clienteles, and modes of behavior. They included conventional political parties that sought power in the electoral arena and through coalitions with other actors; labor unions that

[5] Gabriel A. Almond and James S. Coleman, *The Politics of the Developing Areas* (Princeton: Princeton University Press, 1960), p. 560. Note that these criteria would also eliminate France from the category of modern nations, since the army indubitably played a key role in the events of 1958 as well as in policy making in the international field prior to that time. Perhaps we should revise our conception of political modernity.

sought power through electoral participation, political strikes, conventional lobbying, and, occasionally, violent action; movement-type parties that sought power through the electoral arena, street demonstrations, terrorist and quasi-terrorist actions; military leaders who sought power through such diverse means as civil war, coup d'etat, negotiation, and electoral success; and clerics, students, capitalists, landowners, and other functional groups who sought power through interpersonal and intergroup negotiation, direct action, electoral activity, and other means.

An important characteristic of Argentine political interaction is that the various types of competitors confronted one another directly in various arenas. Demands were not mediated through any single class of competitors. Moreover, the instruments through which these competitors sought to achieve influence were as various as their consequent preferred modes of action: mass support legally expressed, mass support illegally expressed, terrorism, economic sanctions, threats of violence, nationalism, strikes, deprivation of rectitude, and deference were all instruments utilized in the competition for power.

The number and diversity of competitors from 1955 to 1965 were greater than during Argentina's earlier experience with democracy. One important new type of competitor (labor leaders) and one important new power base (the labor unions) reached full development during Perón's tenure. Also, the relative strength of other actors had been altered since the fall of Irigoyen. Industrialists had increased in number, wealth, and prestige; landowners had declined in relative influence and importance. The number of those whom income or occupation defined into the middle class was greater. The old parties of the left had been debilitated by the rise of Peronist organizations that enjoyed massive support of the "new" working class. The range, composition, strengths, and goals of the actors determined the patterns of political interaction. These, in turn, affected the strategies of the actors.

A brief description of the principal competitors during the most recent decade of formal democracy follows.

Conventional Political Parties In Argentina as elsewhere, conventional parties aimed at gaining political power through votes cast in competitive elections and at exercising it through majoritarian legislative procedures. They accepted popular sovereignty, expressed in competitive elections, as the basis of legitimate power.[6]

---

[6] Lasswell and Kaplan have characterized a party as "a group formulating comprehensive issues and submitting candidates in elections," and, further, as

During the period of democratic government, campaigning and organizing were the chief methods by which parties competed for power. During this period conventional parties eschewed violence and valued legality. But in style the conventional Argentine parties remained messianic. They tended to make sweeping claims for their unique moral mission and superiority, and to present themselves as saviors and renovators rather than as representatives. Dozens of such parties existed from 1955 to 1965 and participated in elections. Two hundred and twenty-two parties, most of them conventional, were registered with the Ministry of Interior in 1965, but few of these were national and few had a mass following; only two had any chance of winning a national election. In fact, Argentina has always had one, two, or occasionally three dominant parties. During the years 1955–1965, the conventional parties that were national in character included the Socialists, the Christian Democrats, the Conservatives, and the two chief Radical parties—Unión Cívica Radical Intransigente (UCRI) and Unión Cívica Radical del Pueblo (UCRP, or Popular Radicals). Of these the most important were the Radical parties: the UCRP and the UCRI, whose life histories provide an interesting example of Argentine party development.

The Radical party, whose growth paralleled that of the middle class, had dominated *electoral* politics in Argentina since 1912. While most Argentine parties were provincial in character or very limited in appeal, the Radicals were able to poll over 30 percent of the votes in every election in which they participated. In fact, before Perón welcomed into the electorate Argentina's lowest classes, the Radical party was Argentina's only national party with a broad mass base. But if the extent and durability of Radical support were unique, the chronic institutional weakness that afflicted it was characteristic of other political parties. Like cells, Radical parties multiplied by division. In and out of power, in victory and defeat, in republics and autocracies, before, during, and after Perón, Radical parties split, and split, and split.[7] But—and this is surely significant

---

being "an internal power group whose status has been formalized—it functions as a part of the regime." See Harold D. Lasswell and Abraham Kaplan, *Power and Society: A Framework for Political Inquiry* (New Haven: Yale University Press, 1950), pp. 169, 170.

[7] The experiences of the lean years of Conservative and Peronist rule demonstrate conclusively the ineffectiveness of a *cure d'opposition* for Radical factionalism. In the 1928 presidential elections some seven Radical parties participated. Between 1931 and Perón's rise, leadership quarrels again created factions within factions. Legalistas, Mayoritarios, FORJA, UCR Concurrencista, UCR Unificada, Junta Reorganizadora Nacional, Bloque Oposites, and Junta de Reafirmación Ra-

—these splits apparently had little effect on the Radical identifications of masses of voters.

Electoral prospects could hardly have looked better for the Radicals than in 1956, and Arturo Frondizi, Intransigent leader, moved quickly to secure the Radical presidential nomination and a strong organizational base. Perhaps he moved too quickly. Ricardo Balbín and other leaders of the Nucleo Unidad united with several minor factions to form a new Radical party distinct from Frondizi's. Once again, Radicals split on the rock of personal rivalries. The politics of personal interest divided men largely united on principles of post-Perón policies. The result was a schism that persisted throughout the decade of formal democracy.

After complex wrangles in and out of court, Balbín's Unionists finally took the name Unión Cívica Radical del Pueblo, and the Frondizistas called themselves Unión Cívica Radical Intransigente.

UCRI's history is another instructive example of Argentine party development. Almost immediately after winning the March 1962 elections, two groups of UCRI deputies defected and created two new splinter groups in the legislative chamber. Dissension continued. Finally, on the eve of the 1963 elections, the UCRI literally fell to pieces with one major part backing the National and Popular Front (FNP, a coalition of UCRI, Unión Popular, and four minor parties), another part supporting Oscar Alende as the UCRI standard-bearer, and the various factions battling in the court for control of the party and its name. Before the 1965 elections the UCRI split again, with electoral results that may well have been fatal. Obviously, this factionalism debilitated Radicalism. But it is important to be clear that *its adverse effects did not include significant loss of popular support* for Radicalism generally. Popular identification with a Radical tendency, or a Radical perspective, has shown impressive stability. This relative stability of identifications and instability of organizations demonstrated here is a theme to which I shall return.

Between 1955 and 1965 all major Argentine parties were loosely organized. Links between followers and parties were loose and

---

dical were but the most important Radical factions of the post-1930–pre-Perón years. Still, Radicals managed to win congressional elections in 1937 and 1940. After Perón's rise the process continued with new splits stimulated by Perón's inroads into Radical leadership and supporters. Four distinct factions were represented at the First National Radical Convention after Perón's fall, two of which —the Nucleo Unidad and the Movimiento de Intransigencia Renovación (MIR) —had been the major Radical factions since 1945.

informal; so were links between different units of the same party. Party names varied from province to province to an extent that makes it exceedingly difficult to calculate the national vote or reliably relate provincial party strength to the national scene. All Ministry of Interior election statistics are reported for the provincial level.

Both the birth and the death rates of parties were high. In every election there were new groups bearing new names, as well as old groups under new names. Of the more than thirty parties listed by the Ministry of Interior as having received more than one percent of the vote in Buenos Aires in elections from 1957 to 1965, only five parties appeared in all six elections,[8] and one of these—the UCRI— was the name of a quite different organization in 1965 than in 1958.

New parties sometimes succeeded in getting a substantial number of votes, especially in Buenos Aires. The UCRI was the most successful surge party, but the entirely new UDELPA (Unión del Pueblo Argentino) appeared as a personal vehicle of General Aramburu in 1963 and ran third in a multiparty field with 7.5 percent of the vote. In the same election the Federación Nacional de Partidos del Centro (FNPC, a coalition of Conservative parties) appeared for the first time and won 5.2 percent of the popular vote. The Movimiento Integración y Desarrollo Nacional (MIN) first appeared on the ballot in 1965 and won 6.2 percent of the national vote.

Conventional democratic parties were influenced by their competitors and by the context of their activities. The necessity of responding to the initiatives of competitors operating outside the electoral arena was especially important. Actual and anticipated threats from military leaders repeatedly influenced parties' policies and personnel. Terrorist activities by Tacuara, splinter Peronist groups, Castroites, and others stimulated repressions. Strikes and threats of strikes affected economic decisions. To survive in a political ambiance where conspiracy, violence, and fraud exist alongside competitive campaigns and elections requires that party leaders possess special skills and special talents. Among the most important of these is the ability to negotiate agreements with competitors outside one's own party. President Frondizi won election through his skill in negotiating for Peronist electoral support. To have held off a coup for as long as he did required successfully juggling the

---

[8] UCRP, UCRI, Christian Democrats, Demócrata Progresista, and Partido del Pueblo contested all elections under a uniform name. One or more Peronist parties would have contested all these elections had they been permitted to do so.

often contradictory demands of military groups. In fact, it sometimes appeared that Argentine party leaders were more skilled at compromising differences outside than inside their parties.

Unconventional or Movement-Type Parties Unconventional parties share some but not all the characteristics of traditional parties. They may or may not be legal, that is, part of the structure of the official regime. Their goals are often more revolutionary or comprehensive. The relationship between followers and leaders may be loose or highly structured. It is methods and procedural commitments that distinguish movements from conventional parties. Unconventional parties might welcome achieving power through election but are prepared to engage in various forms of direct action, including strikes, riots, demonstrations, terrorism, and sabotage. Parties of this type are without procedural inhibitions; legitimacy is conceived as unrelated to official procedures. They seek power through terrorism, demonstration, revolution, or *golpe de estado* (coup d'etat). In Argentina, Castroites and such paramilitary rightists as the Tacuara group were (and are) examples. So has been the Peronist movement in some, if not all, of its many organizational embodiments.

The Peronist movement had no reliable commitment to legality, in part, perhaps, because laws regulating the movement were so discriminatory and volatile. Its goals were as ambiguous as those of Perón himself, but there is good reason to believe they did not (and do not) include the determination to preside through majority rule over a constitutional democracy. The movement was not identical with a political party, but various political parties were part of the movement. From 1955 to 1965 it consisted of four main parts: the Peronist trade unions, which are generally believed to have been, and to be, the organizational backbone of the movement; the Unión Popular, which came closest to being the official party; the neo-Peronist parties of the provinces; and the unorganized individuals who identified their electoral preferences with Peronist politics.[9] Some of the provincial neo-Peronist parties appeared to be almost indistinguishable from conventional parties.

Peronist groups employed direct action less frequently in the later years, but during the decade various Peronist factions had repeated

[9] For a discussion of Peronist organization, see Peter Ranis, *"Peronismo* Without Perón, Ten Years after the Fall (1955–1965),"* Journal of Inter-American Studies,* vol. 8, no. 1 (January 1966), pp. 112–128.

recourse to violence. Although it is not easy to distinguish between what Peronist groups have done and what they have been accused of, it seems clear that after 1955 many leaders of the movement were prepared to compete for influence over the personnel and policies of government in various arenas and through such diverse instruments as votes, electoral boycotts, strikes, sabotage, and random acts of terrorism.

The size, tactical flexibility, and resources of the Peronist movement enabled it to influence outcomes in several arenas from 1955 to 1965. A brief look at the movement will illustrate the advantages of this flexibility in the Argentine system.

The Peronist Movement   When Perón took refuge on a Paraguayan gunboat he left behind three tremendously important resources: a powerful Peronist-controlled labor movement, a national political party, and millions of followers who identified their interests with his leadership. The history of the following decade can be written as an account of the efforts of assorted successive opposition leaders to deprive the Peronist movement of these assets and of the efforts of Peronist leaders to use these resources to gain maximum possible influence over the personnel and policies of government.

Government efforts to disarm the Peronists took account of their diverse strengths and capabilities. Efforts to dismantle Peronist organizational strength first aimed at depriving the movement of the capacity to disrupt the economy and control the streets. Another offensive was mounted to prevent Peronist mass support from being translated into victory in the electoral arena. Laws drafted prior to the election of the 1957 constituent assembly aimed with precision at barring Peronist participation. The same statute that guaranteed the free development of political groups banned "totalitarian" parties (whose description bore a not remarkable resemblance to any Peronist organizations) and, in addition, prohibited parties from naming themselves for individuals.[10]

The movement was neither passive nor helpless against the various official offensives. Against each attack, a counterattack was made. Often, where possible or feasible, Peronists struck back violently with acts of rebellion, of sabotage designed to disrupt the public order. Terrorist attacks, presumed to be the work of Peronist "resistance commandos," were especially frequent in the Lonardi-Aram-

---

[10] The use of restrictive legislation to hamstring Peronist electoral participation continued throughout the decade and is described later in this chapter.

buru period and again after Frondizi had "betrayed" the Peronist electors.

Strikes were a major weapon in the Peronist arsenal, and, in 1957 as in the Frondizi period, general strikes, regional strikes, and industry-wide strikes were repeatedly used to protest political and economic grievances or to scuttle a government policy. Somehow General Aramburu's massive offensive against Peronist labor leaders failed, and Peronist control of the "sixty-two unions" [11] survived repeated purges, arrests, occupations, and harassment. Argentina's labor movement remained a resource with which the movement could compete in the industrial arena.

Another arena became available to the Peronists when General Aramburu announced that elections would be held to choose a constituent assembly. It was clear that no Peronist party would be permitted to contest the elections. But at a meeting in Caracas, Venezuela, the Peronist leaders decided to recommend that Peronists make their presence felt in the electoral arena by casting blank ballots.

The more than two million blank ballots cast in the first election dramatized the importance of Perón's mass following for democratic politics in Argentina. Blank ballots outnumbered those cast for any political party. The moral was not lost on non-Peronist politicians. Peronist support could ensure a candidate's victory; free Peronist participation could restore Juan Perón to office. The electoral system prohibited the latter. Dr. Arturo Frondizi, the leader of the UCRI, began his efforts to effect the former. No aspect of modern Argentine history is more controversial than the relationship between the Peronist and UCRI leaderships preceding the elections of 1962. Peronist leaders assert that a deal was made in which Perón agreed to recommend Peronist support for Frondizi in return for which Frondizi, as president, would revoke the statutes barring Peronist participation in Argentine political life.[12]

[11] The sixty-two unions, "Bloc 62," are the Peronist-controlled labor unions in the CGT (Confederación General del Trabajo).

[12] John William Cooke has been identified as Perón's representative, and Rogelio Frigerio as Frondizi's. Peronists purportedly established a tactical command whose function was to communicate to rank-and-file Peronists the decision to support Frondizi's candidacy. The best accounts of this "pact" whose existence has been so vigorously denied but which external evidence strongly supports is found in Ramón Prieto, *El pacto: 8 años de política argentina* (Buenos Aires: Editorial en Marcha, 1963), and Ricardo C. Guardo, *Horas difíciles: septiembre 1955–62* (Buenos Aires: Ediciones Ricardo C. Guardo, 1963).

Frondizi describes *el pacto* as a Peronist fantasy and denies that the agreement ever took place. Certain facts are clear in this disputed episode. The Peronist leadership did announce Perón's desire to have his followers support Frondizi. Frondizi did receive the votes of large numbers of Peronists and was elected. Peronists did feel betrayed by Frondizi's continuation of anti-Peronist legislation. Perhaps most important, the UCRI and Frondizi did win when millions of Peronists voted for him in 1958, and the UCRI did lose elections (in the provinces) after Frondizi was denounced by leaders of the Peronist movement. Peronist power in the electoral arena had been clearly demonstrated. Succeeding events were to prove that it was as durable as it was broad.

Despite the various efforts to eliminate or minimize their influence on elections, Peronist supporters were a major factor in every election after the downfall of Perón, through blank votes that underscored the limits of choice available to Argentine voters, through voting for the various neo-Peronist parties that were sometimes permitted to contest elections, or, once, by bestowing their massive support on another party's candidate at the request of their leader. No electoral system, party registration system, nor appeal by non-Peronist leaders prevented the Peronists' votes from being a major factor in the Argentine electoral arena.

The tendency to factionalism, so clear in the history of Argentine Radicalism, infected the Peronist movement. Soon after his departure, Perón's leadership was threatened from various sources. The electoral possibilities of Peronism without Perón spurred the development of schismatic neo-Peronist parties. Despite the determined efforts of Perón and his representatives to discourage their development, neo-Peronist parties continued to proliferate before the March 1962 elections,[13] in which Peronists were permitted to stand as candidates in neo-Peronist parties.[14] Still other neo-Peronist party groups

---

[13] While new splintering occurred, there were also new efforts at establishing unity. Neo-Peronist unity groups were established for several provincial elections. In Córdoba, Laborista, Justicialista, Tres Banderas, Unión Popular, and Populista parties formed the Junta de Unidad Provincial de Frente Justicialista. In Tucumán neo-Peronist unity moves united the Defensa Provincial Bandera Blanca and the Partido Blanco. Similar efforts in other parties brought limited successes and helped prepare Peronist leaders to seize the opportunity offered by the elections of March 1962.

[14] The principal Peronist party, the Justicialista, continued to be banned, and Juan Perón was denied the right to be a candidate for vice-governor of Buenos Aires.

appeared before the July 1963 elections and were the recipients of approximately half a million votes despite express instructions from the leadership that elections should be boycotted.[15]

Splinter parties persisted even in 1965, when a national Peronist party, Unión Popular, was permitted to contest the election. Although the Unión Popular won the lion's share of Peronist votes, some dozen splinter parties also ran.[16] But the Peronist movement, like the Radical parties, managed to survive its own organizational weaknesses. By 1965 it had demonstrated a durability and versatility that made it a principal competitor for political influence. It could match Radical strength in the electoral arena, and it could compete strongly in the economic arena and in the streets. Its multiple strengths gave it unique potential in the several arenas in which Argentine political decisions are made. No conventional political party could match its versatility. Only one other competitor could match its capacity for violence.

Military Groups   In Argentina as in most of Latin America, military groups have long been major contenders for political power. It should be clear that it is entirely unrealistic to speak of the military as a unit of political action in Argentina because this formulation suggests a unity often lacking in the military establishment. From 1955 to 1965 the armed services contained several groups vying for power within the military establishment and for control of the government. Divisions within the military establishment were a particularly important source of dissension in the immediate post-Perón years. Even after pro-Perón officers had been purged, there remained a deep split between officers who advocated a massive effort to purge Peronist influence from Argentine society (*colorados* or *gorilas*) and those (*azules*) who believed that Peronism without Perón could be integrated into national life provided that harshly repressive measures did not permanently alienate its supporters from post-Perón society. Various minor splits in the military establishment, including personal, provincial, and interservice rivalries, also had repercussions affecting personnel and policies.

[15] The blank vote total indicated the defection of previous supporters to other, non-Peronist political parties. Less than 19 percent of the total electorate followed Perón's request to vote blank—nearly a million fewer than supported Peronist candidates in the 1962 elections.

[16] The more important neo-Peronist parties participating in this election were the Justicia Social, Laborista, Flores-Luyán, Blanco, Provincial (Chubut), Tres Banderas, Movimiento Popular de Mendoza, Movimiento Popular de Neuquén, Laborista Nacional, Blanco, Acción Popular San Luís, and Acción Provincial (Tucumán).

Goals and alliances of military contenders varied greatly. As in the past, military leaders in Argentina made alliances with representatives of the middle class, the working classes, and the land-based aristocracy and with political parties and other types of political movements. Their aims included control of government personnel and policy to the end of maintaining the social and political status quo, and of producing structural changes in government and society. In sum, military groups did not share a single set of goals; their actions were not directed toward the achievement of one goal.

Leaders of the military establishment in Argentina, as in other countries sharing a Mediterranean political tradition, regarded the maintenance of internal order as ultimately a military function. For this reason, severe or chronic disruption of the public order always enhanced the likelihood of increased military participation in politics.

The methods of military groups were more predictable. They did not seek power through elections; [17] they did not compete for influence over public opinion through the mass media or political organizations. They did utilize violence and threats of violence, though their use of violence was typically both economical and stylized. The arenas in which they competed were the armed service organizations, the executive departments of government, and the streets.

The military mode of political action always at least implies violence. Although the military services are part of government, none of their formal legal functions concern the determination of policy or personnel for the whole society; consequently, their activities are simultaneously intragovernmental and extralegal. Despite the repeated predictions of hopeful commentators (largely North American) before General Onganía's accession to power, there was little evidence to support the view that Argentine military officers were about to retire to the barracks. In fact, they had played an increasingly important role in Argentina's politics since 1930.[18]

---

[17] When an individual officer ran for office, as did General Aramburu in 1963, he was not functioning as an actor whose power derived from his military role but seeking an important type of strength not associated with military roles, namely, mass support in the electoral arena.

[18] Edwin Lieuwen, *Arms and Politics in Latin America*, rev. ed. (New York: Frederick A. Praeger, 1961), p. 163. He identified Argentina as one of his Group II Latin nations in which the political roles of the military were in transition, compared with Group I countries in which the military was dominant and Group III countries in which the military was nonpolitical. Among others who expressed, before President Illía's deposition, the view that the Argentine military "have given some indication that they at last are ready to return to their barracks

From 1955–1965, military capacity for violence served as a some-times guarantee, sometimes threat to democratic decision processes. Radical parties, which had no significant violence capacities, could remain in power only so long as military force neutralized Peronist violence capacities. When military leaders ceased to control arenas dominated by violence in behalf of other actors, and instead com-peted in their own behalf to control the personnel of government, the Radicals were ousted and the legal framework of republican decision making collapsed. Military leaders were in this sense responsible for both the existence and the demise of democratic processes.

Other Groups   Labor unions, students, clergy, and other func-tional groups also competed for the power to determine policy and personnel, usually in limited arenas. Their goals were typically limited to policy arenas of direct relevance to their functions, though prolonged or bitter conflict over a limited policy area occasionally resulted in the expansion of their goals to include broad influence on personnel as well as policy. The bitter opposition of the Argentine Catholic hierarchy to Perón is an example of such a comprehensive goal. The clientele of these functional groups comprised members and those dependent on them.   Their methods in the political sphere ranged from garden-variety lobbying to direct action. Labor groups demonstrated readiness to use strikes to achieve political as well as economic goals. The general strike, labor's ultimate weapon, was especially effective when combined with demonstrations and limited violence. Like the military establishment and political parties, the labor movement suffered from internal divisions. After 1955 it was split three ways between the "Bloc 62" Peronist unions (much the largest group), a group of "democratic" unions, and a communist group.

After its participation in the downfall of Perón, the Catholic Church limited its political role to influencing policy concerning education and ecclesiastical rights. Its principal instrument is its presumed relation to rectitude. In addition to conventional lobbying techniques, the Church possesses one unique tool of considerable

---

and leave the solution of political problems to the constitutional civilian govern-ment was the astute historian and student of Argentina Arthur P. Whitaker, in his *Argentina* (Englewood Cliffs, N.J.: Prentice-Hall, 1964), p. 169. Irving Horo-witz took an opposite view, with which I agree, in his essay "The Military Elites" in Seymour Martin Lipset and Aldo Solari, eds., *Elites in Latin America* (New York: Oxford University Press, 1967), pp. 146–189 passim.

efficacy in heavily Catholic Argentina—excommunication plus publicity.

Arenas

An arena may be defined as a site of decision making. The competition for power in Argentina is carried out in diverse arenas and by diverse methods, including peaceful propaganda and various types of violence, ranging from the stylized, minimal violence of the classic coup d'etat and the barracks revolt to rioting and mass demonstrations. Each activity takes place in an appropriate arena. Democratic parties compete in campaigns and elections and act through the mass media, public opinion, and the formal institutions of government. "Movement" parties may take part in these processes and also make their claim for power outside legal institutions—in the streets, in the industrial sphere, pressing their claims through demonstrated capability to mobilize masses or carry out a conspiracy. The principal arena for military action is the military establishment itself. Military groups also act in the executive department against the incumbents of formal governmental roles, removing them or threatening to do so, or act in the streets to counter a show of strength by other competitors. They may lobby government officials in an effort to influence particular policy outcomes. This lobbying takes place neither through the legislature nor through public opinion but directly in the executive department.

The legislature, an arena of prime importance in determining policy in some though not all democratic countries, was not the most significant arena for influencing policy outcomes in Argentina from 1955 to 1965. The most important arena of military and pressure-group activity was the executive branch of government. "Church, agrarian interests, industrial groups, and the labor unions all bring their plaints and their points of view to bear directly on the executive and often upon the leaders of the other power establishments, at best using the legislature as a sounding board and the courts, when possible, as some kind of interim source of juridical legitimacy." [19]

The most important arena of democratic competition was, of course, the electoral. (See Table 3.1.) In 1960, universal adult suf-

---

[19] Silvert, "The Costs of Anti-Nationalism: Argentina," in Kalman H. Silvert, ed., *Expectant Peoples: Nationalism and Development* (New York: Vintage Books, 1967), p. 338.

TABLE 3.1   MAJOR PARTY VOTE, 1957–1965

	UCRI		UCRP		Core Peronist and Blank	
1957	1,849,975	21.7%	2,103,530	24.7%	2,116,031	24.9%
1958	3,761,248	41.8	2,306,995	25.5	743,904 a	8.2
1960	1,841,477	20.6	2,101,089	23.6	2,226,555	24.9
1962	2,442,864	26.4	1,817,452	19.6	2,934,497	31.9
1963	1,593,002	16.8	2,441,064	25.8	1,827,464 b	18.8
1965	407,756	4.3	2,679,251	28.5	2,801,902	29.9

Note: The 1957 election was to elect a constituent assembly; the figures for 1958 and 1963 reflect the votes cast for the presidency; the elections of 1960, 1962, and 1965 were for the Chamber of Deputies. Except for 1965, these election statistics and all that follow are the official figures published by the Ministry of Interior in *Resultados electorales comparativos* and *Elecciones generales del 7 de julio de 1963* (Buenos Aires). The 1965 returns were announced by the Ministry of Interior and published in *La Prensa* (Buenos Aires), March 17, 1965. The use of national Argentine electoral statistics is complicated by the fact that the Ministry of Interior publishes only provincial totals. National totals must be computed by the analyst, whose task is further complicated by minor discrepancies in reporting: for example, some provinces add annulled ballots to blank ballots and report only the combined figure; most report them separately. The totals in the table differ slightly (never more than 1 percent) from those of some other analysts, each of whose figures differ slightly from each other. See, for example, Peter G. Snow, "Parties and Politics in Argentina: The Elections of 1962 and 1963," *Midwest Journal of Political Science*, vol. 9, no. 1 (February 1965), and James W. Rowe, *The Argentine Elections of 1963* (Washington, D. C.: The Institute for the Comparative Study of Political Systems, 1963). Presumably, the discrepancies result from emendations of the returns that are not noted from one mimeographed report to the next.
    a 1958 was the year in which Peronists were instructed to support Frondizi. Blank votes were presumably cast principally by disobedient Peronists.
    b This figure includes blank votes only. It does not include neo-Peronist provincial parties, which ignored the call to cast blank ballots (346,934). It also does not include the annulled ballots of Jujuy and San Juan and Peronist votes thrown to the Conservative party in Chaco.

frage gave Argentina an electorate of almost 12,000,000 out of a population of approximately 20,000,000. Compulsory voting laws requiring virtually all able-bodied adults to vote encouraged voting by providing penalties for nonvoters.[20] The result was a turnout that ranged from 80 to 90 percent, or about 9,000,000 voters. These voters, like the population generally, were heavily concentrated in and around Buenos Aires. Almost one-half of the eligible voters, and

---

[20] Persons not eligible to vote in Argentina included members of the military forces (a touching evidence of the desire to secure their political neutrality), criminals, the insane, and illiterate deaf mutes. There was no general literacy requirement. The only persons excused from the requirement to vote were those over 70, the physically ill, and those who lived far from a polling place; election officials and selected government officials were also exempt.

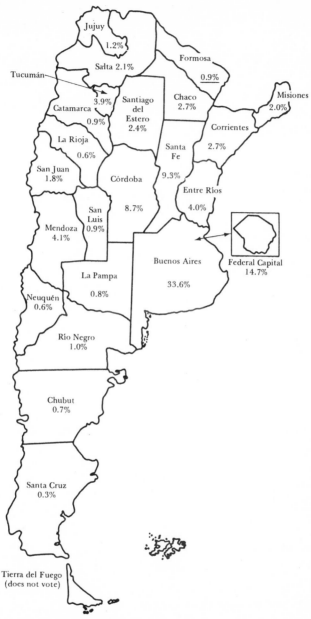

Figure 3.1   Argentina, 1960: Distribution of Electorate by Province (total population: 20,008,945)

somewhat more of the actual ones, were located in Buenos Aires and the Federal District, urban areas of high population density, high industrialization, and high Peronist strength. These two districts, plus Córdoba and Santa Fe, accounted for almost three-fourths of the voters. The remaining one-fourth of the votes were spread over the vast stretches of pampas, plains, and high Andean peaks that make up nearly two-thirds of Argentina. (See Figure 3.1.) Most of the electorate was white (77 percent), literate (87 percent), and urban (65 percent).

Regulation of the electoral system (that is, the terms of competition in this arena) was a subject of bitter conflict about which more will be said later.

Patterns of Interaction

The policies and personnel of government resulted from the interactions of the foregoing competitors. Not all competitors were involved in all interactions in all arenas, but their special strengths, methods, and commitments had to be taken into account at all levels of decision making. The legislative process was determined not only by the positions and unity of the various parties in the Congress and calculations of the effects of alternative actions on public opinion and future votes but also by knowledge or estimates of how the other nonparty competitors for power might react to alternative policy outcomes. So was the executive process of decision making. For example, in the field of economic policy, a president could appoint a minister of economic affairs representing a particular policy position because he believed the policies articulated by this man would win for the administration the support of key military leaders whom he believed were otherwise likely to engage in counter-government plots. The same minister could be discharged by the president because his policies stimulated among labor groups oppositionist activities so intense as to threaten public order and precipitate a coup by military exponents of civic order.

The patterns of interaction are durable, they are repetitive. Slightly different versions existed before the rise and fall of Perón. Most exist today. I do not doubt that most have persisted since the fall of General Onganía. They are different from those of most European democracies and different from those of fascist and communist autocracies. The differences are significant; they define a distinctive mixture of democratic and autocratic, traditional and modern, corporative and individualistic political traditions.

Interactions in the Electoral Arena Every stage of an electoral process is affected by its total political context. It is analytically possible, and often useful, to abstract political party competition, but the resulting oversimplification invites misunderstanding of the relation between elections and politics. This is especially true if the context is unfamiliar, as in Argentina from 1955–1965. In framing electoral laws, implementing them, conducting campaigns, and voting, most of the diverse actors already described were involved at some stage—introducing limitations on electoral choice, violence into a campaign, intimidation into voting. Military leaders participated in the electoral arena by influencing the terms and conditions of competition.[21] Their active role in influencing electoral law from 1955 to 1965 is described in the discussion that follows. Groups also participated in the electoral arena negatively, by *not* naming candidates and *not* voting for actual candidates. The electoral boycott with which Peronists frequently sought to discredit elections from 1955 to 1965 was used by the Radicals both before and after the period of Radical rule from 1916 to 1930.[22]

Elections after 1957 fall into two categories: those from which Peronist organizations (and communists) were legally excluded, and those in which Peronist organizations participated (though under various disabilities). In the elections of 1957, 1958, 1960, and 1963 only conventional democratic parties were permitted to participate. Peronist and communist parties were not permitted to contest these elections. In the elections of 1962 and 1965, Peronists were permitted to name candidates for national office, but Peronist candidates and campaigns were subject to unique and inhibiting restrictions, such as the prohibition against naming a party for one of the Peróns, invoking their names in campaign literature, and naming candidates for the presidency. *All electoral competition after 1955 was limited by laws designed to preclude the possibility of Perón's election to political office or the control of the national government by Peronist leaders.* Limited as it was, party competition was nonetheless an important dimension of the decision process and provided Argentina with two presidents: Frondizi and Illía. Further, after

---

[21] Influencing the terms of competition in any arena was already familiar in the pre-Perón period. In 1931 Popular Radical leaders Alvear and Güemes were barred from becoming candidates by the Uriburu administration, which sought the additional strength that would accrue to it from an electoral victory without risking the possibility of electoral defeat.

[22] In an effort to prevent electoral boycott during Perón's period in office, the Organic Statute of Political Parties (1945) deprived a party that did not run candidates of all rights to engage in any political activity whatsoever.

1955, electoral competition was the most important phase of Peronist competition for power.

The two million blank votes cast in 1957 constituted the most impressive demonstration of popular support mustered for Perón since the days preceding his overthrow—more successful than the general strike of November 1955, more impressive than the episodic sabotage, riots, and plots that punctuated civic life.

Alongside the legal electoral process, *a second type of interaction often took place among unconventional parties both in the streets and in clashes and rioting.* These interactions affected the personnel and policy of government by threatening or destroying public order, demonstrating the government's impotence, and inviting military intervention to restore order. They were relatively rare. Some examples are the riots and street wars between communists and the ultrarightist paramilitary group, Tacuara, in Rosario and Buenos Aires in 1964, during which several persons were killed.

A third type of interaction involved party or government officials and military groups. These interactions occurred when military groups attempted to determine policy or change the personnel of government through violence or threat of violence directed against the government. The following examples of action during the Frondizi regime are by no means a complete list of such interactions but are indicative of their type, range, and efficacy:

1. In July 1959, rebellious naval officers forced the resignation of the secretary of the navy.

2. In September 1959, rebellious generals forced the resignation of the secretary of war.

3. In 1961 the military services forced the resignation of the foreign minister, who was accused of seeking closer relations with the Castro regime.

4. In early 1962 the military secretaries forced a formal break in diplomatic relations with Cuba.

5. Following the elections of March 1962, military commanders successfully insisted on Frondizi's intervening in six provinces.

6. On March 29, 1962, military groups arrested and deposed the president and sponsored a new chief of state. (Since 1955, groups of military officers have forced out of the presidency Juan Perón, General Lonardi, Arturo Frondizi, and Dr. Illía.)

A fourth type of interaction occurred among competing military

groups seeking to control the military establishment. Disunity in
the military sector was endemic. There was often conflict among the
services and within them. The effectiveness of military interyen-
tions against other groups and the government requires at least absence of opposition from within the military establishment. Interactions of this kind lie behind virtually every unsuccessful military
revolt. The following are a few of the many recent examples:

1. Battles between the military forces took place in September
1959, June 1960, October 1960 and continued at an intense level
until the eventual displacement of President Frondizi, whose tenure
in office was prolonged by the internecine quarrels of military
actors.[23]
2. In August 1962 a multisided clash occurred when one army
general rebelled against the secretary of war, demanding his re-
moval. The secretary was deposed and replaced when rebels demonstrated their control of most army bases. The rebels were in
turn opposed by air force officers who forced the resignation of the
replacement. The continuing clash between rival military factions
brought the nation to the brink of civil war in September and was
finally resolved by a victory of the *azules*.[24]
3. In March 1963 a revolt led by army officers and backed by a
portion of the navy failed when the air force remained loyal to the
government.

A fifth type were interactions in which the chief participants were
officers of government and some functional group seeking to deter-
mine policy or effect a change in personnel. These interactions did
not take place through institutions integrated into the structure of
government, such as political parties or the legislature, but through
some type of direct action. Examples drawn from the 1955–1965
decade are

1. a general strike, called by the CGT in November 1961 in an

[23] See Horacio Sueldo, "Fuerzas armadas," in Jorge Parta, ed., *Argentina, 1930–*
1960 (Buenos Aires: Sur, 1961); James W. Rowe, "Argentina's Restless Military,"
in Robert D. Thomasek, ed., *Latin American Politics* (Garden City, N.Y.: An-
chor Books, 1966), pp. 453ff.; and Robert A. Potash, "The Changing Role of the
Military in Argentina," *Journal of Inter-American Studies,* vol. 3, no. 4 (October
1961), pp. 571–578.
[24] See Whitaker, *Argentina,* p. 167, for a description of this clash.

effort to force a change in the Frondizi government's economic policy;

2. a strike of 12,000 physicians attempting to force the government to rescind a hospital appointment; and

3. a general strike in January 1959 designed to prevent the government from enforcing antistrike laws.

A sixth type were interactions in the legislative arenas among elected representatives, which influenced outcomes not only through conventional legislative processes but through using in the legislative arena modes of behavior usually associated with other arenas. Competition within the legislature among conventional democratic political parties had characteristics that distinguished it from the bargaining, speaking, voting activities of Anglo-Saxon legislatures. Party behavior in the constituent assembly of 1957 was notable for its nonconformity to conventional legislative behavior. No sooner had this first democratic assembly of the post-Perón period convened than the 76 left-wing Radicals (UCRI) headed by Dr. Frondizi walked out, alleging that the government had acted illegally in summoning the assembly. This reduced the size of the assembly from 205 to 129. The Frondizistas were quickly joined by 9 UCRP delegates (the Sabatini group), who asserted that in reaffirming the 1853 constitution the assembly had fulfilled its legal function. Their departure left 120 delegates. Ten days later 11 Christian Democratic deputies accused the UCRP majority of totalitarian and socialistic goals, resigned, and left the assembly without a quorum. After an intriguing debate about whether force should be used to secure the return of enough delegates to constitute a quorum, the assembly disbanded.

Finally, there were interactions in which all the types of groups described here were direct participants. These were complex and involved both democratic and nondemocratic processes and modes. They were most likely to occur over important structural questions such as the choice of an electoral system, which activated all the contenders for political power. When these interactions occurred the result was a complex, continuing struggle, carried out in various arenas—the Congress, the streets, the Casa Rosada (presidential residence), the military establishment, and the industrial sphere. The modes of action in the struggle were characteristic of all participants: campaigning, legislative processes, strikes, rioting, terrorism, and the more stylized violence and threats of violence on the part of the military services.

A brief description of the interactions growing out of the continuing controversy concerning the rules governing democratic election processes will demonstrate the complexity of decision making when all contenders are actively involved. Before proceeding, it should be noted that four of the six chief executives Argentina has had since the overthrow of Perón have come to power through a *golpe de estado*. Only two have become president through popular election, and not one constitutional popularly elected government has succeeded another. These facts demonstrate that the basic question of whether Argentina was to have democratically chosen officials was still open. So did the congressional "recesses," the frequent interventions in provincial governments, and the repeated abrogation of elections. They also demonstrate that the controversy about the electoral system was not the most basic open question concerning the structure of the system, but was a second-level question. Nonetheless, it was capable of mobilizing complex, continuing, and violent controversy. The following brief summary illustrates the problems posed by this second-level question of legitimacy, namely, the character of the electoral system.

Historically, manipulation of the Argentine electoral system resulted from several causes, including the problem of finding an electoral system that would produce from the weak and multiple parties workable executive and legislative departments. Behind most of the electoral manipulation since 1955, however, has been the problem of how to contrive elections that could not be won by the followers of Juan Perón. The mass support of the former dictator, plus the divisions among his adversaries, have made this problem acute. Whether and in what form any group supporting Perón should be permitted to compete for office, how to bar Perón's reelection while permitting the people to choose their rulers—these are the questions that inspired electoral reform after reform and conflict after conflict in post-Perón, pre-Onganía Argentina.

In the first two elections after the overthrow of Perón, no Peronista party was permitted to participate. In the July 1957 election for a constituent assembly, support for the former dictator was registered by casting a blank ballot—an act of solidarity performed by over two million voters. In the February 1958 elections an electoral pact between Perón and the UCRI candidate Arturo Frondizi made possible Frondizi's overwhelming victory and demonstrated the power of the Peronists even in a system rigged against them. Again in the provincial elections of 1959 a Peronist party was banned, after the Electoral and the Federal Appeal Courts had rejected its plea for legal standing. Peronists took to the streets with strikes and rioting, and the Frondizi government intensified the search for a formula that would permit their controlled reentry into electoral life. Military pressure against their participation continued to be strong, and the issue remained divisive within the military establishment.

Frondizi shared the *azul* orientation and announced a revised electoral law permitting the limited participation of neo-Peronist parties. At stake in these elections of March 1962 were 86 of 192 seats in the Chamber of Deputies, 14 provincial governorships, and 5 senators and deputies in seventeen provinces. The results were

1. a Peronist victory in which Peronists won the popular vote, 45 of the 86 seats up for election in the Chamber, and 10 of 14 governorships;

2. intervention in six provinces undertaken under military pressure to annul Peronist victories;

3. a military coup that deposed Frondizi, replacing him with Vice-President José María Guido;

4. a decree, demanded by the navy and promulgated by Guido, declaring void all elections held since December 1961 and canceling the projected presidential elections previously scheduled for October 1963;

5. a decree disbanding the executives of all political parties and requiring new party elections within 120 days; and

6. new revisions and contention about the electoral law, and eventually a new electoral law.

In July the cabinet announced that a system of proportional representation would henceforth be adopted in constituent assembly elections. On November 19, 1962, a new decree was announced, aimed at hamstringing the electoral participation of Peronists. Along with it came the announcement of elections for June 1963. The new law attempted to prevent the participation of Peronist parties by providing that any party must register with the national electoral chamber in order to present candidates for national office, for municipal office in the Federal District, or for office in two or more districts. The requirements for registration were framed with formidably detailed attention to prohibiting Peronist participation. This was accomplished by disqualifying (1) any party using the name of a person, or symbols or names of dictators past or present;

(2) any party whose leaders lived abroad or were under judicial indictment, or who had fled the country to avoid prosecution; (3) any party that advocated or attempted to institute a dictatorship or totalitarian regime or a foreign political system; (4) any party that had foreign ties; and (5) any party without a democratic internal organization.

The law also provided that any party that did not obtain 3 percent of the total valid vote, had not presented candidates in three consecutive elections, or introduced military or quasi-military training would lose its registration. The Sáenz Peña system of allocating offices was replaced by the d'Honte system of proportional representation, a change certain to provide increased representation to smaller parties. The law again provided for indirect election of the president and vice-president.

This law did not provide even a temporary respite in controversy over the terms of the next elections. Instead, it set in motion a new chain of reactions. An electoral court ruled that the Peronist Unión Popular could take part in elections. Other political parties requested that Peronists be permitted to participate. Armed forces' secretaries declared their firm opposition. Perón announced his intention of regaining power through a sweeping electoral victory. The government reiterated its intention of banning all Peronist activity. The minister of interior proposed that the Peronist Unión Popular be permitted to join a united front of parties for the election, provided its leaders would agree to claim no more than thirty congressional seats and to nominate no candidates for president, vice-president, and five important governorships. The minister who proposed this pact resigned soon after under military pressure. The government banned from the elections all groups having any alliance or other relations with Peronists, and it annulled a court decision granting recognition to the Unión Popular. On April 11 the new minister of interior decreed that, on pain of loss of all civil rights, (1) all contacts with Perón were prohibited, and (2) the name of Perón must not be used in any form in Argentine political life.

Decisions, revisions, pressures, and counterpressures, judicial actions, and reviews continued up to the time of the elections (July 7, 1963). The Unión Popular and other principal Peronist parties boycotted the election and punctuated the campaign with sporadic violence, street fighting, and riots.

The July elections resulted in the election of Dr. Illía, leader of the UCRP, who polled some 26 percent of the total vote cast. Dr.

Arturo Frondizi, recently amnestied, denounced the election as illegitimate because of the exclusion of Peronists. In November 1964 the Illía government announced its intention to ban no parties in the March 1965 elections for half the Chamber of Deputies. All laws of "repression" of parties affecting Peronists and communists were formally revoked. However, the electoral court nonetheless ruled unconstitutional any use of the former dictator's name.

In the 1965 elections the Unión Popular (Peronist) won a sweeping success, polling almost 3,000,000 votes, or about 30 percent of all votes cast, thus becoming the principal opposition party in the Chamber. Its victories in regional and municipal elections also were sweeping. In October all political activity by the CGT was prohibited.

On June 28, 1966, for reasons only partly related to the outcome of the 1965 elections, a military coup deposed Dr. Illía, placed General Onganía in the Casa Rosada, dissolved the Congress and the provincial assemblies, deposed provincial governors and five supreme court judges, confiscated the property of political parties, banned all political meetings and demonstrations, arrested communist leaders, and proclaimed a new "Statute of the Argentine Revolution" giving the president virtually full powers at the federal and provincial levels.

This short history of electoral manipulations in the post-Perón period dramatizes the multisided conflicts about who shall rule and how rulers shall be chosen. But if recent Argentine experience illustrates the conflict surrounding elections and the tentative, contingent character of their consequences, it also illustrates the importance of elections within this hybrid system, confirming Charles Anderson's observation that "Elections are not definitive in many parts of Latin America. However, they are conscientiously and consistently held, and just as conscientiously and consistently annulled." [25]

In sum, elections were an integral but not a definitive part of the process by which decisions were made and unmade. There was continual conflict about their character, organization, and role. It was a conflict involving all competitors, all arenas, all types of interaction, and it was a conflict as enduring as the democratic framework of government itself. *Basically, it was an extension into the democratic framework of the conflict over who should rule and how those who ruled should be chosen.*

[25] Anderson, *Politics and Economic Change*, p. 94.

Three other aspects of the political system, implicit in the preceding accounts, deserve special note: the ubiquity of violence, the "legitimacy gap," and the pervasive institutional weakness.

The Ubiquity of Violence

Violence was an integral, regular, predictable part of the Argentine political process during the years of democratic government from 1955 to 1965. There was no normal peaceable system occasionally interrupted by violence. Riots, terrorism, demonstrations, and strikes punctuated by violence, coups d'etat, barracks revolts, and threats were part of politics as usual. They were normal modes of the decision process. In Argentina such violence was organized; it was conducted by groups seeking to influence political decisions. Anomic violence was rare.[26]

One characteristic of this violence was that it produced relatively little bloodshed.[27] The stylized violence associated with military coups rarely led to bloodshed. The careful positioning of forces, announcement of strength and intentions, and demonstration of potential more closely resembled chess than war.[28] The bloodiest activities from 1955 to 1965 resulted from the terrorist activities and party warfare.

President Frondizi estimated that 1,566 acts of terrorism were committed in Argentina between May 1, 1958, and June 30, 1961. Intensive terrorist activities preceded the March 1960 elections in Córdoba, where military personnel and installations were the targets of bombings in the wake of which the discovery of a widespread terrorist Peronist conspiracy was announced. This, in turn, was the occasion for announcing the "Conintes Plan," which established Draconian penalties against internal subversion.

There are many other examples of such violence. In May 1962, fighting around the Chamber of Deputies followed President Guido's decree recessing Congress. Repeated violent clashes between armed paramilitary organizations broke out in Rosario in February 1964.

[26] For an interesting discussion and typology of violence in Latin American politics, see William S. Stokes, "Violence as a Power Factor in Latin American Politics," in Martz, *Dynamics of Change*, pp. 140–149. For another typology of violence in Latin politics, see Silvert, *Conflict Society*, pp. 18–22.

[27] Anderson, *Politics and Economic Change*, pp. 96–101.

[28] The 1930 revolution was, for example, described by one observer as "a twelve-hour parade of cadets from the Military School." See George I. Blanksten, *Perón's Argentina* (Chicago: University of Chicago Press, 1953), p. 36.

In July the government announced the discovery of a nationwide Castroite terrorist organization and many arms caches. In September 1966, students clashed violently with police in Córdoba, Tucumán, Santa Fe, Corrientes, and San Juan. In the same year, violence replaced a government based on electoral support with one based solely on military support. The violence associated with the struggle for power *within* the military establishment also was sometimes bloody. In April 1962, for example, fighting between conflicting groups of military personnel resulted in twenty-five killed and thirty-four wounded.

The endemic plots and counterplots against the government by military groups involved violence, however stylized. A distinguished historian has estimated that "there were 34 attempted coups or major crises of one kind or another during Frondizi's tenure, and most of these were the work of military extremists." [29] Most important, the governments of Perón, Lonardi, Frondizi, and Illía were replaced by violence or the threat of violence.

If institutions are patterned behavior, then violence is institutionalized in Argentine politics—a fact entirely compatible with the key role of military groups in the system, for, as Martin Needler has pointed out, "Where force is used, the army necessarily has the last word." [30] But it is the last word in a sentence or paragraph, not the last word in the story. Unity is a prerequisite to the maximum political strength of the military. While modern weapons give the military an overwhelming advantage over other groups, unity is a precondition to the utilization of this advantage, and unity was often lacking. The conflict that afflicted other parts of the system also afflicted the armed forces, undermining their corporate strength. Competition between groups therefore continued, supported by conflict as well as subverted by it. The dissensus characteristic of other institutions also characterized the military establishment. The lack of established, accepted authority characterized these authoritarian institutions just as it did the democratic sectors. Force breeds in the interstices of authority, and these interstices were many and broad.

The presence of violence in a system is often associated with a breakdown in the social order, but when violence is patterned, as in Argentina, it must be considered a mode rather than a disruption of

---

[29] Whitaker, *Argentina,* p. 164.

[30] Martin Needler, "Putting Latin American Politics in Perspective," in Martz, *Dynamics of Change,* p. 25.

the social order. Kalman Silvert has summed up the point with clarity: "some kinds of revolutionary disturbance do not indicate instability. If the normal way of rotating the executive in a given country is by revolution, and if there have been a hundred such changes in a century, then it is not being facetious to remark that revolutions are a sign of stability—that events are marching along as they always have. . . ." [31]

The "Legitimacy Gap"

The persistence of competition between such diverse groups and by such diverse methods obviously demonstrates the continuing lack of agreement in Argentina about the legitimate sources of political authority. No procedure was recognized as *the* legitimate route to power.[32] No group had sufficient power to impose decisions or decision processes for long; no group had sufficient authority to win widespread allegiance to any given decision process.

It can therefore be hypothesized that in such a system political power based on support in a single arena cannot long endure and, conversely, stability in power will result only when a man or group has established and demonstrated supremacy or important strength in several arenas. Perón is the obvious example of a ruler who succeeded, for a time, in winning acquiescence or support in a variety of arenas from a variety of competitors.[33]

Institutionalized Instability

The type of political system described in the preceding pages might accurately be termed a mixed system since it contains characteristics associated with the politics of modern and traditional, democratic and autocratic regimes. But Aristotle long ago preempted the concept of a mixed system and used the term to describe quite a different mix. We might call it a corporative system, but while that term implies multiple power bases and limited power it is often used to describe regimes in which there is no mass par-

---

[31] Silvert, *Conflict Society*, p. 19.

[32] A consequence of the lack of agreement on a legitimate route to power is that various routes are popularly acceptable, for example, military coups as well as electoral success.

[33] General Onganía's concern with winning and retaining labor support suggests that he understood well the need for support from multiple sectors.

ticipation. It seems to me that a new name is needed to designate those political systems in which, through a substantial period of time and regardless of the legal structure of government, diverse and multiple actors (for example, parties, the military, and clerical establishments) compete for political power in diverse and multiple arenas. Such systems might usefully be termed "polyocracies," with "poly" designating the multiplicity of both actors and arenas. Such systems have multiple power bases and no established tradition that distinguishes legitimate authority from possession of political power; that is, they lack traditions of legitimacy that place substantive or procedural limits on the competition for power. They are very likely to suffer from what is conventionally called institutional instability. Since there is no agreement about legitimate arenas of decision making or modes of competition, shifting power relations among actors are likely to be accompanied by structural changes. The actors most vulnerable to institutional changes are political parties, which depend for their strength on mass support expressed through elections. The position of military leaders, labor leaders, church leaders, and terrorist groups is less affected by a shift from a democratic to an autocratic framework of decision than are parties, whose basic mode of participation is by voting.

What are the cultural implications of the persistent conflict over the substance and methods of politics? Does the conflict reflect profound value differences within Argentine society? Or does the conflict involve only superficial bickering superimposed on a unified or different people? To paraphrase, are the Argentines a tranquil people governed by agitated rulers? The relations between mass beliefs and political systems are problematic and relatively unexplored except at the speculative level. The extent to which stable democratic governments require widely shared beliefs about who should rule and to what ends has implications not only for system stability but for pluralism and for political change. Later chapters will explore the nature and distribution of beliefs among Argentines about the legitimacy and efficacy of alternative ways of choosing rulers and using power. These beliefs and values were formed in the context of the political interactions described earlier.

4

Peronists: The Size of the Movement

This chapter will explore the size and electoral stability of the Peronist movement, a task complicated by the organizationally indeterminate character of the movement.

The Peronist population is not identical with the membership of any organization or group of organizations. Restrictive legislation, intragroup rivalries, and the personalist factor in the movement, as well as its tactical flexibility and the absence of its true leader, have all combined to weaken the identification of the movement with any political party. Peronists act in a variety of arenas, each possessing distinctive criteria of strength and determinants of success. In the industrial sphere their success may depend on having sufficient influence on trade unions to produce a walkout that will in turn produce the desired policy outcome. In the streets the relevant measure of strength is their ability to produce a turnout large enough and menacing enough to produce the desired results. In elections it is the ability to get out a large enough vote to affect importantly the election. But no party or combination of parties comprehends all Peronists; no group of labor unions includes all Peronists; no street demonstration rallies all Peronists. No mode of behavior definitely identifies the Peronist universe. Subjective criteria for identifying Peronists are similarly ambiguous. Is a Peronist one who has a good opinion of the former dictator and hopes for his return, although he may never act to bring it about? Or is a Peronist one who intends to vote for the Unión Popular?

The problem of definition is important. Too narrow a definition could result in underestimating the size of the movement, overestimating its homogeneity, and misestimating its political potential. Too broad a definition could produce opposite, equally undesirable distortions. Prudence, therefore, suggests that Peronists be defined operationally as persons who express support for Peronist goals, through such acts as voting or stating in an interview sympathy with Juan Perón or the different groups identified with his name. This definition is consistent with political and organizational realities and will permit the exploration of the entire Peronist universe, which is essentially a universe of shared perspectives, various portions of which can be mobilized by various organizations for various actions in various arenas at various times. The criteria also define the relevant data. Election statistics can be utilized as a guide to the movement's mobilization potential in the electoral arena through time and under several alternative sets of conditions; survey data can provide information about the size, orientations, and distribution of the universe not available through a study of Argentine electorates.[1] By measuring subjective responses to the personalist, organizational, and ideological dimensions and by examining electoral behavior, it should be possible to screen out the full range of sympathetic responses, to establish the parameters of the movement, and to differentiate levels of attachment and mobilization potentials.

Subjective Responses

To illuminate the subjective bases of the Peronist mass vote, I shall examine available survey data concerning (a) responses to Perón personally, and (b) responses to Peronist organizations and parties. Recognizing the integral relationship between the man and the movement, I shall nonetheless attempt to distinguish analytically and existentially between responses to the man and to the movement, looking first at attitudes toward Juan Perón and his record.

The Personalist Factor Latin American politics is famous for its personalist bias. The number of parties and movements that have developed around the person of a dominant leader is legion, with "Fidelismo" being the newest left variant of the personalist form.

---

[1] See Austin Ranney's discussion of the relative utility of aggregate and survey data in the study of electoral behavior for a persuasive argument for the importance of utilizing both types of data. His argument that aggregates are most appropriately used for the study of electorates as a unit of analysis is especially relevant to the use of election statistics in the study of a movement like the Peronist, which contends in various arenas. See "The Utility and Limitations of Electoral Data," in Austin Ranney, ed., *Essays on the Behavioral Study of Politics* (Urbana: University of Illinois Press, 1962), pp. 91–102. For a different view, see Erwin K. Scheuch, "Cross-National Comparisons Using Aggregate Data: Some Substantive and Methodological Problems," in Richard L. Merritt and Stein Rokkan, eds., *Comparing Nations: The Use of Quantitative Data in Cross-National Research* (New Haven: Yale University Press, 1966), pp. 131–167; also C. L. Taylor, ed., *Aggregate Data Analysis: Political and Social Indicators in Cross-National Research* (Paris: Mouton & Co. and International Social Science Council, 1968).

A striking tendency also exists for Latin American political systems to achieve stability through government by "strong men," and for "strong men" to achieve mass support. The popular tyrant is unique neither to the area nor to the period, but the number of Latin American dictators whose popular support has been demonstrated by their having later achieved power through popular election is striking: Vargas in Brazil, the Somozas in Nicaragua, Perón in Argentina, and perhaps Pérez Jiménez in Venezuela are examples.

Peronism is a prime example of a movement that developed around the personality, record, and image of a single man whose personal leadership has been its principal but not its only goal. Despite accumulating evidence that the movement may outlive its leader, as long as Perón is alive and vigorous the appeals of the movement are inextricably related to those of the man.

Perón has achieved the greatest visibility of any political figure in contemporary Argentina.[2] The careful measures designed to prevent his reentry into Argentina, to prevent his participation in elections either in person or symbolically have testified to Perón's opponents' estimate of his continued appeal. So did the various prohibitions surrounding the invocation of Eva Perón. So potent a symbol was Eva Perón that an announcement by the Justicialista party in July 1965 of the intention to place a bust of her in the Congress precipitated public discussion of the likelihood of military action to prevent her statue being placed there.[3]

Several available measures of subjective responses to Perón are useful in determining the size and characteristics of the population that acknowledges responding favorably to him. These measures yielded similar results, indicating that slightly over a fifth of the population positively supported the return of Perón to power.

One question postulated a hypothetical presidential election and inquired for whom among a list of distinguished Argentines the respondent would vote. The responses are given in Table 4.1. Another question inquired whether the respondents would support

---

[2] Survey Research Center authors have commented that "for the electorate as a whole the level of attention to politics is so low that what the public is exposed to must be highly visible—even stark—if it is to have an impact on opinion." See Angus Campbell, Philip E. Converse, Warren E. Miller, and Donald E. Stokes, *The American Voter* (New York: John Wiley & Sons, 1960), p. 60. See Samuel A. Stouffer, *Communism, Conformity, and Civil Liberties: A Cross-section of the Nation Speaks Its Mind* (New York: Doubleday & Company, 1955), for further confirmation.

[3] *Confirmado,* July 9, 1965, p. 15.

TABLE 4.1   PRESIDENTIAL PREFERENCE

	Percentage ($n = 2,014$)
Illía	21.3
Perón	19.7
Aramburu	5.9
Matera	5.6
Thedy	4.8
Frondizi	4.7
Onganía	3.3
Other	3.9
None	17.5
Don't know	13.0

Source: Responses to Question 35 (Appendix B).

a candidate committed to returning Perón to power, and a third question followed inquiries whether, if Perón were permitted to return to Argentina and be a candidate, the respondent would vote for him; 18.1 percent of all respondents asserted they would vote for him. (See Table 4.2.) Thus three queries concerning the respondents' readiness to support Perón's resumption of power as president yielded positive responses of between 18.1 percent and 21.4 percent. Finally, 26.1 percent gave a favorable response to the question, "Do you think it would help or hurt Argentina if Juan Perón were allowed to return to the country?"

This support for Perón is more impressive when interpreted in the context of Argentine modes of response to political leaders. If the four questions just cited can be conceived as measuring response to leaders, then at least a fifth of adult Argentines were without preferences among leaders, which persisted between elec-

TABLE 4.2   RETURN OF PERÓN TO POWER

	Percentage ($n = 2,014$)
Would vote for him tomorrow (alternatives supplied)	19.7
Would support a candidate committed to Perón's return to power	21.4
Would vote for him (no alternative candidate supplied)	18.1

Source: Responses to Questions 35, 17, and 37b (Appendix B).

TABLE 4.3 WITHOUT LEADER PREFERENCES
BETWEEN ELECTIONS

	Response	Percentage ($n = 2,014$)
Would support Perón's return?	Don't know	21.4
Would vote for whom tomorrow? (choice supplied)	No choice	30.5
Would help or hurt for Perón to return to power?	No opinion	23.8
Which leader most harmful to Argentina?	No opinion	24.1
Does national government influence your life?	No or no opinion	30.6

Source: Responses to Questions 17j, 35, 37, 36, and 14 (Appendix B). The last question was taken from *The Civic Culture*.

tions.[4] The percentage of respondents without an opinion on leaders ranged from approximately 21.4 to 30.5 percent (Table 4.3).[5] Compulsory voting laws apparently forced an electoral choice on some persons who were otherwise indifferent to the identity of the ruler.

Therefore, Perón is revealed to have had the support of approximately one-fourth to one-third of the adults with opinions about political leaders. Only President Illía was named by more persons than Perón as a man respondents might vote for "tomorrow." Between them, Perón and Dr. Illía completely dominated the field of political personalities. Note also should be taken of the difference in their respective stations and circumstances at the time of the survey. It had been ten years since Perón was deposed and one year since his abortive effort to return to Argentina. During that decade many assaults had been made on his character, record, and supporters. He was under indictment for statutory rape, condemned

[4] "Don't know" responses are notoriously ambiguous. They may reflect reluctance to answer particular questions, desire to withhold responses generally, indifference, fear, hostility, or genuine ignorance. Analysis of "Don't know" responses to questions of partisan orientation in this survey suggests that (1) they do not reflect general unwillingness to be interviewed or to discuss social and political questions in general (there is, for example, no general unwillingness to criticize the government); (2) they may be safely interpreted in most instances as indicating affective neutrality or uninvolvement in specified dimensions of political life; and (3) affective neutrality is consistent with the pattern of Argentine response to the political world. For a discussion of "Don't know" responses, see Leo Bogart, "No Opinion, Don't Know, and Maybe No Answer," *Public Opinion Quarterly*, vol. 31, no. 3 (Fall 1967), pp. 331–346.

[5] Note that this finding is consistent with the proportion of respondents who did not feel that their personal lives were affected by the national government. Persons who regard themselves as unaffected by the government are unlikely to be concerned about who governs.

by the Church for both personal and policy offenses, and accused of theft from the public treasury. He had been refused entrance by other Latin American governments. Illía, to the contrary, was the president of the Republic and the leader of Argentina's most popular party, 'he UCRP.

The pro-Perón preference of approximately 20 percent of all Argentines, or 25–30 percent of all Argentines with an opinion about leaders, is not only quantitatively impressive but demonstrates the remarkable stability of Perón's personal appeal. The stability of Perón's appeal contrasts sharply with the rapid decline of Arturo Frondizi from popular favor after his electoral victory in 1958 [6] to less than 5 percent in the 1965 survey and in the 1965 election is evidence of rapidly shifting leader preferences among Argentines. A similarly sharp drop in popularity was suffered by President Illía. In a 1965 Argentine public opinion survey, only 51 percent of those who had voted for Illía said they would vote for him in the next election.[7] The duration of Perón's appeal reflects the power of his personality and the strength of the Peronist myth.

The Organizational Factor Respondents closely associated Peronist organizations with Perón. When asked to name the two or three most important political parties in Argentina, *Peronista* was mentioned far more often by respondents than either Unión Popular or Justicialista, despite the laws prohibiting parties from using his name. However, it is also true that as of late 1965 the movement had appeals independent of the appeal of its leader. (See Table 4.4.)

That the distinction between the man and the movement is existentially significant as well as analytically useful is clear from the electoral behavior of the several hundreds of thousands of Peronists who have from time to time disregarded the instructions of the movement's top leadership. In 1963, despite the clear requests of the leadership to vote blank, 628,000 voters cast ballots for neo-Peronist parties. It is also very likely (though it cannot be definitely

[6] Frondizi's showing in the 1958 election was impressive even if the Peronist portion of his support is subtracted.

[7] This finding by the Instituto IPSA was published in *Confirmado*, July 9, 1965, pp. 16–18. The survey revealed generalized dissatisfaction with Illía, who was reproached by a large proportion of dissatisfied former supporters for his failure to handle economic problems adequately, mishandling of his government, and not keeping his promises. Results of public opinion polls by Encuestas Gallup de la Argentina (EGA) in Buenos Aires ($n =$ at least 850) in April and May 1966 indicate that Illía's popularity continued to decline; see EGA, "Argentina," *Polls*, vol. 2, no. 3, (Spring 1967).

TABLE 4.4   MOST IMPORTANT ARGENTINE PARTIES
AS NAMED BY RESPONDENTS

	Percentage ($n = 2,014$)	
Partido Peronista	43.1	
Partido Justicialista	11.0	63.2
Unión Popular	9.1	
Unión Cívica Radical del Pueblo	81.9	
Unión Cívica Radical Intransigente	19.4	
Movimiento Integración Desarrollo Nacional	4.1	
Partido Socialista Argentino	10.7	
Partido Conservador	7.5	
Partido Demócrata Cristiano	5.6	
Partido Demócrata Progresista	4.2	
Partido Comunista	1.0	
Federación Nacional Partidos del Centro	.9	
Unión del Pueblo Argentino	1.2	
Partido Demócrata (no further specification)	2.9	
Partido Socialista Demócrata	.8	
Others	1.5	
Don't know	7.5	

Source: Responses to Question 32 (Appendix B).

proved) that substantial numbers declined to vote for Arturo
Frondizi in 1958 and instead cast blank ballots.

There are various measures of Peronist organizations' appeal. Any
interpretation of these measures is again complicated by Argentina's
distinct pattern of response to political organizations, especially by
the high percentage of respondents who do not identify with a
political party. It is not surprising to find only 3 percent of the
respondents describing themselves as party members, since most
Argentine parties are loosely organized electoral vehicles. More note-
worthy is the fact that only 20 percent of the electorate described
themselves as supporters of any party, and 54 percent of all the
respondents asserted that they did not even "lean" toward any
party. That is, more than half lacked "psychological membership"
of even the loosest kind. This finding could be evidence of reluctance to divulge party identification. Such an interpretation, however, does not appear warranted; respondents did not display general reluctance to divulge information on political preferences.
Furthermore, we have already seen that 20 to 25 percent of the
respondents declined to express preference among potential candidates. In addition, widespread lack of psychological identification
with parties is consistent with other aspects of Argentine electoral
behavior, the whole of which reflects a tenuous relationship between

individuals and political organizations.[8] The evidence suggests that the most likely reason for 54 percent of all informants stating that they had no party preference is that they did not. Lasswell and Kaplan have asserted that "The probability that an aggregate of persons will identify with one another varies with the number and intensity of shared demands."[9] I would add that the probability that they will identify with a political party varies with the number and intensity of demands whose achievements are perceived as positively associated with the power position of a party. In Argentina more than half the electorate did not positively associate demands with any political party.

The existence of numerous persons who expressed no party preference suggests, first, that for many Argentines party identification was not an important psychological link between individuals and the political system; and, second, that party was not the principal determinant of electoral choice for large numbers of Argentines.

It is hardly surprising that for many voters parties did not serve as psychological links to the political system, since in this system elections were but one arena of political competition among many; parties underwent many transformations and divisions; and there were many parties competing for votes in the elections. The shifting rules governing Peronist electoral participation, and the proliferation of Peronist parties, would hardly induce an identification between Peronist goals and any specific organizational mechanism. The Radical position has also lacked a stable organization linking Radical goals to the electoral arena. Radical parties, too, have suffered many splits and mutations.

It is reasonable to suppose that this organizational flux has drastically inhibited the development of psychological attachments to parties and has diminished the importance of parties as the intermediate organizations that either subjectively or objectively link individuals to the political system. The result seems to be that political choices were not generally perceived in terms of political party labels. However, the stability of party organization or attachment does not necessarily affect the stability of partisan loyalties.

[8] José Luis de Imaz, *La clase alta de Buenos Aires* (Buenos Aires: Editorial Universidad de Buenos Aires, 1962), found that among the highest social classes, where education was highest, 18 percent had no party preference; see pp. 65–67.

[9] Harold D. Lasswell and Abraham Kaplan, *Power and Society: A Framework for Political Inquiry* (New Haven: Yale University Press, 1950), p. 19.

TABLE 4.5   PARTY IDENTIFICATION, 1965

| | Percentage ($n = 2,014$) | | |
	Strong	Weak	Total Party Preference
Peronist	8.7	5.1	13.8
UCRP	8.6	7.4	16.0
All others [a]	7.8	8.4	16.2
Without preference	72.9	54.0	54.0

Source: Responses to Questions 28, 28a, 29, and 29a (Appendix B).

[a] The party preferences of the remaining respondents were split among many factions. The party that ranked third in party preferences was the Partido Socialista Argentina, which was preferred by 2.6 percent of the respondents.

Partisan orientations may remain stable amid organizational flux.[10]

In the light of these comments it is possible to assess the scope and character of Argentine orientations to Peronist organizations and the Peronist movement. Like most Argentine parties, Peronist parties were not membership parties but were electoral associations without permanent organization or goals other than winning elections. (Other Peronist organizations were oriented to the accomplishment of other goals in other arenas.) The attachment of pro-Peronist respondents to these electoral vehicles is revealed as weak indeed. Only 8.7 percent of the respondents described themselves as supporters of a Peronist party, and only 5.1 percent more expressed a leaning toward Peronist parties, making a total of 13.8 percent of the respondents who expressed any preference for Peronist parties. However, compared with the general pattern of party identification, the Peronist showing was strong (see Table 4.5). Peronists enjoyed the support of more Argentines than any other group except the Popular Radicals, a finding that is entirely consistent with the spring 1965 elections.[11]

The striking decline of the Intransigent Radicals (UCRI) shown in the 1965 elections is reflected in the survey data, which show the UCRI as lacking a core of voters whose identification with the party

[10] Previous studies, among which François Goguel's work on French electoral geography is notable, have demonstrated that partisan loyalties may be highly stable at the same time that the parties through which they are expressed shift repeatedly. See, especially, *Géographie des élections françaises de 1870 à 1951* (Paris: Librairie Armand Colin, 1951).

[11] For a recent argument that Argentine politics is being polarized despite the fractioning tendencies of their electoral system, see Peter Ranis, *"Peronismo Without Perón, Ten Years after the Fall (1955–1965), Journal of Inter-American Studies,* vol. 8, no. 1 (January 1966), pp. 112–128.

TABLE 4.6   ORIENTATION TO PERONIST ORGANIZATIONS

	Percentage ($n = 2,104$)
Prefer Peronist party	13.8
Approve of Peronist movement	26.2
Generally would support a Peronist-backed candidate	36.6
Would support a Justicialist-backed candidate	36.3

Source: Responses to Questions 28, 29, and 29a, 38, 25h, and 251 (Appendix B).

persisted beyond the moment of electoral choice. The fact that the votes of all Argentine parties far exceeded the number of respondents who expressed identification with them suggests that, for almost half the electorate, preferences expressed in voting reflected a relationship between partisan orientations and political organizations that was established relatively near the time of election and was terminated by the act of voting.

    To summarize, in Argentina lack of party identification did not necessarily imply political neutrality, apathy, indifference, or nonintegration into the political system. While partisan preferences are generally attached to parties and expressed through party identification in countries with stable party systems, in systems such as the Argentine they may not be related to political parties except at election time. At that point, the compulsory voting law doubtless functioned to force voters to identify their partisan preferences with an electoral alternative. Alternative measures of sympathy for the Peronist position demonstrate that large numbers of Argentines of pro-Peronist orientation for one reason or another failed to relate that orientation to their stated party preference (see Table 4.6).

Combining measures of support for Perón's personal leadership with those of support for Peronist organizations, the picture that emerges is shown in Table 4.7. The pattern of affect distribution

TABLE 4.7   RANGE OF PRO-PERONIST UNIVERSE

	Percentage ($n = 2,014$)
Would vote for Perón (no alternatives supplied)	18.1
Would vote for him tomorrow (alternatives supplied)	19.7
Would support a candidate supporting Perón's return to power	21.4
Would help to let Perón return to Argentina	26.1
Approve of activities of Peronist movement	26.2
Would support Peronist-backed candidate	36.6
Would support Justicialist-backed candidate	36.3

Source: Responses to Questions 37b, 35e, 17j, 37, 38, 25h, and 251 (Appendix B).

TABLE 4.8   RANGE OF ANTI-PERONIST UNIVERSE

	Percentage (n = 2,014)
Would not support a candidate supporting Perón's return to power	60.0
Would hurt to let Perón return to Argentina	50.1
Disapprove of activities of Peronist movement	48.6
Against a candidate supported by Peronists	46.1
Against a candidate supported by Justicialists	44.6

Source: Responses to Questions 17j, 37, 38, 25h, and 251 (Appendix B).

reflected in Table 4.7 is reinforced by the results of the examination of negative and indifferent responses to Perón and the Peronist movement shown in Table 4.8.

Analysis of the pro-Peronist universe indicates that the movement's most reliable supporters were those who expressed a personal attachment to Juan Perón. Respondents who said they would vote for Perón also expressed support for the various organizational arms of the movement and approved the activities of the movement. Also, analysis reveals that the characteristics, expectations, and demands that occurred with distinctive frequency among persons sympathetic to the Peronist movement were most common among persons who expressed support for Perón personally. For these reasons, *those who expressed personal support for Perón are termed core Peronists in this study. Those who expressed support for the movement are called pro-Peronists.*[12] Most of the tables in the study utilize this breakdown and terminology. Like most labels, these oversimplify reality (there may be dedicated supporters of the movement who do not support Juan Perón, and less dedicated supporters of Perón who stray from the movement), but the categories are useful for distinguishing broadly between two types of persons who make up the Peronist universe. *When in the text of this study I refer simply to Peronists or to reliable Peronists, it is the core Peronists of whom I am speaking.*

It seems likely that, taken together, responses on the personal and organizational aspects of Peronists demarcate the upper and lower

---

[12] Distinctively Peronist characteristics and orientations that are especially common among persons who said they would vote for Perón (compared with persons who only supported Peronist organizations) include class identification (see Table 5.2); orientations to interpersonal relations (Table 6.5); orientations to group (Tables 6.4, 6.17, and 6.20); orientations to governmental authority; and demands concerning domestic policy. Also see discussion of core Peronist and pro-Peronist demands in chap. 8.

limits of the universe of orientations favorable to Peronism. The data indicate that this universe ranged from 18 to 36 percent of adult Argentines, various portions of which could be mobilized for political action. These findings are strikingly consistent with the Peronist vote in elections since 1957.

Scrutiny of electoral data provides clues to why the movement's strength fluctuated in the electoral arena, and to how various circumstances affected its size (Table 4.9).

The maximum mass support for Peronist causes was available in elections in which Peronist parties were permitted to participate by naming Peronist candidates. The number of voters supporting Peronist candidates substantially exceeded the number casting blank ballots or supporting other candidates on request of the Peronist leadership. Approximately one-fifth of the electorate supported with its votes any effort named by Peronist leaders; almost one-third of the electorate supported Peronist candidates in elections in which they were permitted to run.

The evidence indicates but does not prove that, in 1958, the Peronist leaders were unable to deliver to Frondizi more than two-thirds of their normal electoral support, and that the remainder of potential Peronist voters protested against Frondizi and the UCRI as well as against the exclusion of Peronist candidates by casting blank ballots or voting for other candidates. As Table 4.10 demonstrates, Frondizi's 1958 vote was well below the combined UCRI-Peronist vote in 1962, when Peronist parties were permitted

TABLE 4.9 PERONIST PERCENTAGE OF NATIONAL VOTE, 1957–1965

	Peronist Percentage of Total Vote
1957	24.5
1958	—[a]
1960	24.9
1962	31.9
1963	18.8[b]
1965	29.9

[a] In 1958, Peronist supporters were requested to vote for UCRI candidate Arturo Frondizi, and many did so. Although 8.8 percent of the electorate cast blank ballots, it is impossible to know what portion of these ballots were cast by disobedient Peronists.

[b] This figure reflects only the blank votes cast for president. In the 1963 elections, when Peronists were asked to vote *en blanco,* neo-Peronist provincial parties won 3.6 percent of the national vote. This 3.6 percent figure is not included here.

TABLE 4.10   UCRI-PERONIST STRENGTH IN 1958 AND 1962 ELECTIONS

	Percentage of Total Vote				
	Buenos Aires	Federal Capital	Córdoba	Tucumán	Nation
Frondizi total (1958)	43.3	35.8	43.3	38.8	41.8
Blank votes (1958)	10.2	7.1	5.9	13.7	8.2
Peronist total (1962)	37.8	27.7	32.3	45.5	31.9
UCRI total (1962)	24.0	29.6	19.9	31.7	26.4

to name candidates. But the combined Frondizi vote and blank vote in 1958 was less than the combined UCRI-Peronist vote in 1962.

The request to cast blank ballots had similar effects on the size of the Peronist electoral support. In 1957, 1960, and 1961 the number of blank votes was well below the number of Peronist votes in the elections in which Peronists were permitted to present candidates. Since there was no significant difference in voter turnout, potential Peronist voters who did not cast blank ballots presumably voted for other parties. In 1963, however, the call for blank votes produced a different type of unresponsiveness in substantial numbers of the potential Peronist following, namely, voting for neo-Peronist parties that contested the election in spite of national leaders' instructions to abstain from participation.

In the 1963 election the blank vote dropped to 18.8 percent, which total presumably included an unknown number of UCRI supporters who followed Frondizi's plea to vote *en blanco*. Neo-Peronist parties polled approximately 3.5 percent of the presidential vote and a larger portion of the legislative vote. In some provinces, Perón's instructions to vote blank were massively disregarded in favor of voting for neo-Peronist parties. In nine provinces the total vote for neo-Peronist parties exceeded the blank vote (Table 4.11). The total number of blank ballots *and* votes cast for neo-Peronist parties in 1963 did not equal the Peronist vote in 1962 or 1965. The final figures suggest that some 5 percent of the voters who might have voted for Peronist candidates cast their ballots for candidates of other parties.

Organizational unity is another factor that should be taken into account in estimating the size of the Peronist mass following. Peronist electoral strength is normally estimated on the basis of the

TABLE 4.11 PROVINCES IN WHICH NEO-PERONIST PARTIES'
VOTES FOR DEPUTIES EXCEEDED BLANK VOTES, 1963

| | Percentage of Total Vote | |
	Peronist Parties' Votes	Blank Votes
Neuquén	59.1	11.4
Jujuy	55.8	2.9
Chaco	39.3	4.2
Salta	34.9	5.3
Mendoza	34.8	7.4
San Luis	29.7	2.8
San Juan	20.4	1.8
La Rioja	20.4	13.0
Córdoba	10.5	4.3

total number of votes cast for the various Peronist *and* neo-Peronist parties. These estimates are based on the assumption that partisan orientations are more important than their organizational embodiments, perhaps because of a prior assumption that rank-and-file Peronists are united in their support of Perón.

It may be true that Perón's leadership guaranteed unity transcending the rivalries of his lieutenants. But it should be reiterated that the splintering process that so often afflicts Argentine parties set in among Peronists soon after Perón's fall, and it proceeded apace. Unión Popular emerged as the principal Peronist party, but a number of other Peronist parties quickly developed, some of whom competed with one another for votes. In 1963, Peronist votes in La Rioja were split three ways: 13 percent of the electorate cast blank ballots, 11.2 percent voted for the Social Justice party, and 9.2 percent for the Unión Popular; in the same year in Mendoza, 7.5 percent of the voters cast blank ballots, 18.1 percent supported Tres Banderas, and 16.7 percent the Blanco party. In the 1965 elections Peronists' votes in Entre Ríos were divided between Unión Popular and Tres Banderas. In Buenos Aires the Unión Popular was clearly dominant, but several competing Peronist parties garnered several thousand votes each. In Salta, four Peronist parties contested the election—Justicialista de Salta, Laborista Nacional, Unión Popular, and Partido Blanco, with the first receiving seven times as many votes as the others combined. In Córdoba, Peronist and neo-Peronist parties included Unión Popular, Laborista, and Partido de la Justicia Social, with the first receiving some seventy times more votes than the latter two combined. The results were similar in a number of other provinces.

By 1965 the multiple schisms of the Peronist leadership had not fatally divided the movement. In elections before the suspension of parties, one Peronist party emerged as clearly dominant in most districts, and one group clearly dominant in the nation, but much splintering occurred at the edges and there were some rivalries among the dominant provincial parties. Fissiparous trends were most pronounced in elections that the Peronists were not permitted to contest. This pattern of development was similar to that of Radicalism. Except for the UCRI-UCRP split that divided Radical votes into two large blocs in the elections of 1957, 1960, 1962, and 1963, the Radical vote has been split among one dominant and various splinter parties. And the virtual annihilation of the UCRI between 1963 and 1965 suggested a return to this pattern.

Summary

Peronists, then, were an unorganized collectivity united by positive orientation toward Perón, Peronism, or Peronist organizations. Those positive orientations were expressed through such acts as voting for Peronist parties or expressing identification with or support for Peronist organizations or candidates. The movement could be defined as an aggregate united by the demand that Juan Perón or organizations and persons purportedly associated with him be returned to political power.

The movement had neither definite nor stable boundaries. Its supporters numbered from approximately one-fifth to one-third of adult Argentines. The exact number depended on the issues and the conditions of competition. Peronist electoral strength and unity were greatest in elections in which Peronist candidates were permitted to run. Fewer voters followed leaders' requests to cast blank ballots or to vote for the candidate of another party. But despite followers of uncertain discipline and internal disunity, the Peronist mass base proved broad and durable. Only two partisan orientations —Peronist and Radical—were shared by significant numbers of Argentines. Groups representing these orientations therefore dominated the electoral arena, garnering some 50 to 60 percent of the votes cast. The splintering of other preferences and the rather broad indifference to electoral contests made 20 to 30 percent of the votes a strong (perhaps winning) show of strength in the electoral arena. The Peronist movement had a reliable core of just under one-fifth of the electorate, and this core alone guaranteed the Peronists high rank among Argentine parties. The movement's showing in elections since 1957 demonstrated a durability rare in this country where parties wax and wane like candlelight on a gusty night.

5

Peronists: The Composition of the Movement

El peronismo, en 1955, como expresión del frente nacional que fué en 1946, se había reducido a Perón y a la clase obrera. Es decir, se había sectarizado, había substituido su contenido nacional por el de clase. . . .

Ramón Prieto, *El pacto*

This chapter deals with the composition of the Peronist movement. It attempts to identify the class affiliation, educational and ethnic backgrounds, age, sex, profession, and geographic distribution of rank-and-file Peronists. It is, therefore, chiefly concerned with objective social characteristics of the Peronist movement. It explores the social identity of Peronists and relates it to some influential hypotheses concerning Peronists and the Argentine political tradition.

Class Composition

The alliance between Perón and Argentina's workers has been famous since the march of the *descamisados* on Government House demanding the restoration of Colonel Perón to power in October 1945. Perón's shirt-sleeve, ditch-digging campaign style,[1] his union-building policies in the Labor Ministry, his dramatic presents to Argentina's poor, Eva's flamboyant cultivation of the *cabecitas negras,* and the enduring Peronist control of the largest bloc of Argentine unions all called attention to Perón's widespread support among Argentina's working masses.

The presence and importance of Argentina's lower classes within the Peronist movement are undisputed. Less clear, however, are the extent to which Peronism dominated lower-class politics in Argentina and the extent to which the lower classes dominated the

---

[1] For a colorful description of Perón's early campaigning, see Ruth and Leonard Greenup, *Revolution before Breakfast: Argentina, 1941–46* (Chapel Hill: University of North Carolina Press, 1947), p. 157. For another discussion of Perón's style of mass appeal see Mario Amadeo, *Ayer, hoy, mañana* (Buenos Aires: Ediciones Gure, 1956), pp. 93–108 passim.

TABLE 5.1   SOCIOECONOMIC STATUS: TOTAL SAMPLE
(In percent)

	Interviewer Appraisal [a] (n = 2,014)	Self-Appraisal [b] (n = 2,014)
Upper	0.2	0.7
Upper middle	7.6	25.6
Lower middle	47.7	40.6
Popular or lower	35.8	32.3

Source: Interviewer appraisal (Appendix A), and responses to Question 66 (Appendix B).

[a] 8.7 percent not ascertained.

[b] 0.8 percent declined to answer.

Peronist movement. The findings of the 1965 survey confirm the special attraction of Peronism for Argentina's poorest citizens. They also define the character and extent of the relationship between Peronism and the lower classes.

Two measures of socioeconomic class identification were available in the survey: an interviewer appraisal of the respondent's socioeconomic status (SES), and the respondent's own report of his class affiliation.[2] Comparisons of these two ratings disclose significant information both about the patterns of subjective class identification in Argentina and about the socioeconomic composition of the Peronist mass base.

Tables 5.1 and 5.2 make clear several important facts about the Argentine class structure. First, there obviously existed a marked tendency among Argentines to identify with the middle classes: approximately two-thirds of the nation conceived itself as middle class.[3] This strong subjective identification with the middle class has important implications concerning popular orientations to social goals and groups, relations among the classes, and the political potential of various groups.[4]

[2] For the exact question see Appendix B, Question 66. An explanation of the interviewer appraisal is found in Appendix A, p. 237.

[3] But note that de Imaz found that 91 percent of his sample of the upper class identified themselves with the highest class. See José Luis de Imaz, La clase alta de Buenos Aires (Buenos Aires: Editorial Universidad de Buenos Aires, 1962), p. 7.

[4] Germani and Silvert emphasize the existence of a "self-identifying middle stratum" in assessing the degree of development of systems of social stratification. See Gino Germani and Kalman H. Silvert, "Politics, Social Structure and Military Intervention in Latin America," in Peter G. Snow, ed., Government and Politics in Latin America: A Reader (New York: Holt, Rinehart & Winston, 1967), pp. 301–302.

TABLE 5.2   PERONIST AND UCRP CLASS COMPOSITION
(In percent)

	Interviewer Appraisal			Self-Appraisal		
	Core Peronist (n = 365)	Pro-Peronist (n = 411)	UCRP Voter (n=413)	Core Peronist (n = 365)	Pro-Peronist (n = 411)	UCRP Voter (n=413)
Upper	0.0	0.0	0.0	0.8	1.0	0.2
Upper middle	1.6	7.3	8.2	11.5	19.2	30.5
Lower middle	33.4	42.3	53.3	28.2	42.3	47.9
Popular or lower	56.1	40.9	29.8	58.1	37.0	20.8
Don't know or not ascertained	8.8	9.5	8.7	1.4	0.5	0.5

Source: Same as Table 5.1.
Note: The designations "Core Peronist" and "Pro-Peronist" are defined and discussed in Chapter 4.

Second, there is a discernible tendency among persons conceiving themselves as middle class to identify with the upper sectors of the middle class. The discrepancy between interviewer and self-appraisal concerning the composition and size of the upper middle class indicates a marked tendency to identify upward, to exaggerate or enhance one's social status.[5] While middle-class Peronists demonstrated some tendency to identify upward, lower-class Peronists did not.

Third, survey findings confirm the distinctive responses to Perón and Peronism of different socioeconomic groups. Peronists were confirmed as being disproportionately drawn from among the lower "popular" class. The lower-class character of the Peronist mass base is further emphasized by the clear-cut class identification of lower-class Peronists. Of all political groups, lower-class Peronists showed the least tendency to identify with higher-status groups; lower-class Peronists demonstrated a class consciousness unique among Argentines.[6]

Fourth, while the special appeal of Perón to the poor is estab-

[5] This tendency has been commented on by various writers on Argentine society. See Kalman H. Silvert, "The Costs of Anti-Nationalism: Argentina," in his collection on developing areas, *Expectant Nations: Nationalism and Development* (New York: Vintage Books, 1967), p. 371.

[6] Lipset et al. suggested that class consciousness and distinctive working-class political behavior are a function of the degree of social integration of working classes. See Seymour Martin Lipset et al., "The Psychology of Voting: An Analysis of Political Behavior," in Gardner Lindzey, ed., *Handbook of Social Psychology,* 2 vols. (Cambridge, Mass.: Addison Wesley Publishing Co., 1954), pp. 1124–1175.

TABLE 5.3 SOCIOECONOMIC CHARACTERISTICS AND ORIEN-
TATIONS TO PERONISM

| | Percentage of Class[a] | | |
| | Lower | Middle | Upper |
	($n = 721$)	($n = 960$)	($n = 157$)
Would vote for Perón	32.0	13.0	6.4
Generally approve of Peronist movement	38.7	18.4	12.7
Would support candidate supporting Perón	32.6	15.2	7.0
Perón did most harm to Argentina	19.4	39.5	65.0
Would hurt Argentina for Perón to return	34.8	56.7	77.7

[a] Class characterization based on interviewer appraisal.

lished, it is clear that Peronism is not an exclusively single-class movement. Middle-income respondents are well represented among Peronists, comprising approximately one-third of the persons who supported Perón for president and a larger portion of those with sympathy for the movement. (See Tables 5.3 and 5.4.)

The class image of the Peronist movement coincided closely with its actual composition. Not only were core Peronists chiefly persons of the poorer, least-educated lower classes but the Peronist party was perceived as being the party of the masses. No other Argentine party was so identified.[7] The UCRP tended not to be identified with any class; Socialists and the UCRI had no widely diffused image whatsoever. Almost one-third (31.7 percent) of the respon-

TABLE 5.4 SOCIOECONOMIC STATUS OF PERÓN AND ILLÍA
BACKERS

| | Percentage of Total Class That Would Vote for[b] | |
| | Perón | Illía |
Class [a]	($n = 397$)	($n = 428$)
Upper	6.4	23.6
Middle	13.0	22.6
Lower	32.0	18.7

[a] Class characterization based on interviewer appraisal.
[b] Remainder undecided.

[7] But note that a poll done by Encuestas Gallup de la Argentna (EGA) in Buenos Aires in March 1966 ($n = 1,004$) revealed that 53 percent of *all* respondents believed that the upper classes profited most from the government of President Illía; 63 percent of all lower-class respondents, 50 percent of middle-class respondents, and 27 percent of lower-class respondents expressed this view. See "Argentina," *Polls,* vol. 2, no. 3 (Spring 1967).

TABLE 5.5 PARTY IMAGES (AMONG RESPONDENTS NAMING PERONISTS OR UCRP AS ONE OF ARGENTINA'S MOST IMPORTANT PARTIES)
(In percent)

Image [a]	UCRP ($n = 1,649$)	Peronists ($n = 1,091$)
Party of poor	10.1	31.7
Party of middle class	7.5	—
Party of rich	4.4	—
Democratic	14.4	—
Traditionalist	4.8	—
One that really helps	12.1	4.5
Totalitarian, negative	5.3	6.5
Don't know	17.0	6.2
Not applicable	18.9	48.0

Source: Responses to Question 33 and 33d (Appendix B).
[a] Only those items are listed that were mentioned by more than 4 percent of the respondents.

dents identified Peronists as the party of the poor, for the poor; only 10 percent so identified the UCRP, which had a more diffuse, national, nonclass-oriented image.[8]

The relatively class-bound image of the Peronists was again revealed by responses to questions inquiring into the perceived group basis of parties. One-third of the respondents perceived the Peronist party as representing a particular group, compared with fewer than a quarter who so identified the UCRP. This is, however, less significant than the respondents' spontaneous identification of Peronism with a specific economic category: the poor. (See Tables 5.5 and 5.6.)

Voting patterns in the elections since 1957 confirm the class composition of the Peronist movement. Data permitting a comprehensive analysis of voting habits and the population's socioeconomic characteristics are lacking, but scrutiny of key districts possessing well-defined socioeconomic characteristics illuminates the social correlates as well as the stability of voting habits.

One of the most homogeneous working-class districts is Berisso, a suburb of La Plata, which is about thirty-five miles from Buenos Aires. The Swift and Armour plants make Berisso a center of the meat-packing industry. Workers in these plants are organized into

[8] Party images were elicited by questions following the one inquiring about Argentina's two or three most important parties. For each party named, each respondent was asked what kind of a party it was and what, if any, group it stood for. See Questions 32, 33, and 33d (Appendix B).

TABLE 5.6 CLASS-ORIENTED IMAGES: UCRP AND PERONIST
(In percent)

	UCRP ($n = 1,649$)	Peronist ($n = 1,091$)
Class-oriented description	22.0 [a]	31.7
Nonclass-oriented description	31.3	4.5
Negative description	5.3	6.5
No opinion	17.0	6.2
Not applicable [b]	18.9	48.0

Source: Same as Table 5.5.

[a] This total class-oriented description of the UCRP includes descriptions identifying the UCRP with upper (4.4 percent), lower (10.1 percent), and middle (7.5 percent) classes.

[b] This category comprises the percentage of all respondents who did not name the party as one of Argentina's most important parties.

one of the strongest unions of the Peronist "Bloc 62." Among the workers of Berisso are many immigrants from the interior. In the streets of Berisso, low-cost housing projects stand as tangible monuments to Peronist welfare policies. About half the voters in Berisso voted Peronist when a Peronist party was permitted to contest elections. Approximately one-third voted blank in 1963 when no Peronist candidates or parties were permitted to compete. However, though support for Perón and Peronism was strong here, it dominated but did not preempt the political scene. Unión Popular's half of the votes left it the strongest party by far in the 1962 and 1965 elections; but it polled only half, the other half going to other parties. In 1965 the UCRP was supported by approximately a quarter of the voters of Berisso, with the remaining quarter split half a dozen ways (see Table 5.7).

Avellaneda is another famous industrial district settled in the previous century by Italian, Spanish, and Polish immigrants, some of whom live there today alongside the men from Argentina's interior who have more recently crowded into Avellaneda seeking work.[9] Often they found instead of jobs, only misery to match the deprivations of the countryside. Avellaneda occupies a special place in the history of Perón's romance with the *descamisados*. The historic march of October 17, 1945, that restored Perón to power

[9] Avellaneda is cited by di Tella as a prototype of poor, depressed urban districts, whose inhabitants organize themselves into authoritarian social and political structures to which they were previously accustomed. See Torcuato S. di Tella, *El sistema político argentino y la clase obrera* (Buenos Aires: Editorial Universitaria de Buenos Aires, 1964), p. 17.

TABLE 5.7 BERISSO LEGISLATIVE ELECTION RESULTS, 1962, 1963, AND 1965

	1962	1963	1965
Total vote cast	23,528	24,630	25,684
Party (percentage of total vote)			
UCRI	18.0	12.5	2.62
UCRP	16.3	21.4	26.35
PDP-UDELPA	0.2	5.5	0.40
UP	52.7	—	49.57
Blank votes	1.5	34.1	1.99
Conservative	5.3	6.7	3.44
PSD	2.8	6.2	1.58
PSA	—	5.7	2.09
PDC	0.5	3.0	1.28
Other	2.1	4.8	10.68

Sources: Voting statistics for 1962 and 1963 are from James W. Rowe's analysis, *The Argentine Elections of 1963* (Washington, D.C.: The Institute for the Comparative Study of Political Systems, 1963), pp. 33–34; 1965 figures are from *La Prensa,* March 26, 1965.

began in Avellaneda. Ever since, the district has been a center of Peronist activity. Avellaneda is somewhat more heterogeneous,. ethnically and industrially, than Berisso. Its electoral politics were dominated by Peronist organizations, but other parties found support there. In 1965 the Peronist Unión Popular polled just under half the votes; half went to other parties, among whom the UCRP was the most successful (see Table 5.8).

A similar picture of Argentine voting habits is disclosed by the voting patterns of Vicente López, a fashionable suburb on the outskirts of Buenos Aires inhabited largely by wealthy businessmen

TABLE 5.8 AVELLANEDA LEGISLATIVE ELECTION RESULTS, 1962, 1963, AND 1965

	1962	1963	1965
Total vote cast	169,144	173,626	175,936
Party (percentage of total vote)			
UCRI	22.2	20.4	4.21
UCRP	17.8	25.2	28.15
PDP-UDELPA	0.3	12.7	1.94
UP	44.0	—	46.24
Blank votes	1.2	18.8	1.57
PSD	4.8	5.6	2.76
PSA	2.9	7.0	3.96
PDC	1.2	4.5	2.00
Other	5.5	5.8	9.17

Sources: Same as Table 5.7

and professionals. But Vicente López is not an entirely homogeneous community since some lower-middle-class groups have made homes there. The result is a mixed but predominantly rich suburb in which Peronists do not dominate elections. The strongest political orientation is Radical. The UCRP and UCRI together have sometimes polled 40 to 50 percent of the vote in recent elections. In 1965, however, the Unión Popular drew more votes than the UCRP, and nearly equaled the combined vote of the UCRP and UCRI. The remaining votes were split among half a dozen parties (see Table 5.9).

The specialized appeal of Peronism is clearly visible in Tables 5.7–5.9. Peronist parties did best in low-income industrial areas; but voting patterns confirmed survey findings that, although Perón and Peronism were most attractive to low socioeconomic groups, Argentine politics was not fully polarized on class lines. Perón was most attractive to low-status persons, but roughly as many of the poor rejected him as voted for him. Peronist parties lost votes to the Radicals, but they gained middle-sector votes. It is also clear that some workers were more attracted to Perón than others. The next few pages are devoted to distinguishing who among the lower classes are most responsive to Peronist appeals.

Social Characteristics

Perón's Argentina has been repeatedly characterized as the Argentina of the *gaucho* barbarians from the interior, who lack the culture and civilization of the European-oriented *porteños*. Terms such as

TABLE 5.9   VICENTE LÓPEZ LEGISLATIVE ELECTION RESULTS, 1962, 1963, AND 1965

	1962	1963	1965
Total vote cast	109,617	114,260	116,927
Party (percentage of total vote)			
UCRI	28.5	14.6	2.83
UCRP	20.5	26.3	33.27
PDP-UDELPA	—	20.8	4.26
UP	30.7	—	34.29
Blank votes	1.6	13.5	1.55
Conservative	4.4	2.5	3.67
PSD	7.0	6.6	3.10
PSA	2.5	5.8	3.28
PDC	1.6	6.0	2.29
MID	—	—	4.74
Other	3.2	3.9	6.72

Sources: Same as Table 5.7.

TABLE 5.10   EDUCATION AND PERONIST SYMPATHIES
(In percent)

	Total (n = 2,014)	All Respondents Except Core Peronists (n = 1,649)	Core Peronists (n = 365)
None	3.1	1.8	8.8
Primary incomplete	21.4	18.2	33.7
Primary complete	36.2	35.6	38.6
Secondary incomplete	16.9	18.2	11.2
Secondary complete	12.7	14.1	3.6
University incomplete	5.5	6.1	2.2
University complete	3.7	4.2	1.4
Not ascertained	0.4	—	—

Source: Background information in Question 73 (Appendix B).

nativist, populist, Jacksonian are invoked to communicate a feel for what has repeatedly been described as the distinctive culture and constituency of the Peronist movement. The 1965 survey data confirm the specialized appeal of Perón to these groups and help to define the movement as distinctively attractive not just to the poor but to certain types of poor. Some, but not all, of these other characteristics especially associated with the core Peronists are universally associated with low economic status. Occupational and educational characteristics of core Peronists are also distinctive. Laborers, both manual and skilled, were most numerous. Few businessmen, office workers, or professionals were found among the core Peronists. The uneducated were disproportionately numerous among Peronists, the educated disproportionately few. About four-fifths of the core Peronists had a primary education or less. Fewer than 4 percent had ever attended a university. (See Table 5.10.)

The special appeal of Perón for persons of low education is

TABLE 5.11   EDUCATION, CLASS, AND POLITICAL PREFERENCE
(In percent)

	Persons Having Primary Education or Less	
	Lower Class	Middle Class
Supported Perón	88	68
Supported Illía	79	54

Source: Responses to Questions 35 and 73 (Appendix B), and interviewer class appraisal.

TABLE 5.12   MOTHER'S BIRTHPLACE AND PERONIST
SYMPATHIES
(In percent)

	Total ($n = 2,014$)	Total Non-Peronists ($n = 1,649$)	Core Peronists ($n = 365$)
Argentina	64.1	55.8	73.7
Italy	14.7	15.9	9.0
Spain	12.0	12.7	8.5
Other Latin American countries	2.3	1.9	3.8
Other European countries	6.3	9.6	5.8

Source: Responses to Question 73 (Appendix B).
Note: Somewhat fewer fathers than mothers of the respondents were native-born, but the proportions of the total population and of Peronists with foreign-born fathers were nearly the same: 14.3 percent of the total sample had fathers born in Spain compared with 11.2 percent of the Peronists. Compared with 3.3 percent of the Peronists, 2.4 percent of all respondents had fathers born in other Latin American countries.

confirmed when we control for class. It is clear that in both lower-income and middle-income groups Perón was relatively more popular than President Illía among persons with little education (see Table 5.11).

The survey so confirms the special appeal of Perón and Peronism for indigenous Argentines. Peronists were more likely to be persons with Argentine than with European mothers or fathers (see Table 5.12).[10]

The stereotypical portrait of Peronists as drawn disproportionately from the poor, the uneducated, uncultured natives from the interior is partially confirmed by our data, and is stated in Table 5.13.

Age is also significant in assessing certain aspects of the Peronist appeal. Presumably, the purely personal appeal of Juan Perón would wane as the time after his downfall lengthened. It is therefore particularly interesting that core Peronists were distributed fairly evenly among all ages from the youngest voters to those over 60. The proportion of core Peronists between 30 and 50 is very slightly higher than other age groups. But more important and more con-

[10] Note that, despite the higher percentages of "native" Argentines among the Peronist rank and file, the Peronist elite between 1946 and 1955 contained more sons of immigrants than any government during the period studied by de Imáz (1936–1961). See José Luis de Imaz, Los que mandan, 5th ed. (Buenos Aires: Editorial Universitaria de Buenos Aires, 1966), p. 15.

TABLE 5.13   SOCIAL CHARACTERISTICS OF PERONIST BASE

	Percentage
Less than primary school	+ 22.5
Secondary school or more	+ 14.2
Lowest economic status	+ 18.8
Argentine mother	+ 17.9
Argentine father	+ 12.4
Italian or Spanish mother	− 11.1

Source: Responses to Questions 73 and 35 (Appendix B).
Note: Each cell represents the difference between core Peronists and all other informants.

clusive is the fact that Perón is the preferred political leader of approximately one-fifth of the respondents in all age brackets (see Table 5.14).[11] This finding is consistent with others indicating there is little difference in political orientations among generations, a finding that suggests the stability of political culture, roles, and orientations. The fact of continuity through generations will receive further attention in later chapters. For the moment it is important to note only that the continued influence of the Perón mystique indicates that the appeals of Peronism and its leader did not fade in the absence of personal stimulation of the myth.

Perón's appeal also was strong among both sexes. Women, enfranchised by Perón in 1947, are often said to be especially vulnerable to his masculine appeal. They were not, however, revealed as

TABLE 5.14   AGE AND PERONIST PREFERENCES
(In percent)

	Age Distribution		
	Total Sample ($n = 2,014$)	Core Peronists ($n = 365$)	Pro-Peronists ($n = 411$)
18–24	12.4	11.0	10.9
25–29	10.1	9.9	11.9
30–39	26.4	28.5	27.3
40–49	22.4	23.8	20.2
50–59	16.3	15.6	18.5
60 or more	11.8	11.0	10.5
Not ascertained	0.6	0.3	0.7

Source: Responses to Question 73 (Appendix B).

[11] Confronted with the hypothetical choice for the presidency, the following percentages, by age group, of the total sample asserted they would vote for Perón: 18–24, 19.2 percent; 25–29, 23 percent; 30–39, 19.6 percent; 40–49, 20.4 percent; 50 and over, 18.6 percent.

more Peronist than men. The proportion of strong Peronists of each sex roughly parallels their distribution in the general population, and among pro-Peronists men outnumbered women.

Geographic Distribution

Differences and rivalries between Buenos Aires and the rest of Argentina were important long before there was an Argentina. In the half century after independence, distinctive economic and cultural interests and political ambition kept Buenos Aires outside the nation. Historians, men of letters, and social scientists have described and emphasized the conflict and contrast between the European-oriented *porteño* culture and economy of the capital city and the *gaucho* orientations of the interior that focus on the nation and its Latin neighbors.[12] José Hernández celebrated *gaucho* culture in his famous epic *Martín Fierro;* later, Domingo Faustino Sarmiento, in his equally famous *Facundo,* identified urbanity with civilization, the interior with barbarism, and, as president, promoted immigration to weaken the *criollo gaucho* element in the Argentine nation through the infusion of more European blood. George Blanksten has termed the cleavage between port and interior "basic and tragic," asserting that "hostility between Buenos Aires and the interior is mutual and starts afresh every day."[13] James Scobie proclaimed the importance of the schism in his title, *Argentina: A City and a Nation.*[14]

Each of the two cultures is said to embody a distinctive approach to politics and economics as well as to manners and style. *Porteño* economic orientations are described as directed toward Europe, which was the principal market for exports and the principal source of goods needed to maintain European comforts and life style. *Criollo* economic interests are said to have been focused on Argentina and to have looked to internal development and economic

[12] An interesting contrast between North and South American patterns of status is found in different attitudes toward immigrants. In Argentina, as elsewhere in Latin America, "indigenous" stock (often Indian) is associated with lower-class status. De Imaz reports that 57 percent of his socially elite sample were fourth-generation Argentines, the descendants of immigrants who arrived between 1840–1880. See de Imaz, *La clase alta,* p. 32.

[13] George I. Blanksten, *Perón's Argentina* (Chicago: University of Chicago Press, 1953), p. 18.

[14] James R. Scobie, *Argentina: A City and a Nation* (New York: Oxford University Press, 1965).

independence. The two political cultures are said to be similarly disparate. Since Sarmiento, it has been a convention of Argentine history to identify Buenos Aires with liberal politics and the *gaucho* with authoritarian politics. Rosas is often described as embodying the substance and style of the politics of the interior; Sarmiento himself is cited as an example par excellence of *porteño* politics.[15] According to this stereotype, *porteño* politics is internationalist, liberal, and democratic; *gaucho* politics is nationalist and autocratic. Perón is then a direct descendant of Rosas, and the two of them are either exemplars of nativist, autocratic, barbarian politics of the interior or carriers of an authentic indigenous political style, purer by far than the counterfeit liberal cosmopolitanism of the *porteño*.[16]

The conception of Argentina as embodying two geographically based political cultures shows no sign of waning, only of being updated.[17] In his recent book on the Argentine working class, Torcuato di Tella has emphasized the authoritarian character typical of rural Argentines;[18] another contemporary writer, Arturo López Peña, has described in some detail the *compadre*, carrier of a new variant of *gaucho* culture resulting from the peasants' move from the countryside to the suburbs.[19]

As with many broad social distinctions, the lines between these postulated subcultures are sometimes dim, sometimes wavy, and sometimes both. Owners of large estates, obviously in the interior,

[15] Concerning the *porteño*'s self-estimate, Ysabel F. Rennie has asserted, "the *porteño* mentality . . . may be roughly summed up as the inner conviction that Argentina exists for Buenos Aires, and that all outside the limits of Buenos Aires is outside the limits of civilization." See Ysabel F. Rennie, *The Argentine Republic* (New York: Macmillan Co., 1945), p. 20.

[16] Mario Amadeo, for example, asserts that the "revolution" of 1930 replaced the *porteño*'s skepticism, belief in progress, and principles of the French Revolution with "indigenous traditions," which include Catholicism, "strong" government, nationalism, and "corporativism." He further suggests that the "nationalist revolution" of 1930 served later as an inspiration to Perón, who continued the tradition of indigenous politics. See Amadeo, *Ayer, hoy, mañana*, p. 109.

[17] For recent adaptations of the theme, which relate the "two cultures" to the military, see Rafael Funes, *Reflexiones políticas para militares: hacia una política nacional* (Buenos Aires: Ediciones Relevo, 1963), and Jorge Abelardo Ramos, who also identifies the army with the nationalist anti-*porteño* orientation. See his comments in Silvio Frondizi et al., *Las izquierdas en el proceso político argentino* (Buenos Aires: Palestra, 1959), p. 197.

[18] Di Tella, *El sistema político*, pp. 13–16.

[19] Arturo López Peña, *Teoría del Argentina* (Buenos Aires: Librería Huemul, 1965). This entire essay on Argentine national character is devoted to the differences between *porteño, gaucho,* and *compadre* cultures.

are conventionally described as having shared *porteño* interests in export markets for beef and agricultural products. But selected *estancieros—caudillos* such as Rosas who lived on their land— exemplified *gaucho* political culture. The geographic lines between the two cultures were further blurred when internal migrations from countryside to city transplanted "rural," "interior" attitudes to the fallow soil of burgeoning working-class districts that are then said to have become seedbeds of the new Peronist despotism.

Presumably, if these two Argentinas exist and have significance for mass political behavior, differences between them will be reflected in voting behavior or attitudes toward political objects or both.[20] Although internal migrations would have blurred the pure *porteño* orientations of Buenos Aires inhabitants, one should nonetheless find reflected in the data a provincial, rural subculture spread over the countryside outside the capital city.[21]

Voting patterns neither definitively confirm nor disprove the existence of two geographically based political subcultures. The political identifications and support patterns of *porteños* and provincials show some tendency to split, but the degree of difference is inadequate to support the notion of sharply distinctive political subcultures. One fact with negative implications for the two-culture hypothesis is that *all major parties have support spread over the country*. Since approximately three-fourths of the electorate is concentrated in four districts (Federal Capital, Buenos Aires, Córdoba, and Santa Fe), parties must do well in these districts, but, in fact, the three parties that have shown significant strength in the post-Perón period have all demonstrated substantial strength in most other districts. In 1958 the UCRI-Peronist combination ran first in *all* districts, and the UCRP ran second in all but one. In 1962, when the Peronists were permitted to run candidates, they won elections in eleven of twenty-three districts and ran second in six others. In 1963 the UCRP was victor in sixteen districts. In brief, since 1957

[20] It is possible for distinctive political orientations not to be reflected in electoral behavior and party support patterns, depending on the structure of the party system. The ubiquity of Republican and Democratic labels could cause a foreigner looking at vote distributions in the United States to miss entirely the distinctive, political subcultures that exist in the South, in California, and in the upper Midwest, to mention but three examples. It is also possible that elite subcultures may not be reflected in mass attitudes or behavior but still have significant influence on political life.

[21] Presumably, this subculture would also be found in Buenos Aires' working-class suburbs.

the two Radical parties and the Peronists have proved themselves to be *national parties*, with substantial support in Buenos Aires and the Federal Capital *and* outside it. While internal migrations could account for the support for "interior" styles of politics in Buenos Aires, they cannot be reasonably invoked to account for the *porteño* voting habits in the countryside. Although distinctive political sub-cultures have not been reflected in voting behavior since 1957, Table 5.15 indicates the existence of some differences in political tendencies in the Federal Capital and in the interior. In each election up to 1965 Peronist parties ran somewhat less well in the Federal Capital than in the nation as a whole.

There are other indications of a small but significant difference in the geographic support patterns of the national parties. It has been mentioned that four districts—the Federal Capital, Buenos Aires, Córdoba, and Santa Fe—contain more than 70 percent of the electorate. In 1963, 71.5 percent of all votes were cast in these four provinces. These votes accounted for 77.3 percent of all UCRP votes, 73.9 percent of all Alende votes (UCRI), 86 percent of all Aramburu votes (UDELPA), and only 67.6 percent of all Peronist votes. Similar ratios existed in other elections, demonstrating that while the Peronists were very strong in these districts, as indeed any party had to be to have significant strength in the nation as a whole, they drew relatively more support from other parts of the country. Though not directly germane to the hypothesis concerning Argentina's two graphically based political subcultures, this fact does emphasize the Peronists' strong appeal outside urban areas. In fact, Peronist electoral support after 1957 was strongest in the provinces of Tucumán, Jujuy, Neuquén, Córdoba, and Buenos Aires.

Survey data confirm the geographic support patterns indicated in the foregoing discussion (see Table 5.16).[22] Peronists were somewhat more favorably regarded outside Buenos Aires (see Table 5.17).

TABLE 5.15   PERONIST STRENGTH IN THE FEDERAL CAPITAL AND IN THE NATION IN FIVE ELECTIONS

| | Percentage of Total Vote | | | | |
	1957 [a]	1960	1962	1963 [a]	1965
Federal Capital	18.4	21.5	27.7	12.3	32.9
Nation	24.5	24.9	31.9	18.8	29.9

Source: See note to Table 3.1.

[a] Blank vote only.

[22] It should be borne in mind that for reasons of expense and inaccessibility the sample represents only persons living in towns of 2,000 or more. Truly rural Argentina is not represented. It is, of course, represented in the electoral statistics analyzed.

TABLE 5.16 GEOGRAPHIC DISTRIBUTION OF PERONIST SUPPORTERS
(In percent)

	All Argentines	Federal Capital	Suburbs	Central Provinces	Other
Would vote for Perón	19.7	14.4	18.4	21.2	26.3
Believe Perón should return to power	21.4	16.8	20.8	22.1	26.8
Would help Argentina to let Perón return	26.1	20.4	25.5	26.8	33.1
Would support candidate supported by Peronists	36.6	28.4	34.1	40.8	44.4
Peronist party has good leaders	20.5	17.1	20.1	20.6	24.9
Peronist party has good program	28.8	23.3	28.2	29.6	35.2

Source: Responses to Questions 35, 17j, 37, 25h, 33b, and 33c (Appendix B).

Tables 5.16 and 5.17 suggest a striking and persistent relationship between geographic and demographic factors on the one hand and attitudes toward Peronists on the other. This relationship persisted in slightly modified form when controls were introduced. When education and social class were controlled, geographic and demographic factors were confirmed as having independent influence. Tables 5.18 and 5.19 reflect the results of controlling both educational and class level.

The Peronist support pattern revealed by Tables 5.16–5.19 is consistent enough to be persuasive. Just as previous analysis revealed

TABLE 5.17 DEMOGRAPHIC DISTRIBUTION OF PERONIST SUPPORTERS
(In percent)

	All Argentines	500,000 or More	250,000 to 499,999	50,000 to 249,999	Smaller Towns
Would vote for Perón	19.7	15.4	18.5	21.9	26.3
Believe Perón should return to power	21.4	17.7	21.1	23.7	25.1
Would help Argentina to let Perón return	26.1	20.5	26.1	29.2	31.6
Would support candidate supported by Peronists	36.6	31.1	34.6	39.7	44.9
Peronist party has good leaders	20.5	17.7	20.4	19.8	26.6
Peronist party has good program	28.8	26.9	29.1	28.0	33.3

Source: Same as Table 5.16.

TABLE 5.18 GEOGRAPHIC DISTRIBUTION OF PERONIST SUPPORTERS OF LOW SES AND LOW EDUCATIONAL LEVEL (In percent)

| | Lower Class Having Primary Education or Less | | | |
	Federal Capital	Suburbs	Central Provinces	Other
Would vote for Perón	41.7	54.9	53.4	49.5
Believe Perón should return to power	38.6	50.7	49.6	46.5
Would help Argentina to let Perón return	34.1	48.5	50.3	42.6
Would support candidate supported by Peronists	33.9	45.1	42.3	36.6
Peronist party has good leaders	25.9	33.7	37.1	28.5
Peronist party has good program	25.7	32.2	36.4	27.2

Source: Same as Table 5.16.

that persons of lower class and education were more likely to support Perón than those of higher status and education, this analysis demonstrates that lower-class and less-educated persons outside the Federal Capital were more likely to support Perón than those inside it.

More detailed analysis of class, education, location, and Peronist support indicates that the relationships among these variables are

TABLE 5.19 DEMOGRAPHIC DISTRIBUTION OF PERONIST SUPPORTERS OF LOW SES AND LOW EDUCATIONAL LEVEL (In percent)

| | Lower Class Having Primary Education or Less | | | | |
	500,000 or More	250,000 to 499,999	50,000 to 249,999	10,000 to 49,999	Less than 10,000
Would vote for Perón	35.9	55.0	50.0	71.1	58.2
Believe Perón should return to power	33.0	50.0	48.8	62.2	57.7
Would help Argentina to let Perón return	32.5	48.9	43.0	64.4	53.7
Would support candidate supported by Peronists	31.2	46.0	37.9	51.4	46.1
Peronist party has good leaders	26.4	32.2	32.7	41.8	38.4
Peronist party has good program	24.5	30.3	33.5	44.3	37.0

Source: Same as Table 5.16.

TABLE 5.20 GEOGRAPHIC AND DEMOGRAPHIC DISTRIBUTION OF PERONIST SUPPORT BY CLASS AND EDUCATION (In percent)

	Federal Capital	Suburbs	Central Provinces	Other	500,000 or More	250,000 to 499,999	50,000 to 249,999	10,000 to 49,999	Less than 10,000
Would vote for Perón									
Lower class	50.0	61.5	61.9	54.6	46.7	63.0	55.4	76.3	61.8
Middle and upper class	41.7	33.6	25.4	40.2	39.1	33.0	36.6	23.7	29.1
Primary education or less	71.7	85.2	81.4	76.3	65.2	83.0	84.8	84.2	85.5
More than primary school	28.3	13.9	18.6	22.7	34.8	16.0	14.3	15.8	14.5
Believe Perón should return to power									
Lower class	42.9	57.2	58.5	54.5	39.6	58.8	55.4	70.3	63.5
Middle and upper class	45.7	39.1	26.0	39.4	43.4	37.7	35.5	27.0	28.8
Primary education or less	78.6	82.6	78.0	75.8	69.8	81.6	81.8	86.5	80.8
More than primary school	21.4	16.7	22.0	23.2	30.2	17.5	17.4	13.5	19.2
Would help Argentina to let Perón return									
Lower class	40.0	54.4	58.4	50.0	40.7	55.3	49.7	73.3	58.2
Middle and upper class	49.4	39.6	27.5	41.8	43.1	38.3	41.6	26.7	29.9
Primary education or less	65.9	81.7	78.5	71.3	61.8	80.9	77.9	86.7	79.1
More than primary school	34.1	17.8	20.8	27.9	38.2	18.4	20.8	13.3	20.9
Would support candidate supported by Peronists									
Lower class	40.7	50.9	51.1	42.1	39.8	52.9	43.8	57.1	51.7
Middle and upper class	51.7	44.2	33.5	50.6	44.6	41.7	48.3	41.4	36.0
Primary education or less	63.6	77.9	74.4	64.6	59.1	77.5	73.9	77.1	75.3
More than primary school	34.7	21.7	25.6	34.1	39.8	21.9	25.6	22.9	23.6

Source: Same as Table 5.16.

complex. Support for Perón among middle-class persons or those with education beyond primary school was more common in the Federal Capital than in provincial cities. (See Table 5.20.) The Peronist movement was a more purely lower-class movement in the provincial cities than in the capital. This pattern has interesting implications for the strength of provincial neo-Peronist parties.

These findings clarify the support pattern. They should not obscure the fact that Peronists were relatively numerous outside of Buenos Aires and in relatively smaller cities. These findings provide limited support for the characterization of Peronism as a movement of the interior—the more so when it is recalled that the suburbs of the Capital (an area of significant Peronist strength) are heavily peopled by first- and second-generation internal migrants who are said to have preserved much of the culture of the countryside.

Conclusions concerning the "two Argentinas" must take cognizance of the distribution of other types of political preferences in Argentina. The survey data indicate that persons who supported Illía were also more numerous outside of the Federal Capital (see Table 5.21). While Peronist parties consistently did better outside the Federal Capital than in it in elections as well as in hypothetical races in the survey, the UCRP ran about the same in the Federal Capital as in the whole nation. Both major parties had national support; neither was clearly *porteño* or *gaucho*. Peronism, most often identified with the interior, was indeed most popular there. But more than half its supporters were drawn from the capital city. Many of these may have been first- or second-generation internal immigrants, *compadres* who transplanted *gaucho* culture from the pampas to the sidewalks. But this movement that may have nationalized Argentine political culture also definitively blurred the geo-

TABLE 5.21 GEOGRAPHIC AND DEMOGRAPHIC DISTRIBUTION: PERONIST AND UCRP VOTERS COMPARED (In percent)

	Nation	Federal Capital	Suburbs	Central Provinces	Other
Would vote for Perón	19.7	14.4	18.4	21.2	26.3
Would vote for Illía	21.3	19.0	18.7	27.5	18.7

	500,000 or More	250,000 to 499,999	50,000 to 249,999	Less than 50,000
Would vote for Perón	15.4	18.5	21.9	26.3
Would vote for Illía	20.0	17.2	24.1	25.1

graphic bases of political orientations. So the verdict on the contemporary accuracy of the "two cultures" hypothesis must be an unsatisfactory "not proven."

Summary: Social Characteristics of the Peronist Universe

The preceding analysis gives qualified support for the stereotype that depicts Peronists as undereducated, lower-income indigenous Argentines, but it only demonstrates that these persons were most numerous among Peronists. The mass base of the Peronist movement had a distinctive but not exclusive socioeconomic character. Large numbers of this collectivity shared identical social, ethnic, and economic backgrounds. Persons of primary education and less, of Argentine parentage, and of low income and persons who identified with the lower classes were most numerous among rank-and-file Peronists. Persons from the highest income and education levels were rare. But it was not a single-class movement.

The principal Peronist political organization, Unión Popular, was a national party with a substantial number of supporters drawn from other social categories. The lower classes were most numerous in Unión Popular, just as they were most numerous among British Labourites. Persons drawn from these classes were also relatively more numerous in the leadership of these parties. Both parties were widely perceived as working-class parties. Still, as the Labour party draws from the middle classes of British, the middle classes are also well represented among Peronists, comprising a fourth to a third of the movement's mass base.

The core of the movement, consisting of its strongest, most consistent rank-and-file supporters, was more socially homogeneous than its fringes. The socioeconomic characteristics of the movement's mass base varied with the proximity of issues to Perón himself. Persons who supported the Peronist movement but not the return of Perón to personal power were more socially heterogeneous; that is, persons termed pro-Peronist in this study were less socially homogeneous than those termed core Peronists. Middle-class and relatively more educated backgrounds were more numerous among the former, a finding that at least implies confirmation for the view that the middle classes were more important in the neo-Peronist parties.[23]

---

[23] Peter Ranis emphasizes the aggregative character of the Peronist movement and stresses the middle-class leadership and orientations of some of the provincial neo-Peronist parties. See "Peronismo Without Perón, Ten Years after the Fall (1955–1965)," Journal of Inter-American Studies, vol. 8, no. 1 (January 1966), especially pp. 124–125.

These findings do not imply a necessary or preemptive relationship between social categories and political movements in Argentina. *Most* Peronists are poorly educated and poorly paid. But *most* poorly educated and poorly paid Argentines are not Peronists. Only about half of these low-status persons support Peronist organizations and goals. The preferences of the other half are split among various other groups. Therefore, while Argentine politics in 1965 reflected social cleavages, they were not polarized into a two- or three-class struggle. In this, Argentine mass politics resembles that of such other nations as Britain and the German Federal Republic, each of which has a mass party identified principally with working people but which (1) does not attract the support of all lower-income and lower-status individuals and (2) is less socially homogeneous than the image would suggest.

Three implications of these findings concerning the social composition of the Peronist mass base merit comment. First, we may note that if the durability and solidarity of a movement are favorably affected by a high degree of social homogeneity, its capacities for growth or "permeability" [24] are affected adversely. A movement with a distinctive social or economic clientele (or image that identifies it with such a clientele) will find it relatively more difficult to recruit followers from other social or economic categories. Since the Peronists are widely identified as the party of the poor, while the UCRP is perceived in more general political terms, it seems almost certain that the UCRP will find it easier to draw supporters from all sectors of the society as long as these images endure. This does not suggest that Peronist prospects are bleak. To the contrary, the poor are not only always with us, but they are always numerous. Furthermore, electoral behavior and survey data alike demonstrate that Argentines frequently pass in and out of the political role of Peronist supporters. Therefore, though many Peronists share stable social characteristics, they do not comprise a closed universe with fixed boundaries.

Second, the minimal base of the movement, that is, rank-and-file supporters linked to the movement by stable identifications, was small compared with the stable minimum base of major parties in

[24] "Permeability" is defined by Lasswell and Kaplan as "the ease with which a person can become a participant." It is distinguished from "circulation," which refers to the degree of change in the group membership. See Harold D. Lasswell and Abraham Kaplan, *Power and Society: A Framework for Political Inquiry* (New Haven: Yale University Press, 1950), p. 35.

the United States or Britain but large enough to make Peronists major actors in the Argentine political arena. Fluctuations in the size of the movement beyond the minimum base testify not only to the permeability of the movement but to its rather high rate of circulation.[25]

Third, the fact that Peronists had captured the image, the clientele, and the role of the party of the poor and the working masses posed grim problems for other parties that perceived and presented themselves as working-class parties. Argentina's socialist and communist parties succeeded neither before nor after Perón in recruiting a mass following from among the lower classes. Their growth in numbers, if not in influence, is probably contingent on the collapse or infiltration of the Peronist movement. Perhaps for this reason, communist leaders have been much interested in promoting a united front with Peronist labor and political action groups.[26]

[25] Obviously, circulation rates of political parties vary greatly among political systems. The Peronist circulation rate is rather high compared, for example, with that of the major U.S. parties but notably stable compared with that of other mass parties in the Argentine system.

[26] For a discussion of Argentine communist recruitment problems and a popular front proposal, see Victorio Codovilla, *Por la acción de las masas hacia la conquista del poder* (Buenos Aires: Editorial Anteo, 1963).

6

Orientations to Interpersonal and Group Relations

Verás que todo es mentira
Verás que nada es amor,
que al mundo nada le importa.
yira ... yira ...
Aunque te quiebre la vida,
aunque te muerda un dolor,
no esperés nunca una ayuda,
ni una mano, ni un favor.
From the Tango, "Yira ... Yira ..."

This chapter is concerned with mapping the contours of the social world perceived by rank-and-file Peronists. Its purposes are, first, to delineate some traditional views about how Argentines perceive one another; second, to determine whether there were views about existing and desirable interpersonal relations that were distinctively Peronist, and to describe those views; third, to describe Peronists' views about the allocations of influence and political power in Argentine society; and, fourth, to explore their orientations to a number of politically relevant social aggregates.

Peronists' views on a number of the "big" questions will be investigated here, for these mediate responses to many concrete political and social situations. Whether Peronists are inclined to view the world as benevolent and peaceful or as the arena of a perpetual war of "each against all"; whether they see their society as one run by the few for the few; whom they perceive as the principal contenders for power; whom they perceive as their friends and whom as their enemies; whom they think helps whom; and who represents whom—these are the questions discussed in the following pages.

Interpersonal Relations

In a much-quoted passage, Ortega y Gasset characterized the Argentine as a "man on the defensive":

> In a normal interpersonal relation the Argentine does not abandon himself; to the contrary, when another approaches him, he seals his soul and puts himself upon the defensive. We find ourselves with a man who has mobilized the greatest part of his energy to defend himself. . . . But against whom, or what, if we do not attack him? It is this that surprises us. It is to be expected that one defends oneself when attacked, but to live on the defensive when bothered by no one is an exceedingly strange tendency.[1]

Ortega is by no means the only commentator who, in speaking of the Argentine national character, suggests that interpersonal relations are characterized by mutual distrust, suspicion, and hostility. Simón Bolívar's complaint that "There is no good faith in America, neither between men nor between nations" has often been applied by Argentines to themselves.[2]

Common, too, in literature on the Argentine national character is the emphasis on the related theme of lack of community. H. A. Murena comments:

> *There is no community in Argentina.* We do not form a body, though we may form a *conglomeration.* We behave as if each one were unique and as if he were alone, with the unfortunate consequences which result when that is the situation. The hand knoweth not what the head thinketh, the mouth ignoreth the stomach. . . . *Each organ believes itself the whole, and functions as if it were more important than the whole.* Is there any more succinct definition of sickness? Who is to blame? No one. Everyone.[3]

Fillol shares the view that Argentine society is characterized by

---

[1] José Ortega y Gasset, "Intimidades," in *Obras completas,* 3rd ed., 2 vols. (Madrid: Espasa-Calpe, 1943), p. 668. Without casting doubt on the accuracy of Ortega's characterization of Argentines, we may note that he was very sensitive to the tendency of people to seal themselves off from others and from experience. In *Invertebrate Spain* (New York: W. W. Norton, 1937), he describes Spaniards as hermetically sealed. Elsewhere he describes this as an important quality of mass men in *Revolt of the Masses* (New York: W. W. Norton, 1932).

[2] See, for example, Alfredo Galletti, *La realidad Argentina en el siglo XX: la política y los partidos,* vol. 1 (Buenos Aires: Fondo de Cultura Económica, 1961), p. 201.

[3] Quoted in Tomás Roberto Fillol, *Social Factors in Economic Development: The Argentine Case* (Cambridge, Mass.: The M.I.T. Press, 1961), p. 22; Fillol's emphasis.

lack of community and mutual distrust. In his effort to describe Argentine value orientations he comments:

Two characteristics emerge clearly: first, that the dominant value orientations of the Argentine population are basically *passive;* second, that this particular value-orientation profile is inimical to the emergence of social relationships which would enable individuals to act concertedly in the pursuit of common goals.[4]

McGann restates the point in his book on Argentina:

The most fundamental question confronting the Argentine people was not political, economic, or social. It was psychological. It was the crisis of national character, long discussed by intellectuals and even politicians, but now a reality so clear that any citizen could feel and see it—in the fragmentation of political life, in the clash of classes, in the rampant pursuit of power whether economic or political, in the breakdown of national consensus. . . .[5]

Mario Amadeo strikes the same theme when he discusses the mutual hostilities that riddled Argentina in the pre-Perón period. Hate, he says, dominated relations between rich and poor, leader and led, learned and ignorant, oligarch and plebeian.[6] In a similar vein, Kalman Silvert comments, "Argentina's class-bound politics assume that no public measure can be good for almost everybody, that the benefit of one group is the automatic loss of all others. Life is an inelastic pie, and a bigger piece for *fulano* necessarily means a smaller piece for *sutano.*"[7]

These remarks are typical of the characterizations of the Argentine national character and will have a familiar ring for students of Mediterranean cultures generally. Lack of community is a recurrent theme in the literature on Latin cultures. In these cultures, family is often described as the only unit whose members are united by trust, affection, and empathy; the family is usually described less

[4] Ibid.

[5] Thomas F. McGann, *Argentina: The Divided Land* (Princeton, N.J.: D. Van Nostrand Company, 1966), p. 60. McGann's view that consensus broke down implies that it existed at some earlier time. Most students of Argentina doubt that.

[6] Mario Amadeo, *Ayer, hoy, mañana* (Buenos Aires: Ediciones Gure, 1956), p. 109.

[7] Silvert, "The Costs of Anti-Nationalism: Argentina," in Kalman H. Silvert, ed., *Expectant Peoples: Nationalism and Development* (New York: Vintage Books, 1967), p. 350.

as an intermediate unit linking the individual to larger groups than as a fortress in which the individual can protect himself against society. Fillol commented, "in Argentina this loyalty is carried to such an extreme that family is considered practically the *only* institution on which an individual can depend, and at the same time the only institution toward which an Argentine feels obligation and (almost always) manifests loyalty." [8] Interpersonal relations outside the family are said to be dominated by mutual suspicion and distrust, and the polity to be dominated by *incivisme*.

Few empirical studies have explored interpersonal relations in Latin cultures, nor is much evidence available for assessing differences between Latin and other cultures. [9] So far as I am able to determine, the 1965 survey provides the first quantitative national data concerning Argentine views of interpersonal and group relations.

Several questions elicited views concerning orientations toward "others." Three items inquired into informants' views about existing interpersonal relations; other questions explored the qualities most valued in others. [10]

Together, Tables 6.1, 6.2, and 6.3 constitute a rough measure of Argentine and Peronist expectations concerning interpersonal relations.

Table 6.3 reveals that there were few differences between socioeconomic classes; certainly the differences were not adequate to account for the greater differences between core Peronists and non-Peronists. Education, however, turned out to be a more important variable than class in Argentina as well as in the countries studied

---

[8] Fillol, *Social Factors in Economic Development*, p. 21; Fillol's emphasis. He also comments that the extended family organization has been broken down somewhat by increased mobility, but that it remains strong.

[9] Almond and Verba report that distrust is higher among Italians, Germans, and Mexicans than among respondents from the United States and Britain. See Almond and Verba, *The Civic Culture*, pp. 266–269 passim. Edward Banfield investigates relations between family and community in *The Moral Basis of a Backward Society* (New York: Free Press, 1959).

[10] The questions concerning the three items testing views about prevailing interpersonal relations also occur in Almond and Verba, *The Civic Culture*. These items appeared originally in Morris Rosenberg's questionnaire investigating the relationship between "faith in people" and democratic and nationalist views. The Rosenberg scale, utilized by Almond and Verba, consisted of five items. I have utilized only three of these, feeling that they were adequate to measure the dimension. The exact wording of the relevant parts is given in Question 15 (Appendix B).

TABLE 6.1   INTERPERSONAL TRUST AND DISTRUST
(In percent)

Agree	Core Peronists ($n=365$)	All Others ($n=1,649$)	All Argentines ($n=2,014$)
People will take advantage of you	89.9	82.4	83.8
No one much cares what happens to you	75.3	63.8	69.1
People generally help one another	65.2	59.4	63.9

Source: Responses to Questions 15b, 15h, and 15e (Appendix B).

by Almond and Verba.[11] Confidence in the environment was significantly lower among persons with only primary education, certainly lower than among those who went very far beyond primary school. More than half (54 percent) of all respondents with no education beyond the primary level agreed with both statements attributing indifference and malevolence to others; only 36 percent of the respondents with more education agreed with both of these statements. The less educated were almost, though not quite, as distrustful of their human environment as were the Peronists (see Table 6.4).

TABLE 6.2   INTERPERSONAL TRUST AND DISTRUST: CROSS-NATIONAL
(In percent)

Agree	All Argentines ($n=2,014$)	United States	United Kingdom	Germany	Italy	Mexico
People will take advantage of you	84	68	75	81	73	94
No one much cares what happens to you	69	38	45	72	61	78
People generally help one another	64	80	84	58	55	82

Sources: Same as Table 6.1; the comparative figures are from Almond and Verba, *The Civic Culture*, p. 267. Response set may be a factor here, but there are significant cross-national differences.

[11] Almond and Verba, *The Civic Culture*, p. 268.

TABLE 6.3   INTERPERSONAL TRUST AND DISTRUST BY CLASS
AND PROFESSION
(In percent)

Agree	All Others ($n=1{,}649$)	Core Peronists ($n=365$)	High ($n=157$)	Class (SES)[a] Middle ($n=960$)	Low ($n=721$)
People will take advantage of you	82.4	89.9	83.4	82.6	85.0
No one much cares what happens to you	63.8	75.3	58.0	68.5	71.6
People generally help one another	59.4	65.2	59.9	63.9	67.1

Agree	Housewife ($n=724$)	Laborer ($n=410$)	Profession Business, Professional ($n=248$)	Clerical ($n=301$)	Other ($n=331$)
People will take advantage of you	84.0	87.8	85.1	82.1	78.9
No one much cares what happens to you	71.7	70.7	69.8	66.1	63.4
People generally help one another	66.6	59.8	59.3	66.1	64.7

Source: Same as Table 6.1.
[a] Interviewer appraisal of class identification.

TABLE 6.4   DISTRUST, EDUCATION, AND POLITICS
(In percent)

Agree	Education Primary or Less	More than Primary	Politics Core Peronist	All Other
People will take advantage of you *and* No one much cares what happens to you	54	36	60	40

Source: Responses to Questions 15b and 15h (Appendix B).

Several other breakdowns according to social categories are interesting because they identify factors that were not significantly correlated with expectations of environmental hostility and indifference.
Sex, mobility, religious practices, and union membership were not
significantly related to perception of environmental hostility. The
size of city of residence, geographic region, parents' origins, and
views about the political role of the military were only slightly
correlated with distrust. The difference was in no case as great as
the difference between Peronists and others, and especially the differences between Peronists and Popular Radicals (see Table 6.5).

These findings indicate that core Peronists had a distinctive
orientation toward interpersonal relations, but this distinctive orientation did not (a) characterize the entire universe of core Peronists, or (b) distinguish them from the majority of the rest of the
population. Still, the expectation of indifference and profiteering in
interpersonal contacts was more common among Peronists than in
the population as a whole, and more common among them than
among persons of other political orientations.

Turning from interpersonal expectations to the qualities most
admired in others, it is clear that, although indifference and profiteering were widely expected, the personal qualities most admired
by Argentines in general, and core Peronists in particular, were
generosity and consideration of others. Like their expectations,
Peronists' preferences concerning human traits were similar to those
of other Argentines but showed some small but consistent differences in degree if not in direction. From a list including job performance, social service, generosity, respect for others, and psychological self-protection, a majority of all Argentines, including

TABLE 6.5   INTERPERSONAL TRUST AND DISTRUST BY
ORIENTATION TO PERONISTS
(In percent)

Agree	Core Peronist ($n = 365$)	Pro- Peronist ($n = 411$)	Non- Peronist ($n = 1,238$)	UCRP Voter ($n = 413$)
People will take ad- vantage of you	89.9	82.0	77.7	77.2
No one much cares what happens to you	75.3	70.8	63.8	61.7
People generally help one another	65.2	60.6	59.4	63.4

Source: Same as Table 6.1.

TABLE 6.6   MOST ADMIRED QUALITIES
(In percent)

	UCRP Voters
Job-oriented virtues	+ 3.1
Interpersonal consideration[a]	+ 9.4
Self-protection	− 2.8
Social service	+ 3.2

Source: Responses to Questions 3 and 3a–3i (Appendix B).
Note: Each cell represents degree of deviation from attitudes of reliable Peronists.
[a] Generosity plus respect.

Peronists, most often identified interpersonal consideration as the most admired characteristic (see Table 6.6). Nonetheless, it was less frequently ranked as most important by Peronists than by persons who voted for the UCRP.

More important than Peronists' relatively high concern with interpersonal consideration was their lack of agreement concerning the most desirable human traits. Their views were widely divided; no more than 26.3 percent of core Peronists agreed about the desirability of any trait. The implications of this disagreement are interesting. First, there was less agreement among core Peronists and among Argentines generally about what kind of interpersonal relations ought to prevail than about which kind actually prevail; second, there was no agreement among Peronists or among Argentines in general about the most valued personality traits. This indicates that rank-and-file Peronists did not share one. component of wholistic ideologies, namely, acceptance of a model personality embodying preferred traits, predispositions, and attitudes.

Orientations to Social Aggregates

The social process is most often perceived in terms of aggregates even when those aggregates are not organized. A great deal of thinking about politics and society involves the attribution of attitudes and activities to collectivities perceived to have common interests. The "they" invoked to explain social events is often an unorganized aggregate, which may in fact be entirely incapable of activity.

Much of Argentine history, like that of most other nations, is written today with social aggregates as the principal actors. The military, the Church, the *estancieros*, the *saladeros*, the immigrants, the middle class, the working class are the chief actors in many historians' accounts of the development of the nation. Individuals appear on the scene and influence it but tend to be identified with some social aggregate or group that they are said to serve, symbolize, or represent. These same characters people contemporary events as described by journalists and often by political scientists. In fact, these unorganized collectivities have become so important a currency for thinking about social events that they may be said to have achieved an independent existence. If "they"—the unorganized aggregates—are not in reality social and political actors, the fact that they are so widely believed to be gives them undoubted importance for political events and analysis.

In popular ideologies, social aggregates—organized or unorganized —achieve a visibility and prominence that is often denied persons and organizations that do act directly in the political sphere.[12] Issues tend to be perceived in terms of aggregates—the Negroes, the poor, the rich, the *descamisados*—and reacted to in the context of views about the aggregates.

This section deals with several aggregates that there is reason to believe are politically relevant, either because of their activities or because of the perception of the aggregate by others. These include organized aggregates (the military, the Church, trade unions), unorganized aggregates (middle classes, foreigners), and semiorganized aggregates (large landowners). I shall be concerned with how the respondents perceived themselves in relation to these various aggregates (are they members or nonmembers? aware or unaware? hostile, friendly, or indifferent?), and how they perceived the actual and desirable role of the aggregates in the political arena. The purpose of the analysis is to develop a model of politically relevant social orientations of Peronists and to determine the distinctive characteristics of Peronists' perspectives.

Questions included in the survey were designed to elicit the respondents' perspectives concerning the power of various aggregates, both organized and unorganized, in the society and in the political arena. Other questions were aimed at measuring identification and affect relating individuals to these collectivities. Table 6.7 reflects

---

[12] Philip Converse has commented on the centrality of aggregates for the ideologies of masses, asserting that what he terms "visible social groupings" have a "high centrality in the belief systems of the less well informed" and that "groups as attitude objects (groups *qua* groups) have higher centrality in the belief systems of the mass than of the élite." See Philip E. Converse, "The Nature of Belief Systems in Mass Publics," in David E. Apter, ed., *Ideology and Discontent* (New York: Free Press, 1964), pp. 234–235.

the respondents' views about which group exercised the greatest influence in Argentine society.

The responses shown in Table 6.7 make it clear that there was no very wide agreement about which single aggregate in Argentine society was most influential. One-third were convinced that the military had most influence, but two-thirds were unconvinced. Though there was relatively little agreement about which aggregate was the most powerful, there was greater agreement about which were powerful and which were not. The military, the Church, the big landowners (the partners of the traditional "oligarchy") were seen as most influential, with Peronists and labor unions in second rank and entrepreneurs and the middle class in third place. The middle class was the only aggregate about which there was significant disagreement (see Table 6.8).

Peronists' perceptions of the distribution of power approximated that of the rest of the society, with one notable and significant exception: they were much more likely to rate highly the power of the Peronist movement. Almost one-fourth of the Peronists described the movement as the most influential group in the society. Only 5 percent of the other respondents so described it.

The marked tendency of Peronists to perceive their movement as

TABLE 6.7 THE STRUCTURE OF SOCIAL INFLUENCE
(In percent)

| Group | Most Powerful | | Least Powerful | |
	All Argen-tines (n=2,014)	Core Peronists (n=365)	All Argen-tines (n=2,014)	Core Peronists (n=365)
Military services	33.8	28.8	0.6	0.6
Church hierarchy	14.6	9.6	2.4	2.4
Big landowners	10.1	11.0	1.1	1.1
Peronists	8.3	24.4	2.7	2.7
Labor unions	8.3	6.6	3.9	3.9
Argentine entrepreneurs	4.5	1.9	0.8	0.8
Middle-class Argentines	4.4	3.0	12.3	12.3
Agricultural workers	2.2	1.9	10.2	10.2
University students	1.4	1.1	2.1	2.1
Argentine communists	1.0	1.9	11.7	11.1
Foreigners	0.9	0.8	10.2	10.2
Justicialists	0.6	0.8	1.5	1.5
Intellectuals	0.6	—	11.0	11.0
Bureaucrats	0.2	—	12.3	12.3

Source: Responses to Questions 24 and 24a (Appendix B).

TABLE 6.8   SCALE OF SOCIAL INFLUENCE: ARGENTINE AND PERONIST PERCEPTIONS OF MOST INFLUENTIAL

Group	All Others ($n = 1,649$)	Core Peronists ($n = 365$)
Military services	602	487
Church hierarchy	371	304
Big landowners	187	216
Peronists	135	428
Labor unions	190	186
Argentine entrepreneurs	141	67
Middle-class Argentines	117	76

Source: Responses to Question 24.
Note: Each ranking of group as *most* influential was computed as 3, second most influential as 2, third most influential as 1. The totals were then weighted to take account of the difference in the number of respondents.

most influential or very influential (more Peronists also ranked the movement as second or third) suggests that the rank and file saw the movement as the center of the social universe (see Table 6.9). There was no comparable difference between others' evaluation and the self-evaluation of the influence of other groups. The meaning of the difference between Peronists' and others' evaluation of Peronism is somewhat problematic. It cannot prudently be explained as an example of overcompensation by the powerless. It would be dangerous to classify it as evidence of a tendency to aggrandizement among rank-and-file Peronists because, in fact, the movement was and is very influential.

There are some suggestive though not great differences in perception of the power structure by different social classes. Landowners were perceived as more powerful by more lower- than upper-class respondents; so were labor unions, and so, especially, were the

TABLE 6.9   PERCEPTION OF PERONISTS AS MOST POWERFUL BY POLITICAL CATEGORY

	Percentage
Core Peronists ($n = 365$)	24.4
Pro-Peronists ($n = 411$)	9.0
All others ($n = 1,238$)	5.3
UCRP voters ($n = 413$)	2.7

Source: Same as Table 6.7.

Peronists. The power position of the military services, on the other hand, was more impressive to upper- than to lower-class informants.

Peronists and Argentines alike perceived that social power is not necessarily translated into political power, and saw that the distribution of social and political influence is not identical. Two questions were included that inquired into respondents' conception of who controlled the government. One asked: "One sometimes hears that some people have so much influence over the way the government is run that the interests of the people are ignored, and only the needs of the influential people receive attention. Do you think this is true or not?" A probe inquired of those who answered the question affirmatively, "Which are the groups that have that influence?" Of the core Peronists, 53.4 percent, and 40.6 percent of all other respondents, agreed with the statement that the government was run by and for a few influential people; 19.5 percent of the Peronists and 29.6 percent of all other respondents disagreed. Later chapters will explore some implications of the fact that only about 30 percent disagreed with the view that the government was the property of "special interests"; at this stage it is important to identify the groups that were believed to have determinative influence over government. Once again the military was ranked first, with 15.5 percent of the whole sample and 17.8 percent of the Peronists identifying it as the group that controlled and profited from the operation of government. Entrepreneurs, it will be remembered, were not named by many as one of the most influential groups in the society, yet they were believed by 12.2 percent of the whole sample and 17 percent of the reliable Peronists to be the people who *really* decide who gets what and to be the ones who do most of the getting. Next came professional politicians, identified by 9.8 percent of all respondents and 12.1 percent of the Peronists, as the group controlling and profiting from government. The Church, the big landowners, and the Peronists were perceived by very few as enjoying the privileged relationship to government described in the question. A comparison of the respondents' perceptions of social and political power hierarchies is reflected in Table 6.10.

Several aspects of the perception of determinative political influence deserve comment. First, the belief that the military *and* the professional politicians run the government for their own profit was almost certainly an expression of general suspicion of government as well as of these groups, since these are the groups that did in fact control the machinery of government and make the decisions.

TABLE 6.10   SOCIAL INFLUENCE AND POLITICAL CONTROL
COMPARED
(In percent)

| | Who Has Greatest Influence | | Who Controls and Profits | |
	All Argentines ($n = 2,014$)	Core Peronists ($n = 365$)	All Argentines ($n = 2,014$)	Core Peronists ($n = 365$)
Military services	33.8	28.8	15.5	17.7
Church hierarchy	14.6	9.6	2.3	3.0
Big landowners	10.0	11.0	2.3	3.6
Peronists	8.3	24.4	0.7	0.5
Labor unions	8.3	6.6	—	—
Entrepreneurs	4.5	1.9	12.2	17.0
Professional politicans	—	—	9.8	12.1

Source: Responses to Questions 23a and 24 (Appendix B).

Second, it is significant that, while the Church and the big landowners were perceived by many as having great influence, few conceived them as wielding determinative political power or of being
the principal beneficiaries of government policy. This finding is the
more interesting since it concerns two of the three members of the
traditional "oligarchy." Entrepreneurs, not big landowners, were the
only economic group conceived by many as the special beneficiaries
and controllers of government. This probably represents an accurate
perception of the effective political power of both the Church and
the landowning class. De Imaz's study, *La clase alta,* revealed that
the members of the social elite perceived themselves as enjoying far
more status than power; in fact, they perceived themselves as possessing little political power.[13] Most expert observers believe the
political power of the Church has declined greatly in recent years,
despite the undoubted influence of its anti-Perón campaign.

The near absence of Argentines who perceived the Church and
the *estancieros* as wielding determinative power demonstrates that
the image of the nation as ruled by the traditional "oligarchy" for

[13] José Luis de Imaz, *La clase alta de Buenos Aires* (Buenos Aires: Editorial
Universidad de Buenos Aires, 1962), p. 55. The study was limited to a carefully
selected group of the social elite. Asked how much importance the group had in
the nation's political life, 70 percent said they had little influence, 16 percent said
they controlled it; 14 percent said they did not know. Asked who *did* control political life, the responses of this group were as follows: 36 percent, the middle
class plus workers; 29.5 percent, the middle class only; 18 percent, only the upper
class.

their own interest is dead, if indeed it ever existed at the level of popular opinion.

Third, although core Peronists viewed the movement as influential in Argentina, they had no delusions about its power in the government.

Groups in the Political Process

The last section explored views about the relative power and influence of various social aggregates. This section also deals with orientations to aggregates, but here attitudes toward important collectivities will be investigated in greater detail. The military establishment, the Church, owners of large estates, trade unions, and other politically relevant groups and aggregates are examined in an effort to determine how Peronists relate to each. Enough description of each is provided to clarify the meaning of orientations toward it.

The Military Services Debate about the proper political role of the military forces is a continuing aspect of the discussion of Argentina. Since 1930, military officers have intervened in Argentine politics with increasing frequency.[14] As Pendle points out, "Five of the seven Presidents between Irigoyen and Perón were generals." [15]

[14] Germani and Silvert have suggested that the explanation of the increasing frequency of military intervention in Argentina may be related to that country's transition from a limited to a fully participatory democracy. See Gino Germani and Kalman H. Silvert, "Estructura social e intervención militar en América Latina," in Torcuato S. di Tella, Gino Germani, Jorge Graciarena y colaboradores, *Argentina, sociedad de masas* (Buenos Aires: Editorial Universitaria de Buenos Aires, 1965), pp. 239–240; translated into English, "Politics, Social Structure and Military Intervention in Latin America," in Peter G. Snow, ed., *Government and Politics in Latin America: A Reader* (New York: Holt, Rinehart & Winston, 1967), pp. 299–318. For an interesting analysis of the military roles and growing professionalism, see Merle Kling, "Toward a Theory of Power and Political Instability in Latin America," in John D. Martz, ed., *The Dynamics of Change in Latin American Politics* (Englewood Cliffs, N.J.: Prentice-Hall, 1965). However, for the view that long-range trends in Latin America are away from military participation in the political sphere, see Edwin Lieuwen, *Arms and Politics in Latin America*, rev. ed. (New York: Frederick A. Praeger, 1961), p. 171; John J. Johnson, *Political Change in Latin America: The Emergence of the Middle Sectors* (Stanford: Stanford University Press, 1958), pp. 192–193; Victor Alba, "The Stages of Militarism in Latin America," in John J. Johnson, ed., *The Role of the Military in Underdeveloped Countries* (Princeton: Princeton University Press, 1962).

[15] George Pendle, *Argentina* (London: Oxford University Press, 1963), p. 118.

Then came Perón. Since his overthrow, three generals have ruled Argentina after having achieved power through military force (Lonardi, Aramburu, Onganía); three governments have been deposed by military coups (Lonardi's, Frondizi's, Illía's); innumerable policies concerning both domestic and foreign affairs have been altered in response to military demands; and attempted coups, almost too numerous to count, have punctuated the efforts of successive presidents to rule the nation. Obviously, military officers are important and often victorious competitors for political power.[16] De Imaz has commented that "The military establishment has been perceived by all political groups as the potential instrument needed to achieve their particular objectives." [17] This statement may or may not be literally true, but it is demonstrably true that during this century Argentina's military officers have acted on behalf of a number of different political causes. They have overthrown both fraudulent and genuine democracies, and they have overthrown a dictator—Perón—and then established a constitutional democracy. They have also deposed and replaced each other.[18] In addition to

[16] This participation is often regarded by writers, especially North American writers, as reflecting some sort of social pathology. Germani and Silvert, for example, have commented: "Military intromission in the political power structure always indicates, of course, at least a relative inability of other social institutions to marshal their power effectively, and at most an advanced state of institutional decomposition." See "Politics, Social Structure and Military Intervention," p. 300. Note also a variation in this interpretation in the view of Almond and Coleman that military intervention in politics does not occur in "developed" systems. See Gabriel A. Almond and James S. Coleman, The Politics of the Developing Areas (Princeton: Princeton University Press, 1960), p. 560. For a different approach see, among others, Lucian W. Pye, "Armies in the Process of Political Modernization," in Johnson, Role of the Military, pp. 69–89.

[17] José Luis de Imaz, Los que mandan, 5th ed. (Buenos Aires: Editorial Universitaria de Buenos Aires, 1966), p. 84.

[18] A large literature exists on the political roles of Latin American military establishments; much of it identifies the military with conservative politics; for example, Robert Scott, "Political Elites and Political Modernization," in Seymour Martin Lipset and Aldo Solari, eds., Elites in Latin America (New York: Oxford University Press, 1967), p. 121; Irving Horowitz, "The Military Elites," in ibid., pp. 147–149; Lieuwen, Arms and Politics, p. 163; and Gino Germani, Política y sociedad en una época de transición: de la sociedad tradicional a la sociedad de masas (Buenos Aires: Editorial Paidos, 1962), p. 139. Peronists also view the military as the instrument of reaction; see Ramón Prieto, El pacto: 8 años de política argentina (Buenos Aires: Editorial en Marcha, 1963), pp. 18–19. But there is also growing note of the varying political roles available to and played by the military. See, for example, Lieuwen, Arms and Politics, p. 129. See also John J. Johnson, "The Latin-American Military as a Politically Competing Group in Transitional Society," in Johnson, Role of the Military, pp. 91–129; Horowitz, "Military Elites," p. 147; and Germani and Silvert, "Estructura social e interven-

this key role in the succession process, they have repeatedly and effectively intervened to determine policy.

The relationship between Perón and the military establishment underwent many changes in the years after 1943 when the then Colonel Perón entered politics as a junior member of a military junta. The failure of Perón's various efforts to make his officers loyal servants of the Peronist regime has been demonstrated again and again. Military officers forced the withdrawal of Eva Perón as a candidate for the vice-presidency; military pressure played its role in stimulating Perón's conservative retreat in economic policy; and in 1955 the military establishment drove Perón from the presidency and ever since has guarded all accesses to power against his return.

Since 1955 the Peronist movement has been the subject of repeated disagreements within the military establishment, but opinions have ranged only from hostile to very hostile. Among the leaders of Argentina's political parties, there have been many expressions of support for broader Peronist participation in the nation's political life, but again and again civilian initiatives have met the determined opposition of military officers, so that Peronist exclusion from power since 1955 can be traced directly to the dominant factions of the military establishment. Peronists therefore might be expected to have especially strong feelings about those who have purged their leaders, banned their parties, deposed their allies, annulled their electoral victories, and guarded the borders against the return of their leader.[19]

---

ción militar," p. 242. Increasingly, the political role of the military is related to the predominantly middle-class background of the officer corps. Recent empirical studies establishing the middle-class backgrounds of many officers are de Imaz, whose *Los que mandan* provides the largest amount of data on Argentine military recruitment; Liisa North, *Civil-Military Relations in Argentina, Chile, and Peru* (Berkeley: University of California, Institute of International Studies, 1966), which studies the backgrounds of several Latin nations' officer corps; and José Nun, "A Latin American Phenomenon: The Middle Class Military Coup," in University of California, Institute of International Studies, *Trends in Social Science Research in Latin American Studies* (Berkeley, March 1965), pp. 55–91. Alberto Belloni, *Peronismo y socialismo nacional* (Buenos Aires: Ediciones Coyoacán, 1962), pp. 9–11, also stresses the middle-class character of the Argentine military establishment.

[19] The antimilitary feelings of the Peronist supporters may to some extent be offset by the tendency to associate military participation in politics with the nativist, indigenous politics, as opposed to the policies of the "liberal *civilizados*" who are, it will be remembered, also viewed as the arch enemies of Peronism. See, among others, Rafael Funes, *Reflexiones políticas para militares: hacia una política nacional* (Buenos Aires: Ediciones Relevo, 1963), especially pp. 1–35 passim. Very similar arguments concerning the military as carriers of the authentic

The 1965 survey data provide a description of how Peronists in particular and Argentines in general viewed the military sector on the eve of the last venture that brought a general from the barracks to the Casa Rosada. Unfortunately, data are lacking to test adequately de Imaz's guess that, while 100 percent of Argentines are against military intervention in general, 100 percent desire a military intervention to support their own viewpoints on national affairs. But it is important to remember his warning not to mistake attitudes toward "the military" in the abstract for attitudes toward any particular officer or action. Many other students of Argentine politics believe the feeling against the idea of military intervention in politics is widespread among Argentines. The 1965 survey data bear this out. While opposition is not universal, it is high among all population categories and especially high among Peronists.

Several questions eliciting views about political activities of military officers reveal that there was little support for military participation in politics. Specifically, more than three-fourths (78.2 percent) of Argentines opposed military intervention in principle, approximately two-thirds (63.9 percent) denied that military interventions had saved the country from chaos, and 57.2 percent said they would oppose a party supported by the military. On each of these, Peronists showed somewhat greater opposition to the military than others.[20] The Peronists' antimilitary position must, of course, be interpreted in the context of the military background of their own leader. There is some indication that once an Argentine (and perhaps a Latin) military figure achieves the presidency, his identification with the military establishment is attenuated and he is perceived as a political leader.[21]

About 11 percent of the core Peronists identified Perón as a military leader in a question inquiring if there was any military figure they admired.[22] This number is small enough and the hostility of Peronists to the military widespread enough to indicate that most

national tradition are found in the writings of others of nationalist persuasion, for example, Jorge Abelardo Ramos in Silvio Frondizi et al., *Las izquierdas en el proceso político argentino* (Buenos Aires: Palestra, 1959), pp. 197–220.

[20] Intensity of opposition is also important; so are the consequences of opposition. Some writers are impressed with the passive resignation with which Argentines confront military intervention, for example, Gerald Clark, *The Coming Explosion in Latin America* (New York: David McKay Co., 1963).

[21] It would be interesting to know at what point, if ever, President de Gaulle, who came to power by a quasi-coup, lost his identification as a military leader and acquired the image of a civilian leader.

[22] The exact question is given in Appendix B (Questions 27 and 27a).

rank-and-file Peronists did not conceive Perón as a military leader. He was viewed as a victim rather than a representative of the military establishment. Another evidence of the lack of identification of Perón with the military by Argentines is that, while 2.7 percent of all respondents identified him as a military leader they especially admired, 7.9 percent named him as an admired world figure.

All categories of the population shared a generally antimilitary orientation, but there are some suggestive differences among them in the degree of antimilitary sentiment. More upper- than middle- or lower-class respondents supported the military's activities in politics, more women than men, more among those who were strongly religious than those with weak religious attachments, and more UCRP supporters than Peronists (see Table 6.11).

Age, national origin, and mobility did not correlate with attitudes toward the military. Region and size of city of residence were ambiguously related. Persons in middle-sized interior cities in the Federal Capital were somewhat more favorable to the military than were those elsewhere.

To a question inquiring if any military leader was especially admired by respondents, approximately 18 percent replied negatively. General Onganía, not then president, was the most widely admired military leader: 7.5 percent of the total sample named him; approximately 4 percent named Isaac Rojas; 2.7 percent named Perón; and less than 2 percent named General Aramburu, who in the election earlier that year had conducted an unsuccessful campaign for the presidency. General Onganía had some following among all categories of people but was almost twice as frequently admired by upper-class as by lower-status respondents.

The Church The Church, in Argentina as in other Latin American countries, is of course the Roman Catholic Church; it has played a principal role on that continent since missionaries arrived with the *conquistadores*. From that time, also, the roles of ecclesiastical and civil authority have been intertwined.[23] As an Argentine Jesuit put it, at the same time church and state were being separated in Europe, "in America there developed through Spanish influence a

[23] For a general discussion of the role of the Church in Latin America, see, among others, Frederick B. Pike, ed., *The Conflict Between Church and State in Latin America* (New York: Alfred A. Knopf, 1964); J. Lloyd Mecham, *Church and State in Latin America: A History of Politico-Ecclesiastical Relations* (Chapel Hill: University of North Carolina Press, 1934); and Frank Tannenbaum, *Ten Keys to Latin America* (New York: Alfred A. Knopf, 1962), pp. 53–65.

TABLE 6.11   ATTITUDES SUPPORTING POLITICAL ROLES OF MILITARY
(In percent)

	Class			Religion			Peronists	UCRP Voters
	Upper (n = 157)	Middle (n = 960)	Lower (n = 721)	Strong (n = 467)	Moderate (n = 634)	None (n = 913)	(n = 365)	(n = 413)
Supports military intervention	15.3	11.8	10.0	15.0	9.3	11.1	10.7	12.8
Military saves nation from chaos	31.2	21.5	9.1	26.3	23.2	18.0	17.0	25.9
Welcomes military's support of candidate	36.3	28.0	26.6	34.0	28.1	25.6	27.4	36.1

Source: Responses to Questions 17i, 26, and 25f (Appendix B).

new Christianity deeply rooted in the institutions of the civil order." [24]

The influence of the Church on the political life of the nation has been seminal and continuing, breeding both a clerical and an anticlerical tradition.[25] Like the Spanish, the Argentine political tradition has until recently juxtaposed "liberal" and "Catholic" politics with the "liberal" tradition associated with democratic institutions, enlightenment philosophy, and anti-Catholic legislation. Nationalism, authoritarian institutions, and unity of civil and ecclesiastical authority were traditionally linked to "Catholic" politics. Of the wave of anticlerical legislation sponsored by "liberal" rulers at the turn of the century, Father Anduriz commented, "The Catholic conscience developed a reactive resistance against the liberalism of the civil order . . . [and] there grew at the deepest levels of our Catholicism an increasing anti-liberalism which secretly sought opportunities for expression in the institutions of the civil society." [26] According to Father Anduriz, Perón was believed to be the opportunity for that expression.

The short, tumultuous relations of the Church and Perón are well known. Perón wooed and won the support of ecclesiastical authorities with legislation that gave the Church new and desired privileges in the civil order; eventually, this happy relationship deteriorated into open enmity and war, until "every act of adhesion to the Church constituted, simultaneously, a public repudiation of the [Peronist] regime." [27]

At the time of his downfall, Perón's enemies invoked many Christian symbols. General Lonardi, leader of the coalition that deposed Perón, was a strong Catholic and nationalist. Christian symbolism was central in his coup: the papal flag flew beside that of Argentina in his triumphal entrance into Buenos Aires; saluting aircraft formed a cross; and he adopted *Christus vincit* as a slogan.

[24] Joaquín Anduriz, "Religion," in *Argentina, 1930–1960* (Buenos Aires: Sur, 1961), p. 423.

[25] The principal cause of contention between civil and ecclesiastical authorities has been the "school" question, specifically, whether there should be religious (Catholic) instruction in the public schools. A comprehensive account is found in John J. Kennedy, *Catholicism, Nationalism and Democracy in Argentina* (Notre Dame, Ind.: University of Notre Dame Press, 1958), pp. 169–216 passim.

[26] Anduriz, "Religion," p. 424. Kalman H. Silvert makes the same point in *The Conflict Society: Reaction and Revolution in Latin America*, rev. ed. (New York: American Universities Field Staff, 1966), p. 31.

[27] Anduriz, "Religion," p. 429.

TABLE 6.12   CATHOLIC IDENTIFICATION
(In percent)

	All Argentines ($n = 2,014$)	Core Peronists ($n = 365$)	Pro-Peronist ($n = 411$)	Political Orientation Not Favorable to Peronism ($n = 1,238$)	UCRP ($n = 413$)
Yes	86.7	86.8	86.1	86.8	86.4
No	13.2	13.2	13.9	12.9	13.6

Source: Responses to Question 63. (Appendix B).

He then appointed a government of Catholic nationalists and set about canceling Perón's anticlerical legislation.

One consequence of the split between Perón and Church authorities was to precipitate rethinking by many clergy and laymen of questions concerning the "good" civil order. Another was to introduce a new discordant element into relations between the Church and the lower classes. It was widely predicted that this schism, added to the preexisting image that identified the Church and the rich, would precipitate the de-Christianization of the Argentine urban poor as the French working classes had been de-Christianized.

Attitudes toward the Church are therefore particularly important for assessing the relations of Peronists to the "establishment" and to other sectors of the population. De Imaz has asserted "that Catholics are numerous in all sectors of the society." [28] The survey data tell us whether they are as numerous among Peronists as in other sectors, and whether Peronists conceive the Church to be an instrument of class politics. They also illuminate the perceived relationship between religion and political behavior, and the role of the Church in civil society.

The first rather striking fact revealed by the data is that in regard to religious identifications there was virtually no difference between the core Peronists, pro-Peronists, and non-Peronists. The responses to the query "By the way, are you a Catholic?" are given in Table 6.12.

While Catholics were found in approximately equal proportions among core Peronists, pro-Peronists, UCRP voters, and others, there were differences in religious identification between social classes, between union members and nonmembers, and between inhabitants of large and small cities. Some, but not all, of these differences are

[28] De Imaz, *Los que mandan*, p. 166.

incompatible with common assumptions. Fewer (79 percent) of the upper than lower (88.1 percent) social strata identified themselves as Catholics; fewer union members (79.2 percent) than nonmembers (88 percent); fewer (78.1 percent) residents of the Federal Capital than of other areas; more (94.1 percent) residents in towns under 50,000 than in cities over 500,000 (80 percent).

Turning from identification to practice, 56.5 percent of the respondents said they had not gone to Mass in the four weeks preceding the survey;[29] the percentage of Peronists who had not was slightly higher (59.5 percent) and the percentage of UCRP supporters slightly lower (54.5 percent), but the difference is small. However, there are interesting and significant class differences. Although the percentage of persons not identifying with Catholicism was highest among the upper social stratum, the percentage who had not been to Mass in the previous four weeks was lowest in this stratum and highest among lower-class informants (see Table 6.13). The same relationship holds for the city size. Large cities had the highest percentage of nonidentifiers and the lowest number of nonpracticers; they also contained the larger portion of persons who felt they discharged all their religious obligations.

It is clear that the lower classes had not departed from the Church. The fact that the lower classes were somewhat less likely to fulfill their religious obligations regularly does not signify schism. The conflict between Perón and the Church did not result in significant alienation from the Church among rank-and-file Peronists.

It is equally clear that, however important clerical issues may have been from time to time, Argentina's mass politics did not reflect religious splits. The Peronists were not drawing their supporters disproportionately from the non-Catholic portions of the lower classes, and neither were the Radicals, their anticlerical traditions to the contrary notwithstanding.[30]

Identification with the Church did not entail approval of its political role in Argentina. About 14 percent of the very devout—those who fulfilled all obligations—characterized its political activities as "bad," a percentage only slightly smaller than that deploring the Church's political activities within the whole population. Pero-

[29] The exact question asked is given in Appendix B (Question 63a).

[30] The relation of politics and religion in Argentina is more like that in the United States than that on the Continent. For a recent summary of the relation of religious and political issue orientations, see *Gallop Opinion Index: Special Report on Religion* (Princeton, N.J., 1967).

TABLE 6.13 CATHOLIC IDENTIFICATIONS AND PRACTICES
(In percent)

	Class			Political Orientation			
	Upper (n = 157)	Middle (n = 960)	Lower (n = 721)	Core Peronist (n = 365)	Pro-Peronist (n = 411)	Not Favorable to Peronism (n = 1,238)	UCRP (n = 413)
Are you a Catholic? Yes	79.0	86.9	88.1	86.8	86.1	86.8	86.4
Have not been to Mass in 4 weeks	36.9	55.6	63.5	59.5	58.4	54.9	54.5
Discharge all religious obligations	33.1	22.1	20.4	21.6	21.2	24.3	24.2
Rarely discharge religious obligations	19.7	31.3	35.5	30.1	36.5	30.8	29.3

Source: Responses to Questions 63, 63a, and 63b (Appendix B).

TABLE 6.14   JUDGMENT OF CHURCH'S POLITICAL ACTIVITIES
(In percent)

| | Class | | | | Political Orientation | | | |
	Upper (n = 157)	Middle (n = 960)	Lower (n = 721)	Core Peronist (n = 365)	Pro-Peronist (n = 411)	Not Favorable to Peronism (n = 1,238)	UCRP (n = 413)
Good	36.3	32.7	27.2	23.3	30.2	33.7	37.3
Bad	21.7	16.6	16.8	27.9	19.0	15.0	13.6
Neither	17.2	14.7	11.2	11.5	17.5	14.5	15.7
Don't know	24.8	30.0	44.8	37.3	33.3	37.1	33.4

Source: Responses to Question 64 (Appendix B).

nists' views of these activities were more negative than those of non-Peronists. Peronists were the only political aggregate identified in which there was more disapproval than approval of the political activities of the Church. However, even among Peronists the disapproval was not massive. Less than a third said they believed what the Church had done in the political sphere was "bad" (see Table 6.14).

Consistent with other findings concerning women and the Church, Argentine women were revealed to be more often Catholic, more devoutly Catholic, and more approving of the Church's political activities than were the male respondents. However, though the difference was marked, it was not great.

Perhaps the most surprising finding concerning the popular perception of the Church's political activities was that more than 50 percent of the respondents had no views on the subject. This withholding of judgment does not appear to have resulted from general reticence to discuss religion; almost no one declined to reveal his religious status or degree of fidelity in fulfilling his obligations. Neither does it appear to reflect generalized lack of views (or reticence in expressing them) about activities of influential groups; there was no comparable group without opinions about the activities of the military. Perhaps approximately one-half of the Argentines simply had not thought about the Church's role in the political sphere. Perhaps in the popular mind the Church is not as involved with politics as some scholars assume. In fact, 47.9 percent of all the respondents asserted that Catholicism had little or no influence on the conduct of politicians. About one-third disagreed and believed it had significant relevance to public affairs.[31]

Among all respondents, nevertheless, the most common criticism directed against the Church was that it was involved in politics at all. Among Peronists (as among others) few respondents complained specifically of its role in deposing Perón; instead, the reproach was general, simply asserting that the Church should not be involved in politics at all. The most approved political activity of the Church was in promoting peace (see Table 6.15).

Another question aimed at exploring the social role and identifications of the Church, asking which groups had been helped least by the Church. Sixteen percent of all respondents, 19 percent of the Peronists, and 16 percent of the lower-class respondents identi-

---

[31] The exact question asked is given in Appendix B (Question 63c).

TABLE 6.15   EVALUATIONS OF CHURCH'S ACTIVITIES
(In percent)

	All Argentines (n = 2,014)	Core Peronists (n = 365)
Works for peace	14.2	9.3
Has done much to help poor	9.5	6.3
Never gets involved in politics	3.4	3.3
Everything it does is good	4.7	3.3
Supports democracy, opposed Perón	1.0	0.5
Church should not be involved in politics	16.0	19.7
Was wrong to oppose Perón	1.1	2.7
Has done bad things (general)	4.7	6.0

Source: Responses to Question 64a (Appendix B).

fied the workers or the poor and needy as that group.[32] However, almost as many Peronists as lower-class respondents answered that it helped all equally, and again, nearly half (44.8 percent) said they did not know. It seems clear that while a tendency existed to regard the Church as indifferent to the poor, this tendency was not salient and was not a dominant part of the Church's image (see Table 6.16).

There is one other measure of attitudes toward the political role of the Church: a question inquiring about respondents' reactions to support by the hierarchy for a political party. The results again revealed mixed feelings about the Church in politics, with no distinctive Peronist reaction and fewer unfavorable reactions among lower- than upper-class informants.

In sum, notwithstanding Peron's quarrels with the Church, rank-

TABLE 6.16   PERCEIVED ATTITUDE OF CHURCH TOWARD POOR
(In percent)

	All Argentines (n = 2,014)	Core Peronists (n = 365)	Upper (n = 157)	Class Middle (n = 960)	Lower (n = 721)
Has done much to help poor	14.2	6.3	5.1	10.7	8.6
Does least for poor	16.1	18.9	14.6	15.5	16.1

Source: Responses to Questions 64a and 65 (Appendix B).

[32] The exact question asked is given in Appendix B (Question 65).

and-file Peronist attitudes were generally favorable to the Church.[33] Peronists did not recruit disproportionately among non-Catholics. Their attitudes toward the Church's political activities were only slightly more negative than those of other political groups. Most important, Peronists' reactions to this pervasive institution of hispanic culture and the hierarchy associated with it were entirely comparable to the reactions of the rest of Argentine society. *Religion* —and reactions to religion—*did not separate Peronists from the rest of society, nor did it reinforce political identifications.*

Landowners The third and senior member of the "oligarchy" was the great landowning class. It was their interests that, according to conventional interpretations, the Church sanctified and the military protected. These interests were, as previously stated, different in Argentina than in some other Latin American nations. The broad pampas, which encouraged cattle raising and made beef the principal Argentine export, also created a different style of life and some unique interests. The *gauchos* of the nineteenth-century *Martín Fierro* and *Facundo* alike differed from the peasant of *hacienda* culture. And the *ganaderos* developed a unique interest in export markets for their beef. Agricultural interests developed, but they coexisted with cattle raisers' interests. They did not displace them. The great Argentine landowners had other distinctive characteristics. Many were absentee owners, who in fact did not play the quasi-feudal roles of *hacendados,* serving as lawgivers as well as patrons of their estates. Many lived in the cosmopolitan, luxurious, literate, and sophisticated milieu of Buenos Aires. De Imaz has commented, "People have the impression that Argentine rural society" is identical with the "high class of Buenos Aires.[34] He has also pointed out that *"La clase alta* of Buenos Aires never was authentically conservative"[35]—in part because of its urban residence, in part because of its liberal ideology, in part because of its cosmopolitanism, and in part because these led to its association with selected upward mobile immigrants.

Nonetheless, Argentina's landowners shared some characteristics

---

[33] Note that Perón himself always emphasized that his quarrel was not with the Church but only with certain reactionary members of the hierarchy. For a recent statement of his strong attachment to the Church, see Esteban Peicovich, *Hola Perón* (Buenos Aires: Jorge Alvarez Editor, 1965).

[34] De Imaz, *Los que mandan,* p. 85.

[35] Ibid.

with those of other Latin American nations.[36] Their indifference or opposition to industrial development is one such characteristic. Their undoubted prestige and social leadership is another.[37] Their habits and preferences provided the flavor and set the styles of Argentine society, not only among the rich but, we are told, also among the middle classes.

Juan Perón was the first ruler of Argentina to display open hostility toward this class. Pendel has commented of Perón, "He despised the old-fashioned 'colonial' occupation of farming and cattle raising. . . ." [38] He despised them for their cosmopolitan style, their *vendepatria* economics, their indifference to national development, their continued snubbing of his wife.

Perón's reckless economic policies probably harmed the landowners more than his deliberately planned efforts.[39] But there is little doubt than his symbolic revolution of class relations left the landed aristocracy weakened in both the social and the political spheres.[40]

Obviously, Argentines believe the landowners have been debilitated. We have already seen that virtually no respondents perceived landowners as the power behind the junta, controlling policies for their own benefits. On the other hand, we have also seen that the landowners were still believed to have substantial influence in Argentine society.

The survey provides two other measures of attitudes toward the *estancieros:* in responses, first, to a question about attitudes toward a political party identified with big landowners, and, second, to a

[36] On the traditional landowner, see Tannenbaum, *Ten Keys to Latin America,* pp. 77–94. On the influence of the values of a land-based aristocracy, see William S. Stokes, "Social Classes in Latin America," in Snow, *Government and Politics,* pp. 64–69.

[37] See de Imaz, *La clase alta.*

[38] See Pendel, *Argentina,* p. 106.

[39] See Fillol, *Social Factors in Economic Development,* p. 31; Arthur P. Whitaker, *Argentina* (Englewood Cliffs, N.J.: Prentice-Hall, 1964), p. 149; and Silvert, "Cost of Anti-Nationalism," p. 367, for estimates of the effects of Peronist policies on the large landowners. Wags commonly called Perón's Instituto Argentino de Promoción del Intercambio (IAPI) the Institute for the Destruction of Argentine Agriculture.

[40] The changed structure of landownership has also had its effects. See de Imaz, *Los que mandan,* pp. 93–103 passim. His two chapters devoted to landowners are an indispensable source on this important social category. For another recent discussion of landowners and cattle raisers, see José Alfredo Martínez de Hoz, "Agricultura y ganadería," in *Argentina, 1930–1960,* pp. 189–211.

TABLE 6.17   LANDOWNER SUPPORT AND OPPOSITION
(In percent)

Attitude	All Argentines (n = 2,014)	Core Peronists (n = 365)	Pro-Peronists (n = 511)	Not Favorable to Peronists (n = 1,238)	UCRP Voters (n = 413)
Toward party supported by landowners					
For	12.1	0.9	15.8	11.6	14.0
Against	70.3	78.9	76.4	65.8	64.6
Don't know	17.6	11.5	7.8	22.7	21.3
Toward expropriation and redistribution of large private estates					
For	63.9	81.6	74.0	55.3	60.0
Against	20.7	9.9	13.9	26.1	22.5
Don't know	15.4	8.5	12.2	18.6	17.4

Source: Responses to Questions 25a and 17f (Appendix B).

question about respondents' views concerning the expropriation of privately owned lands.[41] Both confirmed the existence of widespread hostility to the landowning class. Seventy percent of all respondents said they would oppose a party identified with landowners. Almost two-thirds of all respondents favored expropriation of private lands for redistribution to landless farmers. On both questions, Peronists were particularly anti-*estanciero* (see Table 6.17).

The marked hostility of all sectors of Argentine society and especially of Peronists to large landowners is probably symptomatic of the widespread rejection of the past, of which there are many symptoms in Argentine society. Further, the special antipathy of reliable Peronists to the big landowners reflects a continuation of hostility to this class typical of the Peronist era. As principal members of the *"vendepatria* oligarchy," landowners functioned as the worst of the "bad guys" in the symbolism of the Peronists' populist nationalism. Obviously, this part of Peronist agitational ideology was widely shared among rank-and-file Peronists. But here again we see that Peronist attitudes differed in degree but not in kind or direction from those of the whole society.

[41] The exact questions asked are given in Appendix B (Questions 17 and 17a–17j).

Trade Unions A long-time student of Latin American labor movements, Robert Alexander, comments near the beginning of his book on the subject: "From its inception organized labor in Latin America has been highly political." [42] In this respect, as in others, the Argentine movement is prototypical of South American trade unions. As in other Latin nations, Argentina's oldest unions date from the last decades of the nineteenth century, when they were established by and for immigrant workers who poured in from Italy, Spain, and elsewhere. Socialist, and especially anarcho-syndicalist influences were strong, giving the union movement the flavor and style of some of its continental counterparts and associating labor with the specter of "alien extremism." [43]

During the early period socialists, syndicalists, anarcho-syndicalists, communists, and their schismatic institutional progeny pursued political goals, usually those of comprehensive social revolution, through labor associations. This phase of labor history is said to have lasted through World War I, when it was succeeded by a reformist stage that in turn ended with the rise of Perón. [44]

The workers whom Juan Perón was able to forge into the lever that hoisted him into supreme power were not the workers who had organized themselves into revolutionary trade unions. There was, as Alexander asserts, "a change in the nature of the working class itself." [45] This change had three principal facets: a rapid growth in the urban and industrial sector, which resulted in a greatly increased urban population available for organization; a decrease in immigration and in the proportion of workers with experience in continental labor movements; and a massive migration from the countryside to the capital (and to provincial cities). Whitaker points out that the percentage of internal immigrants living in greater Buenos Aires increased from 12 percent in 1936 to 29 percent in 1947, by which year "for the first time in history foreign immigrants were outnumbered in Buenos Aires by Argentina's own migrants from the

[42] Robert J. Alexander, *Organized Labor in Latin America* (New York: Free Press, 1965), p. 13.

[43] See Moisés Poblete Troncoso and Ben G. Burnett, "Labor and Politics: Problems and Prospects," in John D. Martz, ed., *The Dynamics of Change in Latin American Politics* (Englewood Cliffs, N.J.: Prentice-Hall, 1965), p. 253, for further comment on this association.

[44] Raúl Puigbó's work on the Argentine labor movement describes five historical phases through which the movement has passed. Puigbó's phases are described in some detail by de Imaz, *Los que mandan*, pp. 208–211 passim.

[45] Alexander, *Organized Labor*, p. 41.

back country. During this decade approximately 96,000 rural migrants settled each year in Buenos Aires." [46] The result was an entirely new working class, some of whose members were in trade unions by the time Perón became minister of labor and social welfare in November 1943, and many of whom were organized by him into new unions. The number of organized workers in Argentina grew from 200,000 in the late twenties to 4,000,000 in the late forties.[47]

The intense and lasting (albeit somewhat troubled) romance between Juan Perón and the Argentine labor movement is famous. Perón's welfare policies, labor legislation, and wooing of Argentina's workers are all a matter of public record. Some, like Fillol, believe the workers followed Perón for psychological as well as material reasons: "Perón gave the workers *recognition,* the *feeling of being valued,* and the conviction that the government was genuinely interested in his needs and wishes." [48] Certainly, he catered to them, and they benefited from his policies. Nominal wages increased five times from 1940 to 1950, and though inflation consumed a good part of this raise, improvement in the workers' material well-being was substantial. And, of course, the workers, organized into massive Peronist unions, reciprocated support.

In 1965, more than a decade after the downfall of their leader, despite the "interventions" (read purges) of the Aramburu government, the manipulations of Frondizi, and the efforts of the Radicals, communists, socialists, and anti-Peronist unionists, Peronists still dominated Argentina's labor movement.

The leadership of "Bloc 62," and much of the leadership in the CGT were clearly identified with Peronist politics. There were grounds, however, for questioning the intensity and operational consequences of Peronist sentiments at the base. Labor did not turn out with the massive ferocity hoped for in 1955. Its ranks were not mobilized when the government blocked Perón's entry in 1965. On the other hand, rank-and-file unionists gave heavy electoral support to the Unión Popular.

The next few pages describe the relationship between Peronists and trade unions. We shall be interested in Peronist perceptions of the trade-union movement, in the extent to which Peronist and trade-union identifications were overlapping or identical, and in

[46] Whitaker, *Argentina,* p. 106.
[47] De Imaz, *Los que mandan,* p. 214.
[48] Fillol, *Social Factors in Economic Development,* p. 85; Fillol's emphasis.

views about the actual and desirable role of the trade-union movement in politics.

It is easy to summarize the survey findings concerning the orientations of Peronists toward trade unions. *They were more pro-union in attitude and perspective than any other population category. They were more pro-union than were union members themselves; more pro-union than laborers in general; more pro-union than lower-class respondents as a whole. Peronist responses were highly distinctive on questions concerning union roles and activities.*

It seems clear that the labor movement had an ideological significance for Peronists that was distinct from simple economic interest and did not simply reflect economic roles, but instead reflected views and commitments that Peronists held as Peronists. Political commitment functioned here as an independent variable and conditioned responses to labor's role in the polity.

It is readily demonstrable that Peronist perspectives on labor did not simply or directly reflect economic roles and class status. It is also clear that while there was much overlapping membership, Peronists and trade unionists were by no means identical. First, less than one-fifth of trade-union members were reliable supporters of Perón. Almost another fifth were generally favorable to the movement. The political preferences of the remaining three-fifths were distributed over a wide political spectrum. Conversely, approximately one-half of the core Peronists were drawn from trade-union families. On a wide range of questions, the proportion of pro-labor responses significantly exceeded the proportion of trade-union members and the pro-labor responses of laborers as a whole (see Table 6.18). The ideological commitment of Peronists to organized labor was most dramatically revealed by the contrast between their opinions about trade unions and the opinions of trade-union members themselves (see Table 6.19).

TABLE 6.18   LABOR-UNION MEMBERSHIP, BY FAMILY
(In percent)

	All Argentines ($n = 2,014$)	Core Peronists ($n = 365$)	Pro-Peronists ($n = 411$)	Not Favorable to Peronists ($n = 1,238$)
Yes	11.6	16.7	17.5	8.2
No	82.0	78.1	77.1	84.7
Don't know	6.4	5.2	5.4	7.1

Source: Responses to Question 59 (Appendix B).

TABLE 6.19   PERONIST AND UNIONIST ATTITUDES
(In percent)

	Core Peronists ($n = 365$)	Union Members ($n = 234$)
Unions have played constructive role	66.0	55.6
Labor has been treated fairly by government	18.9	34.6
Unions should have important part in politics	37.3	27.8

Source: Responses to Questions 57, 56, and 58 (Appendix B).

More Peronists than others believed labor has played a constructive role in Argentine society in recent years.[49] More Peronists than others regarded unions as a positive political reference group, saying they would support a party supported by trade unions. More Peronists than others would turn to labor leaders for needed information on public affairs.[50] Among all the population categories tested, more Peronists than others believed the labor movement had been treated unfairly by the government (see Table 6.20).[51] More Peronists favored the participation of the labor movement in politics and, to the extent that they perceived the movement as controlled by a political party, believed it to be desirable.

There were marked differences among social classes in their perceptions of labor affairs. Both beliefs and attitudes differed about the actual and the desirable role for trade unions. For example, a question of fact (whether the labor movement was controlled by a political party) revealed sharp differences of opinion among upper-class respondents on the one hand and middle- and lower-class respondents on the other. Differences on this question of fact were as great as those on attitudes toward the desirability of political association with labor (see Table 6.21).

The organized labor movement is then a subject on which there were sharp class cleavages and political cleavages. Though the lower class is an important source of Peronist rank and file and leaders,[52] the movement's pro-labor orientations were more marked than were its lower-class composition, indicating a widely shared ideological

[49] The exact question asked is given in Appendix B (Question 57).

[50] The exact question asked is given in ibid. (Question 48). Slightly more than one-fourth (26.6 percent) of the Peronists, compared with 5.7 percent of all other respondents, asserted they would turn to union leaders for information on public affairs.

[51] The exact questions asked are given in ibid. (Questions 56 and 56a).

[52] De Imaz, *Los que mandan,* p. 13.

TABLE 6.20 ATTITUDES TOWARD LABOR
(In percent)

	All Argentines (n = 2,014)	Core Peronists (n = 365)	Pro-Peronists (n = 411)	Not Favorable to Peronists (n = 1,238)	UCRP Voters (n = 413)	Lower Class (n = 721)	Laborers (n = 410)
Unions played constructive role (1)	− 30.1	0	− 17.6	− 43.1	− 36.0	− 24.0	− 16.2
Labor treated unfairly by government (2)	− 30.9	0	− 24.6	− 42.1	− 43.7	− 34.1	− 19.7
Labor *should* be involved in politics (3)	− 23.7	0	− 18.2	− 32.3	− 32.2	− 23.2	− 19.4
Would support party supported by labor (4)	− 21.1	0	+ 0.5	− 33.7	− 27.6	− 12.4	− 10.8

Source: Responses to Questions 57, 56, 58, and 25c (Appendix B).
Note: Each cell represents the difference between the percentage of reliable Peronists taking the position stated and the percentage of the designated subgroup taking the same position. For proposition (1), 0 = 66 percent; for proposition (2), 0 = 68.8 percent; for proposition (3), 0 = 58.4 percent; for proposition (4), 0 = 93.7 percent.

TABLE 6.21   LABOR AND CLASS
(In percent)

Agree	Upper (n = 157)	Class Middle (n = 960)	Lower (n = 721)	Core Peronists (n = 365)
Labor movement is controlled by political party	59.2	36.4	32.0	32.6
Would support party supported by labor	56.7	68.8	81.8	93.7

Source: Responses to Questions 55 and 25c (Appendix B).

commitment to organized labor. This fact, along with the differences in elite composition, helps explain why Peronist parties had such a strong working-class image. While the UCPR drew substantial support from laborers and the lower classes, a pro-labor orientation was by no means as widely shared among UCRP voters as among rank-and-file Peronists. These distinctively pro-labor orientations of Peronists are also consistent with the more marked class consciousness of lower-class Peronists.

Two additional facts should be noted about responses to the labor movement: first, pro-labor aggregates were more favorable to labor participation in politics, and vice versa; and, second, while there were distinctive class reactions to the labor movement, there was no marked or general class-based antagonism toward labor. To the contrary, large portions of both upper and middle classes exhibited friendly, positive responses to organized labor.

Orientations to Groups and Aggregates: An Overview

Table 6.22 depicts the affective orientations toward several collectivities as political participants. Several interesting relationships are revealed concerning both social relations generally and distinctive Peronist orientations.

Landowners and communists were the clear winners of a negative popularity contest. They were the only groups that inspired near-universal opposition. The fact that they represented opposite ends of the conventional right-left political spectrum invites the inference that Argentines overwhelmingly rejected the political extremes.[53] The military establishment and the Church ranked well behind both

[53] Communists who believe in the inevitable victory of the party as the wave of the future might decide that Argentines reject both past and future.

TABLE 6.22   POLITICAL REFERENCE GROUPS: POSITIVE AND
NEGATIVE
(In percent)

Support	Core Peronists ($n = 365$)	All Argentines ($n = 2,014$)	Lower Class ($n = 721$)	Laborers ($n = 410$)
Big landowners	9.6	12.1	10.1	9.0
Agricultural workers	84.1	78.1	82.7	82.0
Labor unions	93.7	73.1	81.8	83.4
Argentine entrepreneurs	47.1	54.4	49.8	48.3
Argentine communists	10.4	5.6	7.5	8.8
Military services	27.4	28.4	26.6	29.3
Intellectuals	68.4	68.5	68.0	65.1
Peronists	98.5	36.6	32.9	50.2
Church hierarchy	43.8	41.6	44.5	40.0
Middle-class Argentines	86.3	86.0	86.1	86.6
Bureaucrats	85.8	80.9	82.7	80.0
Foreigners	36.4	37.7	37.9	38.3

Source: Responses to Questions 25a–25n.

landowners and communists as negative reference groups; military
officers were not perceived as the most objectionable actors. More
than five times as many respondents in the total sample and two
and a half times as many reliable Peronists rejected associations
with the communists than with the military. More than twice as
many Argentines in general and approximately three times as many
Peronists saw landowners as less desirable associates than the military establishment.

The "foreigners," who were often identified as synonymous with
"imperialists," are also on the low end of the political acceptability
scale. But again it is striking that they were not as universally
opposed in fact as in the rhetoric of nationalist spokesmen. And
more than a third of both the total sample and the Peronists expressed willingness to have the "foreigners" as political associates.

Turning to the highly regarded social categories, it is interesting
to note that the middle classes, rural workers, and trade unionists
were all widely approved by Argentines generally and by Peronists.
This finding clearly indicates the absence of any widely perceived
conflict between bourgeoisie and working class. This, plus the widespread hostility to landowners, indicates a system of class relations
far from the Marxist model for modern industrial societies. But
Argentina is a highly industrialized, highly urban society. It is surely
significant that the principal class cleavages separate the great

majority from the dominant class of the preindustrial past.[54] Do the higher mutual regard and lower hostility among other classes indicate the diminution or attenuation of class cleavages? Or is this configuration an example of cultural lag? De Imaz's study of the highest class indicated that landowning still enjoys the highest status and that members of the highest class see themselves as a social elite without important economic or political power.[55] Does the widespread dislike of this class reflect contempt for a group whose status outstrips its power? Or whose prestige exceeds its functional importance?

The fact that the middle classes were more widely approved by Argentines generally than any other category is consistent with the widespread tendency to identify with the middle class noted earlier. It is also consistent with the high upward mobility between lower and middle classes and is one among several indications that Argentina is well on its way to becoming a middle-class society—a possibility whose political implications are less clear than is sometimes assumed.

Finally, the foregoing analysis clearly demonstrates that Peronists shared dominant attitudes toward social aggregates. Their reactions were both qualitatively and quantitatively similar to those of Argentines in general. Broadly speaking, they shared with other Argentines views about the identity of positive and negative reference groups, indicating that Peronists had the same general perspective as others on socially desirable traits and roles. Nonetheless, there were some interesting differences in degree. While Peronists shared the general consensus about the identity of the heroes and villains, they diverged on the question of who—among the "good guys"—is best, and who—among the "bad guys"—is worst. Big landowners rather than communists were most objectionable; trade unions rather than the middle class were most widely supported.

Compared with UCRP supporters, Peronists were more favorable to rural workers, trade unions, and domestic communists; they were less favorable to large landowners, domestic entrepreneurs, the

[54] Everett E. Hagen, "The Entrepreneur as Rebel Against Traditional Society," *Human Organization,* vol. 19, no. 4 (Winter 1960–1961), pp. 185–187, discusses the role of business leaders in industrial development. For a famous, progressive Argentine entrepreneurial career, see Thomas C. Cochran and Ruben E. Reina, *Entrepreneurship in Argentine Culture: Torcuato Di Tella and S.I.A.M.* (Philadelphia: University of Pennsylvania Press, 1962).

[55] De Imaz, *La clase alta,* p. 55.

TABLE 6.23   PERONIST-UCRP GROUP SUPPORT PATTERNS
(In percent)

	UCRP Deviation
Big landowners	+4.4
Agricultural workers	− 7.6
Labor unions	− 27.6
Argentine entrepreneurs	+ 13.7
Argentine communists	− 6.5
Military services	+ 8.7
Intellectuals	+ 5.9
Church hierarchy	+ 2.2
Middle-class Argentines	+ 5.5
Bureaucrats	− 0.6
Foreigners	+ 5.7

Source: Same as Table 6.22.

Note: Each cell represents the difference between UCRP and Peronist support for the indicated group.

military services, intellectuals, the Church, the middle classes, and foreigners (see Table 6.23).

The configuration of group orientations characteristic of Peronists reveals that there were relatively more Peronists than UCRP supporters for whom class was an important and divisive factor. *Peronist class consciousness was higher than that of other members of the working class, a fact that acquires special significance in the context of a society moving toward middle-class homogeneity*. While others were tending to place themselves in an undifferentiated middle class, lower-class Peronists affirmed their class identifications. Add to this a pro-labor ideological commitment and an almost equally strong tendency to see labor as unfairly treated, and there exists the psychosocial basis of a combative ideology. The somewhat greater frequency of antilandowner, antientrepreneurial orientations are further evidence of the presence among rank-and-file Peronists of divisive class orientations that are distinctive in Argentine society.

It must, however, be emphasized that this trend is suggestive, not preemptive. Rank-and-file Peronists did not conceive themselves as soldiers in a class war. Their widespread positive orientations to the middle class alone prove nonconformity to the Marxist model of exclusive class loyalties and mutual class hatred.

Finally, the favorable orientation of a large majority of all Argentines to public employees is interesting. It obviously does not indicate generalized antistate attitudes sometimes impressionistically associated with Latin American political orientations. Berger's suggestive hypothesis that postulates a correlation between prestige of bureaucratic officials and level of social development comes to mind, but data adequate to test it are lacking; so is a scale indicating which levels of development are compatible with which levels of prestige.[56] Argentina is a highly developed country when measured against most criteria. By many contemporary criteria of political development, however, its political system reflects a lower level of development than its society and economy.[57] The pattern of intergroup relations is similarly ambiguous in its implications for assessing social development.

[56] Morroe Berger, *Bureaucracy and Society in Modern Egypt: A Study of the Higher Civil Service* (Princeton: Princeton University Press, 1957).

[57] See, for example, Phillips Cutright, "National Political Development: Measurement and Analysis," *American Sociological Review*, vol. 28, no. 2 (April 1963), p. 261. This discrepancy between economic and political development has been most recently commented on by Darío Canton, *El Parlamento Argentino en épocas de cambio: 1890, 1916 y 1946* (Buenos Aires: Editorial del Instituto, 1966), pp. 103–150 passim.

7

Peronists and Political Authority

In the first place [spoke the law of Athens to Socrates], . . . did
we not bring you into existence? Your father married your mother
by our aid and begat you. . . . Well, then, since you were brought
into the world and nurtured and educated by us, can you deny in
the first place that you are our child and slave, as your fathers were
before you?

Plato, *Crito*

In a word, it is the perspectives of the mass which confer authority
on the governors.

Lasswell and Kaplan, *Power and Society*

This chapter deals with Peronists' perceptions of government and
their relations to it. Relations between government and individuals have, of course, stimulated much of the best writing about and
analysis of politics throughout recorded history. In classics of political philosophy, citizen relations to political authority have been
repeatedly identified as a principal determinant of the quality of
the polity. The concepts of citizen, subject, foreigner, and slave
were developed to describe possible relationships between individuals and political authority.[1] Similarly, around the notion of
political obligation a large body of literature has developed, which
explores the several and reciprocal duties of individuals and governments. Contemporary discussions of nation-building continue a
tradition already developed by the fifth century B.C. Plato, Machia-
velli, and Rousseau are but three among many who believed that
subjective identification with the polity was the most certain ground
of obligation to rulers and to law. Contemporarily, the lack of
identification of the self with the polity is often said to underlie
some of the most stubborn problems of new nations, in which sub-

[1] Contemporary emphasis on the normative component of the classics tends to
obscure the existence and importance of the descriptive, analytic, and predictive
components in the "great tradition."

national groups—tribal, linguistic, regional, and kinship—are the effective units of identification and the foci of obligation.[2] In such societies, cognitive conceptions that relate the individual to the nation are often lacking. Lack of identification is also said to afflict older nations in which sectarian, class-bound politics announces the state to be the property of a particular class.[3] Such lack of identification, tinged with hostility, is called alienation and is said to result from long-endured, consciously perceived inequity suffered from the rulers.[4]

The objective relations between citizens and polity in Argentina in recent decades make especially interesting the investigation of the perceived roles of Argentine citizens. Since the beginning of mass participation in politics, Argentines have lived with political fluctuations that defined them in and out of the decision-making process. From 1916 to 1930 Argentine citizens were participants in the choice of rulers and, indirectly, of policies. From 1930 to 1943 they were at first formally, then informally and fraudulently excluded from the process of deciding who should rule. From 1946 to 1954 they were again admitted as participants, but in a context that imposed unusual limits. From 1955 to 1957 they were again defined out; from 1957 to 1965 they were in again; from 1966 to the present they are once more subjects rather than participants. More than three decades of objective fluctuation between the roles of citizen and subject have almost surely had subjective conse-

[2] The problem of transferring identification from traditional parochial units to the new national units of political organization is viewed as a central problem of nation-building by much of the literature on developing areas; see, among others, Karl W. Deutsch and William J. Foltz, eds., *Political Parties and National Integration in Tropical Africa* (Berkeley and Los Angeles: University of California Press, 1964); Edward A. Shils, "On the Comparative Study of the New States," McKim Marriot, "Cultural Policy in the New States," and David E. Apter, "Political Religion in the New Nations," in Clifford Geertz, ed., *Old Societies and New States* (New York: Free Press, 1963); David E. Apter, *The Politics of Modernization* (Chicago: University of Chicago Press, 1965); Myron Weiner, "Political Integration and Political Development," in Jason L. Finkle and Richard W. Gable, eds., *Political Development and Social Change* (New York: John Wiley & Sons, 1966); Almond and Verba, *The Civic Culture*, especially pp. 3–42; and Gabriel A. Almond and G. Bingham Powell, Jr., *Comparative Politics: A Developmental Approach* (Boston: Little, Brown and Company, 1966), especially pp. 42–72.

[3] Silvert, among others, emphasizes the class-bound character of Argentine politics before and after Perón in Kalman H. Silvert, ed., *Expectant Peoples: Nationalism and Development* (New York: Vintage Books, 1967), pp. 344–372 passim.

[4] The assumption that exploitation had alienated Europe's working classes underlay the surprise of many Marxists of the First International at workers rallying to support their respective nations in World War I.

quences. So presumably have the multiple interventions invalidating decisions in which citizens took part. Argentina is an excellent but not unique example of a system in flux between decision processes that permit (and, through compulsory voting laws, require) mass participation and processes that permit no participation.[5] It is an excellent testing ground for hypotheses dealing with this type of system instability. Either democratic expectations or cynicism, or both, could result from such prolonged alternation in roles. So might comprehensive alienation. The subjective consequences of experience with such mixed systems, which we tend to think of as transitional,[6] have been little investigated despite their relatively large number.

Within the system I shall, of course, be particularly interested in the attitudes of Peronists. Followers of a popular dictator, victims of electoral manipulation designed to prohibit the victory of their leader, largely lower-class carriers of purported authoritarian characters, Peronists are sometimes said to constitute a large antidemocratic core within the political system, and a good deal of the discussion of their "integration" or "reintegration" into political life assumes that the problem is one of transforming them from the mass supporters of a nondemocratic Caesar into supporters of a democratic role system and processes. Modern Caesars, like ancient ones, often find their support among masses more concerned with outcomes than with procedures; more interested in reaping benefits than in sharing decisions; more concerned with the distribution of goods than of influence, and unable to see a connection between the two. The followers of Perón are often so characterized.

This chapter delineates Peronists' (and other Argentines') perceptions of the distribution and structure of political influence, including (1) *who* makes decisions, and (2) the role of the individual citizen in the decision-making process with regard to (a) influence, (b) deference, (c) competence, and (d) obligations. The chapter also describes Peronists' perceptions of selected outcomes, with regard to equity and competence. Throughout, focus is on the distinctiveness

[5] Germani and Silvert suggest that the nation's prolonged political instability may be an incident in the transition to a society that permits full mass participation. See Gino Germani and Kalman H. Silvert, "Estructura social e intervención militar en América Latina," in Torcuato S. di Tella, Gino Germani, Jorge Graciarena y colaboradores, *Argentina, sociedad de masas* (Buenos Aires: Editorial Universitaria de Buenos Aires, 1965), p. 240.

[6] It is by no means clear what they are in transition *to*—presumably to modern "participatory" systems that can be either democratic or totalitarian in nature.

of Peronists' perceptions of the decision process, both inputs and outcomes.

Present knowledge of the subjective correlates of political systems and movements on the one hand and of the Argentine political system on the other suggests the following expectations as reasonable:

1. Widespread cognition of the fact that the national government affects individuals' lives is to be expected. Awareness of this link is a prerequisite to all other attitudes concerning the self in the political system. Modern national integration requires building structures objectively linking individuals to national governments and communicating the existence of such a link to individuals. Argentina is not a new nation. Its populace is largely urban and overwhelmingly literate. An advanced technology permits a national communication system. Universal compulsory suffrage has existed intermittently for decades. Welfare politics has touched the lives of individuals unable to grasp abstract relationships. Because of all these factors, one would expect to find a widespread but not universal sense of the relevance of government to individuals' lives.[7]

2. One would also expect to find relatively widespread doubts concerning the efficacy and influence of individuals in the decision process. Among Peronists, who have been subjected to special, discriminatory electoral disabilities, skepticism about the influence of individuals on decisions should be especially high.

3. Relatively low expectations of equal or fair treatment were to be expected among Peronists since the survey took place after sweeping, widely publicized purges of Peronist officials from all branches of government.

4. Also to be expected was fairly widespread familiarity with some mechanisms through which individuals can act to influence political decisions, since mass support has been a factor in determining Argentine political decisions for several decades—through elections, demonstrations, strikes, and other forms of collective action. It should be noted here again that the demonstration of mass support has been a factor in political decisions in nondemocratic as well as democratic periods.[8]

---

[7] On research on the development of popular politics, see Daniel Lerner, ed., *Public Opinion Quarterly*, special issue, *Attitude Research in Modernizing Areas*, vol. 22, no. 3 (Fall 1958), pp. 217–420.

[8] See chap. 3 for further discussion.

TABLE 7.1   PERCEIVED INFLUENCE OF GOVERNMENT ON SELF
(In percent)

	All Argen- tines (n = 2,014)	Core Pero- nists (n = 365)	UCRP Voters (n = 413)	Upper (n = 157)	Class Middle (n = 960)	Lower (n = 721)
A lot	41.1	39.5	40.2	52.2	40.3	39.9
A little	28.3	29.3	30.8	21.7	28.8	26.5
Not at all	22.6	22.2	24.9	18.5	22.7	24.7
Don't know	8.0	9.0	4.1	7.6	8.2	8.9

Source: Responses to Question 14.

Influence of Government on Individuals

A question, borrowed from *The Civic Culture,* inquired: "Thinking about what the national government does—the laws it makes, etc.—about how much effect do you think it has on you in your personal life? Would you say that what they do affects you personally a lot, some, a little, or not at all?" Table 7.1 describes the responses.

That almost one-third of all Argentines either believed the government had no effect on their lives or were not sure should, I suppose, come as no surprise to students of mass publics and readers of *The Civic Culture.* That study revealed that the number with this view was nearly as great in the United Kingdom and Germany as in Argentina, and a good deal larger in Italy and Mexico.[9] Despite the high incidence among Peronists of lower-class, lower-education respondents from the hinterlands, Peronists were not notably less aware of the influence of government (at least at the abstract level) than were supporters of the UCRP. The explanation is probably the obvious one, that those with defined political preferences inevitably overrepresented that portion of any social aggregate that is most sensitive to the role of government in the society.

Contemporary literature has made it clear that awareness of a relation between government and one's self is not a prerequisite to being politically mobilized. Recent studies argue that in some new nations mobilization often precedes cognition of the goals toward

[9] Almond and Verba, *The Civic Culture,* p. 80. In Argentina, as in the other countries, awareness of the influence of government is related to class, region, and education.

which the group activity is directed.[10] An unknown portion of Perón's *descamisados* may have marched before they noted the effects of government on their lives. But Peronists in 1965 were as aware, and unaware, of their relation to government as were Argentines generally, and the awareness presumably reinforced their political interest.

Influence of Individuals in the Decision Process

Several questions were included in the survey to elicit respondents' perceptions of how much influence people in general and they in particular had on the way the government was organized.[11] Responses were mixed, and their interpretation is in some respects problematic. While approximately 80 percent of all Argentines and 86 percent of the Peronists agreed that "the way people vote is the main thing that decides how things are run in this country," almost half of all respondents expressed doubts elsewhere that average citizens have any influence "on what the government does," and among Peronists this disbelief in the influence of average citizens was particularly widespread. Follow-up questions exploring anticipations concerning treatment and influence in specific situations confirmed the expectation of negligible or small influence among about two-fifths of the population.

Juxtaposition of the findings in Tables 7.2 and 7.3 suggests that while there was wide acceptance of the abstract idea that voters determine policy, this was not necessarily regarded as giving average people significant influence over government. The inconsistency is logical rather than existential. In democracies, voters as a whole can and do wield significant power—collectively. Individual citizens may be and usually are without any other influence on decisions.

Daniel Goldrich has commented that the political mode of the poor is "one of immediacy, . . . [the poverty stricken have] an alertness only to what is closely related to the needs of the moment, . . . electoral process is unlikely to have meaning for the impoverished because its very nature is gradualist and abstract. . . ."[12]

[10] Apter, *Politics of Modernization*. Demonstrators who can be hired by the head are a good example of mobilization independent of cognized political goals or of cognitions linking the activity to the goals.

[11] The questions on political competence were taken from Almond and Verba, *The Civic Culture*.

[12] Daniel Goldrich, "Toward the Comparative Study of Politicization in Latin America," in Peter G. Snow, ed., *Government and Politics in Latin America* (New York: Holt Rinehart & Winston, 1967), p. 255.

TABLE 7.2   AVERAGE CITIZEN'S INFLUENCE ON GOVERNMENT
(In percent)

	All Argentines (n = 2,014)	Core Peronists (n = 365)	Pro-Peronists (n = 411)	Not Favorable to Peronists (n = 1,238)	UCRP Voters (n = 413)
Votes decide how things will be run	79.9	85.8	80.5	77.9	80.6
Average citizen has *no* say about what government does	53.3	64.9	54.0	48.1	40.0
Average citizen has *no* influence on government	42.1	47.4	46.0	39.3	32.7

Source: Responses to Questions 15a, 15f, and 8 (Appendix B).

Approximately half of all Argentines and somewhat fewer Peronists felt average citizens did influence government, expected that they could affect a decision of the national legislature, and expected that they would receive "proper" consideration in expressing their views to a government office or court.[13]

---

[13] Compared with *The Civic Culture* findings on perceived ability to do something about a national regulation, Argentina ranks below the United States and Great Britain but above Germany, Italy, and Mexico. See Almond and Verba, *The Civic Culture*, p. 185.

TABLE 7.3   PERSONAL IMPOTENCE VIS-À-VIS GOVERNMENT AGENCIES
(In percent)

	All Argentines (n = 2,014)	Core Peronists (n = 365)	Pro-Peronists (n = 411)	Not Favorable to Peronists (n = 1,238)	UCRP Voters (n = 413)
Could do nothing about national legislature's action	39.0	38.1	42.1	38.2	35.8
Would get little or no hearing from officer of government	39.5	42.7	42.1	37.8	34.6
Would get little or no hearing from court	34.8	37.5	32.6	34.1	29.1

Source: Responses to Questions 9, 11, and 13 (Appendix B).

TABLE 7.4   CITIZEN's PERCEIVED IMPORTANCE IN GOVERN-
MENT DECISIONS
(In percent)

	All Argentines (n = 2,014)	Core Peronists (n = 365)	UCRP Voters (n = 413)
Average citizen has no say	53.3	64.9	40.6
People like you and me have no influence on government	42.1	47.4	32.7
Government run by a few interests who ignore majority interests	42.5	53.4	37.3
I could not influence national legislature	39.0	38.1	35.8
I would not get a proper hearing from government	39.5	42.7	34.6
I would not get an adequate hearing from court	34.8	37.5	29.1

Source: Responses to Questions 8, 15f, 23, 9, 11, and 13 (Appendix B).

The figures in Table 7.4 make clear that approximately two-fifths of all Argentines did not conceive themselves as effective participants in governmental decisions, either of general decisions at the national level or of decisions in which they were personally involved. The percentage of Peronists who doubted the influence of average citizens generally, and themselves specifically, is consistently higher than the proportion of UCRP voters. The survey was done during the administration of President Illía. It is possible that having supported the incumbent, that is, seeing one's man in office, may have heightened their sense of political power and efficacy. In this case the difference would be transient. Later analysis will reveal whether the perception of impotence was related to other perceptions and preferences that cast doubt on democratic assumptions and views, or whether these perceptions of the impotence of average citizens (and the self) were independent of policy and structural preferences.[14]

Inquiry into *how* individuals might attempt to influence a decision of the national legislature (1) confirms the view that the vote

[14] These findings on perceived competence are roughly, though not exactly, comparable to *The Civic Culture* category, "Neither national nor local competence." The percentage of Argentines who felt neither is similar to that of Italy (47 percent felt incompetence) and Mexico (43 percent felt incompetence). The portion who felt incompetence is lower in the United States (15 percent), the United Kingdom (19 percent), and Germany (34 percent). See ibid., p. 186.

TABLE 7.5   PERCEIVED MODES OF INFLUENCE ON NATIONAL
DECISIONS
(In percent)

	All Argentines (n = 2,014)	Core Peronists (n = 365)	UCRP Voters (n = 413)
Unite with others to protest	12.2	9.0	13.8
Protest (not otherwise specified)	10.6	13.2	13.8
Make public opposition (radio, TV)	7.2	7.1	7.5
Speak to or write representative	6.1	6.0	5.8
Use vote	2.7	2.5	3.1
Make demonstrations	2.3	4.1	1.2
Do not support it	2.5	2.7	2.9

Source: Responses to Question 9 (Appendix B); taken from *The Civic Culture.*

was not widely regarded as an effective means of wielding influence
on decisions; (2) indicates reasonably widespread knowledge of
forms of individual political action; (3) indicates that approximately
the same possible courses of action occurred to persons of different
political views, and in approximately the same proportions (Peronists showed only slightly more inclination to suggest direct action
than supporters of the UCRP); and (4) demonstrates that formal
channels between individuals and government were not widely perceived as efficacious—parties were barely mentioned as channels of
influence, and contacts with representatives were mentioned far less
frequently than more direct and less specific forms of action (see
Table 7.5).

The perception of impotence does not entail a demand for more
power, though it is consistent with such a demand. There is some
indirect evidence that not all Argentines who perceived themselves
as without influence in government decisions desired a greater voice.
Approximately two-thirds of all respondents (and three-fourths of
all Peronists) agreed that "politics and government are so complicated that the average man cannot really understand what is going
on." [15] Approximately one-fifth felt they personally did not understand "important national and international issues facing the
country" at all; another two-fifths said they did not understand them
very well. Peronists less frequently made claims to adequate understanding than did UCRP supporters and, perhaps significantly, were

[15] The exact question asked, taken from *The Civic Culture,* is given in Appendix B (Question 45).

TABLE 7.6   REASON FOR BEING UNINFORMED
(In percent)

	All Argentines ($n = 2,014$)	Core Peronists ($n = 365$)	UCRP Voters ($n = 413$)
Average man does not understand	67.9	75.1	68.5
I do not understand issues [a]	56.7	62.5	51.2
Problems too complex	28.1	24.1	30.0
People not interested	26.6	15.9	33.4
Those in power do not help	39.5	56.2	31.2

Source: Responses to Questions 47, 47a, 47b, and 47c (Appendix B); taken from *The Civic Culture*.

[a] Those who said they did not understand issues very well plus those who said not at all.

almost twice as likely to blame government officials for their felt lack of understanding. There is, of course, no necessary connection between views about one's information and about the role one ought to have in the decision-making process. While one model of democratic process equates good citizens with well-informed ones, not only is this model under contemporary attack as providing unrealistic, unattainable, and spurious standards of democratic citizenship,[16] but it also is radically different from the principal justifications for mass participation in decision making found in the classics. Aristotle and Bentham, to name two rather reluctant friends of democracy, found the justification for mass participation in the competence of the average man to know his own interests and "when the shoe pinches. . . ." They did not expect citizens to have comprehensive information about public policy. Still, the modern association of understanding public issues with political competence is widespread, and one cannot assume that respondents did not regard it as relevant. Of course, Peronists' strong tendencies to blame the government for their lack of information psychologically freed them from the implications of any responsibility for personal incompetence (see Table 7.6).

Comparing Peronist responses with those of the lower socio-

---

[16] E. E. Schattschneider, *The Semisovereign People: A Realist's View of Democracy in America* (New York: Holt, Rinehart & Winston, 1960), is a particularly effective modern attack. On the same subject, see V. O. Key, Jr., with the assistance of Milton C. Cummings, *The Responsible Electorate* (Cambridge, Mass.: Harvard University Press, 1966); Joseph A. Schumpeter, *Capitalism, Socialism and Democracy* (New York: Harper and Brothers, 1946), pp. 250–302 passim; and Robert A. Dahl, "Further Reflections on 'The Elitist Theory of Democracy,'" *American Political Science Review*, vol. 60, no. 2 (June 1966).

TABLE 7.7 BLAMED AUTHORITIES FOR LACK OF INFORMA-
TION

	Percentage
Peronists ($n = 365$)	56.2
Lower class ($n = 721$)	40.5
Laborers (n = 410)	42.0
UCRP voters (n = 413)	31.2

Source: Responses to Question 47 (Appendix B).

economic class and with all laborers reveals a distinctive political factor operating in their reproach to authorities for failing to help inform them (see Table 7.7). It is not a lower-class attribute; it is a Peronist attitude. The notion that it is the responsibility of those in power to help citizens acquire information suggests a communication network in which information flows from the leader (or patron) to the followers.[17]

Equal treatment has no necessary relation to democracy. Inmates of a prison may be equal in impotence; so may subjects of a dictator. And though two citizens may each have the right to vote, one may get better treatment by police, or a government office, or a party official because of bribery, kinship, or other reasons. Nevertheless, equal treatment by political authorities and by the government is a value independently desired by many. The feeling that one is discriminated against or is treated unfairly is widely regarded as an evil by citizens of democracies and autocracies alike. In Argentina approximately two-thirds of all respondents said they would expect fair treatment from a government official. A similar number of all respondents would expect fair treatment from the courts. Relatively more UCRP supporters than Peronists expected equitable treatment from both administrative and judicial officials (see Table 7.8).

About as many Argentines expected fair treatment from government agencies as believed they had a voice in government decisions (about 60 percent). Approximately 40 percent of the reliable Peronists had neither a sense of participation nor an expectation of equal treatment. Concerning both potential influence and equal treatment, Peronists' expectations diverge slightly from average responses and sharply from those of UCRP supporters. I have suggested that the existence of a UCRP administration at the time of the survey may

[17] A suggestive study of communication patterns and their relation to the development of a modern political system is Daniel Lerner, *The Passing of Traditional Society: Modernizing the Middle East* (Glencoe, Ill.: Free Press, 1958).

TABLE 7.8   EXPECTATION OF FAIR TREATMENT
(In percent)

	All Argentines ($n = 2,014$)	Core Peronists ($n = 365$)	UCRP Voters ($n = 413$)
From government officials	65.8	61.6	73.4
From the courts	65.5	56.7	75.8

Source: Responses to Questions 10 and 12 (Appendix B); taken from *The Civic Culture*.

account for the higher expectations of Popular Radical supporters. However, trend data would be required to determine the importance of this factor. In the absence of trend data it is virtually impossible to determine the extent to which differential responses reflect realistic (and temporary) historical factors. It does seem very likely that differences between perceived distribution of power and felt competence reflected more than transient topical conditions such as the fact that a Popular Radical government was in power and that existing electoral laws subjected Peronists to unique disabilities.

Most Peronists' responses were the same as most UCRP supporters' responses, and a substantial minority of UCRP supporters, 23 to 30 percent, responded in the same way as a larger Peronist minority. That is, the responses of Peronist and UCRP supporters were more similar than dissimilar, despite the substantial difference in the objective positions of their parties. This broad overlapping of orientation between respondents of different partisan orientations would be expected in any political community that was not deeply divided. Only if political differences build on and reflect comprehensive subcultures would one expect to find comprehensive differences in kind rather than in degree.

Perception of Obligations to Government

The preceding section dealt with the perceived distribution of influence; this section deals with the perceived distribution of obligations. One of the most important aspects of the political socialization process is the preparation of the child for his role as a member of the polity. Patriotic rituals and routines, the rights and duties of citizenship, models of appropriate civic behavior are all culturally transmitted from generation to generation.[18] So, of course, are patterns of evaluation and cathexis. Depending on the homogeneity of the culture and the variations of orientations to citizenship, one of several conceptions of citizenship may emerge.

The range of demands made by states on citizens has varied greatly through time and space; so have conceptions of the duties of citizens. It is one of the hallmarks of the modern state, as of the Greek city-state, that individuals stand in some direct relationship to political authority. The modern participatory state demands loyalty to selected symbols as well as the performance of selected duties such as paying taxes and military service.

Democracies are often believed to require a higher sense of duty and dedication to the polity than autocratic systems.[19] Anglo-Saxon democracies are sometimes said to place especially great stress on civic virtues, to encourage voluntary associations to promote collective goals, and to emphasize cooperation as a desirable mode of interaction.[20] The famous *incivisme* of modern France is, on the other hand, said to result from a culture that stresses the rights of individual and family and speaks little of shared duties and common goals.[21]

[18] The subject of political socialization has recently enjoyed a renaissance that features more systematic investigation of the transmission of political culture; see, among others, Fred I. Greenstein, *Children and Politics* (New Haven: Yale University Press, 1965), and Herbert Hyman, *Political Socialization: A Study in the Psychology of Political Behavior* (Glencoe, Ill.: Free Press, 1959). See also Harold D. Lasswell, "Political Constitution and Character," *Psychoanalysis and the Psychoanalytic Review*, vol. 46 (1960), pp. 1–18, for a translation into contemporary analytic terms of Plato's views on the relation of political socialization to changing constitutions; also *Annals of the American Academy of Political and Social Science*, special issue, *Political Socialization: Its Role in the Political Process*, vol. 361 (September 1965).

[19] See, among others, Jean Jacques Rousseau, *The Social Contract*, trans. with intro. by Willmoore Kendall (Chicago: Henry Regnery Co., 1954), bk. 3, chap. 4, pp. 72–75, and *Considerations on the Government of Poland*, trans. Willmoore Kendall (Minneapolis: Minnesota Book Store, 1947), especially chap. 3, pp. 6, 7; Baron de Montesquieu, *The Spirit of the Laws*, trans. Thomas Nugent (New York: Hafner Publishing Company, 1949), bk. 3, chap. 3, pp. 2–22; and John Stuart Mill, *On Representative Government* (New York: E. P. Dutton and Company, 1950); chap. 4, pp. 292–305.

[20] See, among others, Alexis de Tocqueville, *Democracy in America*, 2 vols. (New York: Alfred A. Knopf, 1945).

[21] See Herbert Leuthy, *France Against Herself* (New York: Fredrick A. Praeger, 1955), and Stanley Hoffmann et al., *In Search of France* (Cambridge, Mass.: Harvard University Press, 1963).

Models of citizenship are, of course, provided in a nation's heroes, who reflect valued personality types and preferred styles of political behavior and admired accomplishments. For this reason, analysis of a nation's great men is very useful for understanding a national political culture. Most useful of all, however, is to know average citizens' concrete conceptions of their duties and obligations, because these most accurately reflect operative rather than ideal standards of civic behavior.

Survey questions were included that inquired both directly and indirectly into respondents' views concerning their obligations as citizens. One series of questions inquired into their conceptions of their obligations to the national and local communities (see Tables 7.9 and 7.10). Another concerned their views about priorities among various obligations. Related questions inquired into personality traits and patterns of activity admired by respondents, permitting them to rank civic virtues in relation to other categories of admirable activities. All the questions in this series were taken from *The Civic Culture.*

Responses indicate the existence of broad differences within the Argentine community regarding the obligations of citizens. Lack of consensus about these obligations and how, if they exist, they can best be discharged is perhaps consistent with a political system in which there is broad disagreement about legitimacy and conflict resolution.

First, concerning obligations to activity in local affairs, about 56 percent of all Argentines and 50 percent of Peronists said they believed that "the ordinary person ought to play a part in the local affairs of his town or district." The remainder were unevenly divided between persons who did not believe there was any such obligation and those who did not know. Views about how these obligations could be discharged were understandably vague, but suggestive; the idea of cooperation is central in them. A few respondents mentioned an obligation to inform themselves; still fewer mentioned voting (perhaps because compulsory voting laws made the obligation to vote so clear that it was assumed, but perhaps because it was not regarded as significant participation). The major emphasis was on participation in group activity and on general "cooperation" or "work" for the community.

The obligation to participate was much more frequently expressed by upper-class respondents than among others; group activity most frequently occurs to upper-class respondents as an appropriate mode

TABLE 7.9   OBLIGATION TO PARTICIPATE IN LOCAL AFFAIRS
(In percent)

	All Argentines (n = 2,014)	Core Peronists (n = 365)	UCRP Voters (n = 413)	Upper (n = 157)	Class Middle (n = 960)	Lower (n = 721)
Ordinary person ought to take part in local affairs	56.3	50.7	61.5	75.8	56.3	49.9

Source: Responses to Question 6 (Appendix B).

of participation. The distinctive class responses indicate that the participatory model of citizenship was dominant only among the upper classes and that, despite highly organized trade-union activities, upper-socioeconomic respondents were much more likely than others to think of participation in public affairs through groups.

Readers of *The Civic Culture* may remember that, of the five countries surveyed, only in the United States did half the respondents say they felt citizenship obligated one to take part in local affairs.[22] But the coincidence of Argentine and U.S. findings does not necessarily indicate identical models of citizenship. Only 5 percent of the Argentines identified activity in social and political

TABLE 7.10   MODES OF PARTICIPATION: LOCAL LEVEL
(In percent)

	All Argentines (n = 2,014)	Core Peronists (n = 365)	UCRP Voters (n = 413)	Upper (n = 157)	Class Middle (n = 960)	Lower (n = 721)
Join and work for parties, other groups	23.1	17.8	26.9	38.2	22.4	18.3
Work, cooperate	22.9	21.9	23.7	29.3	24.3	21.6
Inform self	2.8	1.6	2.7	5.1	2.9	1.7
Complain, protest	1.1	1.4	0.5	0.6	1.3	1.1
Vote	1.1	1.6	1.0	—	0.9	1.2
Other (under 1 percent)	4.0	3.6	4.8	5.1	3.8	3.7
Don't know	3.4	4.9	4.1	1.3	2.7	4.6
No obligation to participate	43.7	49.3	38.5	24.2	43.8	50.1

Source: Responses to Question 6a (Appendix B) from those responding affirmatively to Question 6; see Table 7.9.

[22] Almond and Verba, *The Civic Culture*, p. 169.

affairs as a trait most admired in others. Personal characteristics that relate to skill, social progress, interpersonal consideration, thrift, and even self-protection were more often named as admired traits and behavior than was social or political participation. Furthermore, public activity was less highly rated among Peronists (and lower-class informants) than among UCRP supporters and upper-class informants. In addition, although almost half of all respondents asserted that citizens have a duty to participate in local affairs, only 7 percent had ever actually participated in any political activity. Fewer Peronists believed they had a duty to participate, but more reported having actually engaged in political activity than did UCRP supporters or Argentines generally. The greater currency of participatory values among upper-class respondents was complemented by their substantially higher levels of actual participation in political activity, though the discrepancy between the acknowledged duty and the level of actual political activity was still great.

Actual participation in political affairs is everywhere very limited. What has been called the "rationalist-activist" model of democratic citizenship has more reality as a hortatory slogan than as a description of how political affairs are conducted in democracies. Voting is the only civic activity that is in fact engaged in by masses in democratic societies. Totalitarian states, with their requirements for ideological participation, make more demands on citizens for activity. It is difficult to assess the meaning of attitudes toward participation and patterns of participation (see Table 7.11). Widespread acquiescence in the principle of participation may be more

TABLE 7.11   POLITICAL PARTICIPATION: OBLIGATION
AND PERFORMANCE
(In percent)

	All Argentines ($n =$ 2,014)	Core Peronists ($n =$ 369)	UCRP Voters ($n =$ 411)	Upper ($n =$ 157)	Class Middle ($n =$ 960)	Lower ($n =$ 721)
Ordinary person ought to take part in local affairs	56.3	50.7	61.5	75.8	56.3	49.9
Have ever participated in *any* type of political activity	7.1	10.4	9.7	12.1	6.3	6.2

Source: Responses to Questions 6 and 30 (Appendix B).

TABLE 7.12   OBLIGATIONS OWED ONE'S COUNTRY
(In percent)

	All Argentines (n = 2,014)	Core Peronists (n = 365)	UCRP Voters (n = 411)
Work hard to help progress	52.3	54.2	54.2
Obey, respect laws	20.4	17.0	18.6
Complete military service	22.5	25.8	17.9
Serve country (general)	14.8	13.7	17.5
Love country	7.8	9.9	7.3
Contribute to social improvement	4.7	4.4	6.1
Vote	2.7	2.7	3.9
Others	1.2	1.1	0.7
Don't know	2.5	0.8	3.4
Not obligated to do anything	0.7	1.1	0.2

Source: Responses to Question 7 (Appendix B).

significant and relevant as an index of integration of masses into a single political society than as a measure of democratic political culture. That is, participation may well be more closely related to modern industrial than to democratic political culture.

In any event, it is clear that Argentina's political culture is ambiguous about the duty of citizens to participate actively in public affairs. Over half of all Argentines said they believed it to be a duty, but actual participation was limited to about 5 percent of the total population, and the participant was not a widely admired personality type. Peronists' attitudes toward participation did not diverge significantly from those of the whole population; their actual participation was somewhat higher.[23] Unfortunately, survey questions inquiring into citizens' duties vis-à-vis the national level are not entirely comparable to those concerning local affairs.[24] Responses to the inquiry into citizens' obligations to the nation do, however, again show half of the respondents subscribing to an activist conception of the citizen's role, believing that citizenship requires something other than obedience to laws (see Table 7.12). Conversely, they confirm that about half of all respondents and Peronists did not share the activist conception of citizens' obligations.

[23] It seems likely that leadership attitudes and directives are more important in mobilizing groups than are rank-and-file beliefs about participation.

[24] These questions, like those concerning the duties of citizenship, were taken from *The Civic Culture. The Civic Culture* analysis (pp. 161–179), like this one, suffers from certain deficiencies because of lack of comparable inquiries into views on local and national affairs.

TABLE 7.13   ORGANIZATION OF AND PARTICIPATION IN
POLITICAL POWER
(In percent)

	Peronists' Perceptions
People like you and me have *no* say in government	+ 24.9
Average citizens have *no* influence on government	+ 14.7
I could not affect national legislature	+ 2.3
I could not get hearing at government office	+ 8.1
I could not get hearing in court	+ 8.4
I *would* get equal treatment from government official	— 14.8
I *would* get equal treatment from court	— 19.1
Average citizen's duty to take part in local affairs	— 10.8
I don't understand national and international issues	+ 11.3
The government is to blame for failing to inform me	+ 25.0

Source: Responses to Questions 15f, 8, 9, 11, 13, 10, 12, 6, 46, and 47c (Appendix B).

Note: Each cell represents the deviation of frequencies of Peronists' responses from UCRP voters' responses.

Summary

The findings reported in this chapter have broad significance for the student of Argentina or the Peronist movement. They demonstrate, first, that most Peronists shared dominant perceptions of government and their roles in it; but, second, that there was a consistent pattern of divergent responses among Peronists, indicating a limited but significant variation in orientation among rank-and-file Peronists and rank-and-file UCRP supporters. The frequency with which these two groups differ about the structure of influence, the accessibility of power, and their own political efficacy indicates the existence of distinctive, though not mutually exclusive, political orientations. Orientations believed to be indicative of a democratic culture occurred with greater frequency among UCRP supporters than among Peronists.[25] Peronists were less likely to believe in their potential influence over political events; they were less likely to expect a fair hearing or fair treatment from officials. They were less likely to believe they understood public affairs and more likely to blame the government for their informational inadequacy. Fewer

[25] Nonetheless, the tentative quality of our knowledge of the cultural and psychological concomitants of democratic institutions should be borne in mind. See, among others, Ernest S. Griffith, John Plamenatz, and J. Roland Pennock, "Cultural Prerequisites to a Successfully Functioning Democracy: A Symposium," *American Political Science Review,* vol. 50, no. 1 (March 1956); also Almond and Verba, *The Civic Culture.*

Peronists than UCRP supporters believed they had an obligation to take part in local politics, though more Peronists had actually participated. Table 7.13 summarizes these findings, which, taken together, suggest a degree and direction of distinctiveness that is significant for the student of Argentine political movements.

Outcomes

The foregoing profile of political perceptions is one of marginal disbelief in the existence and efficacy of popular participation and of skepticism about the chances of getting equal treatment. It does not indicate a radically distinctive Peronist perspective on the political world. It does not reflect massive or comprehensive dissatisfaction with the distribution of power.

It also does not tell us how much importance Peronists attached to the political sphere or how much they cared about what they perceived to be inequities in the distribution of power. Obviously, the feeling of political impotence does not necessarily entail dissatisfaction. The belief that average citizens do not have influence on government may or may not be accompanied by the additional belief that they should have influence on government. In fact, there is evidence indicating that Peronists were more likely than others to prefer a political system with a highly unequal distribution of power. Their enthusiastic loyalty and support for Juan Perón is itself persuasive evidence, and the number who agreed that "a few strong leaders would do more for this country than all the laws and talk" demonstrates strong (57 percent of Peronists as opposed to 35.1 percent of UCRP voters) support of autocratic leadership in principle, not just in one concrete instance.

Other evidence in the survey indicates that Peronists were in fact relatively less concerned with the organization of power in the community, and far more interested in the uses than in the structure of power. Dissatisfaction with outcomes was especially strong among Peronists. Their reaction to the distribution of goods was stronger and more distinctive than their reaction to the distribution of power.[26]

[26] A principal pitfall of survey research is the danger of imposing the researcher's frame of attention, then mistaking it for the respondents' own views of priorities. See, among others, Claire Selltiz, Marie Jahoda, Morton Deutsch, and Stuart W. Cook, *Research Methods in Social Relations,* rev. ed. (New York: Holt, Rinehart & Winston, 1962), pp. 566–574; Herbert H. Hyman, with William J.

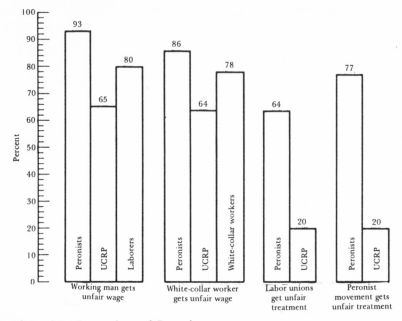

Figure 7.1   Perceptions of Inequity
Source: Compiled from responses to Questions 53, 54, 56, and 39 (Appendix B)

Peronists, we shall see, were much more concerned with concrete bread-and-butter questions than with questions of politics.[27] Overwhelmingly, they saw the important problems facing Argentina as

Cobb, Jacob J. Feldman, Clyde W. Hart, and Charles Herbert Stember, *Interviewing in Social Research* (Chicago: University of Chicago Press, 1954), pp. 58–66; and Hadley Cantril, *The Pattern of Human Concerns* (New Brunswick, N.J.: Rutgers University Press, 1965), pp. 21–26.

[27] Michigan Survey Research Center studies have revealed American voters' very low levels of attention to politics and explored some of the implications of this finding. See Angus Campbell, Philip E. Converse, Warren E. Miller, and Donald E. Stokes, *The American Voter* (New York: John Wiley & Sons, 1960), pp. 60–63. Yet to be fully explored are the theoretical implications of the widespread prominence of concrete personal economic issues and the much lower level of attention accorded political problems. The many recent considerations of democratic culture have not reexamined the question of how much attention to politics is desirable in democratic institutions. Aristotle, it will be recalled, suggested that a populace that had too much time free for politics created less desirable citizens of a democracy than a populace principally occupied with private affairs. The question has not been systematically explored since, although the "rationalist-activist" model assumes an answer. See Aristotle, *The Politics*, bk. 4, chap. 6, trans. with intro. by Ernest Barker (London: Oxford University Press, 1946).

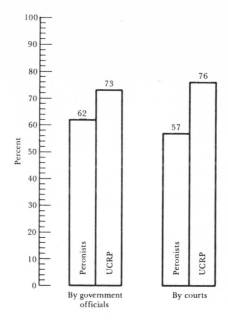

Figure 7.2 Expectations of Equitable Treatment
Source: Compiled from responses to Questions 10 and 12 (Appendix B)

economic problems, and they defined their movements—Peronist parties and unions and other organizations—in terms of economic goals. For these reasons it would be a mistake to attempt to assess Peronists' orientations to the political system apart from their perceptions and evaluations of outcomes, that is, of the consequences of the existing distribution of power and structure of decision making.

While disbelief that a citizen can participate in power may not indicate dissatisfaction, disbelief in the equity of a system is a sure sign of dissatisfaction. Peronists were especially convinced of inequities in the economic sphere, that is, on those questions with which they were most concerned (see Figures 7.1 and 7.2). Consensus among Peronists was also much broader on outcomes than on questions concerning the organization of political power, suggesting that specified economic outcomes constituted central issues on which there was solidarity as well as distinctiveness. The next chapter is devoted to these issues.

8

Peronist Demands

An opinion aggregate is the more likely to attain solidarity the more highly controversial the opinion, and the more the aggregate is in a minority.

Lasswell and Kaplan, *Power and Society*

This chapter deals with demands shared by Peronists. Political demands may be defined as preferences that are felt to be and may be asserted as claims on the collectivity. Demands may relate to the preservation or change of existing value allocations. They may concern any area of human experience. A political actor's demands define his notions about the purposes of political authority. A demand for the restoration of religious instruction in public schools necessarily implies views about the propriety of using the coercive power of government to support a religious position. The content of a group's demands defines the group's purposes. The number, character, and intensity of its demands determine its cohesiveness and durability. Rank-and-file demands constitute rank-and-file understandings of the group's purposes. Elite demands constitute elite understandings of the group's purposes.

Demands are that part of a political ideology that can be shared by elite and rank and file. There is impressive evidence to support Converse when he asserts, "It cannot . . . be claimed that the mass public shares ideological patterns of belief with relevant elites at a specific level any more than it shares abstract conceptual frames of reference." [1] But the evidence also suggests that mass and elite can and in some situations do share demands. Making demands does not require ideological or cognitive sophistication. Sharing demands does not entail sharing frames of reference or comprehensive belief

[1] Philip E. Converse, "The Nature of Belief Systems in Mass Publics," in David E. Apter, ed., *Ideology and Discontent* (New York: Free Press, 1964), p. 231.

systems.[2] The demands may be perceived and articulated as discrete and isolated. They can be, and are, made by persons lacking a comprehensive rational political orientation.[3] A principal function of demands is to link individuals without comprehensive ideologies to candidates, parties, and political movements,[4] which may be usefully conceived as demand aggregates.[5]

The demands of mass publics reflect their understanding of both possibilities and responsibilities (however realistic or unrealistic these may be). Available evidence suggests that a population with a contemplative orientation to problems makes few demands, conceiving few possibilities of change, whereas a population that conceives its situation as a problem capable of resolution may make many demands. Conversely, the number and content of demands made by masses may be viewed as an index of the extent of manipulative orientations in that society. Are only problems of economic security the subject of demands? Are demands made concerning health, education, longevity? This chapter is concerned with the content, range, and intensity of the demands of rank-and-file Peronists.

Earlier chapters have indicated some social and economic characteristics of Peronists. It is not surprising to find close relations between these and the demands that define the movement. We have seen that the movement drew heavily from the lower classes, and

[2] Gabriel A. Almond, in *Appeals of Communism* (Princeton: Princeton University Press, 1954), explores differences between communist rank-and-file and elite ideologies, especially pp. 62–183 passim. Converse examines the same dichotomy in "Nature of Belief Systems," p. 231.

[3] Hadley Cantril, *The Pattern of Human Concerns* (New Brunswick, N.J.: Rutgers University Press, 1965), provides a comparative study of aspirations that are of course relevant to, but not identical with, demands.

[4] Michigan Survey Research Center authors comment, "If ideology in a sophisticated sense is not widespread in the population, there must be surrogates to act *as though* propelled by ideological concerns." See Angus Campbell, Philip E. Converse, Warren E. Miller, and Donald E. Stokes, *The American Voter* (New York: John Wiley & Sons, 1960), p. 217; emphasis in original. Demands, I suggest, are the chief surrogates, linking the politically sophisticated to the unsophisticated.

[5] This conception of groups does not suggest that they are bound together by knowledge of or sophistication about issues of public policy. It does, however, suggest that, by definition, all demand aggregates—that is, persons with a shared claim on the collectivity—are issue-oriented, providing we define an issue as the subject matter of a demand. Furthermore, when political groups are defined as demand aggregates, the entire controversy about the issue orientations of large groups is bypassed.

that Peronists comprised the most class-conscious portions of the lower classes. We have seen, too, that Peronists saw labor as the collectivity most worthy of support and most unfairly treated under the existing allocation of goods. (A demand is implicit in the characterization of a group's treatment as unfair.) It is therefore not surprising to find, first, that Peronist demands related principally to redressing economic wrongs to the lower classes and, second, that the manifest content of Peronist demands concerned distributions of economic rather than political goods. The image of Peronists as comprising a class-oriented movement is confirmed and underscored. Although social class was not assumed to be a principal variable in explaining the Peronist movement, its centrality has been empirically established, and social class emerged as a core identification around which there were clusters of demands.

Peronists defined the organizations identified with the movement in terms of demands for economic betterment and for redressing economic wrongs. These characterizations of Peronist organizations are the more significant because they emerged as unprompted responses to open-ended questions. Separate questions inquired whether respondents had heard of Peronist political parties, "Bloc 62," and justicialism and were followed by questions inquiring about the goals or principles of each. Both the knowledge and the consensus of respondents were impressive. The party, the movement, "Bloc 62," and justicialism were all overwhelmingly defined by Peronists themselves in terms of helping the lower classes and the workers and improving their standards of living (see Table 8.1).

Peronists, sympathizers, and others all perceived the movement

TABLE 8.1   SELF-PORTRAIT OF PERONIST MOVEMENT

	Specific Mentions of Economic Goals
What kind of party is it?	120 $(n = 282)$ [a]
In what does Peronist movement deserve support?	311 $(n = 365)$ [b]
What are the goals of "Bloc 62"?	130 $(n = 255)$ [c]
What does justicialism stand for?	239 $(n = 279)$ [d]

Source: Responses to Questions 32 and 33, 42, 43 and 43a, and 44 and 44a (Appendix B).

[a] More than half (54 percent) of all respondents named the Peronists or Justicialista party as one of Argentina's two or three most important parties; among these were 282 core Peronists. Item one in the above table reflects their responses.

[b] $n =$ number of core Peronists.

[c] $n =$ number who had heard of "Bloc 62."

[d] $n =$ number who had heard of justicialism.

TABLE 8.2   CORE PERONISTS' VIEWS OF MAJOR PROBLEMS
FACING ARGENTINA

	Total Number of Mentions by Core Peronists
Economic	602
Domestic political	75
Social services	21
Moral	23
Foreign policy	9

in terms of economic goals. The self-definition in terms of class-oriented economic demands most unambiguously demonstrates the demands that unite Peronists. The self-image is clear. It is focused. It states the organization's raison d'être. Political goals are subordinate. They are mentioned by Peronists only 22 times in response to the question "In what respects does the Peronist movement deserve support?" compared with 311 mentions of economic improvement or helping the workers.

Peronists' focus on demands for economic betterment and the welfare of the poor is consistent with their perception of the principal problems facing Argentina. Overwhelmingly they perceive these to be bread-and-butter problems relating to specific economic problems. Peronist emphasis on these problems is shared by Argentines generally, but the lack of distinctiveness does not make less important the high agreement of Peronists about the priority of these issues.

Table 8.2 depicts the general responses to the question, "What are the principal problems that Argentina faces these days?" [6] The economic problems that Peronists conceived as most important in responses to the same question are those given in Table 8.3.

Although Argentines of all political and social categories agreed about the priority of economic problems,[7] there are some interesting

[6] Question 16 (Appendix B), which preceded all others concerning issues of public policy.

[7] A poll conducted by Encuestas Gallup de la Argentina (EGA) in March 1966 in greater Buenos Aires ($n = 1,004$) revealed a similar emphasis on economic problems in responses to an open-ended question, "What do you consider the most important internal problem this country is facing at present?" The high cost of living and the general economic situation were most often named. Concern with unemployment had dropped but was ranked third among lower-class respondents. Reported in EGA, "Argentina," *Polls*, vol. 2, no. 3 (Spring 1967), p. 23.

TABLE 8.3 ECONOMIC PROBLEMS ENUMERATED BY CORE PERONISTS

	Total Number of Mentions by Core Peronists
High cost of living	197
Lack of jobs, employment opportunities	111
Bad economy, general	98
Low or unstable salaries	85
Lack of housing	59
Poverty, misery, hunger	30
Lack of devaluation, monetary stability	22

differences in degree among social classes. Upper-class respondents more frequently cited political problems and were more inclined to cite general than specific economic problems.[8] They also most frequently cited educational deficiencies as a prime problem.[9] Middle-class problem perceptions predictably fell between those of the lower and upper classes.[10]

One explanation for the salience of bread-and-butter problems and demands is available in the Peronists' pessimistic evaluation of their situations and prospects (see Table 8.4). Peronists and Argentine laborers generally were neither happy with the present nor sanguine about the future. Approximately half of all Peronists believed they were economically worse off at the time of the survey than they had been a year earlier, and almost 30 percent anticipated that their situation would worsen in the coming year. Peronists' pessimistic expectations were shared by lower classes and laborers generally. Class differences in evaluation of situations and prospects

[8] But note, in the Gallup survey just cited, lower-class respondents most frequently mentioned political problems.

[9] Upper-class respondents most often and lower-class respondents least often stressed the need for improving the educational system and facilities. This finding is consistent though not identical with those of H. H. Hyman, "The Value Systems of Different Classes," in Reinard Bendix and Seymour Martin Lipset, eds., Class, Status, and Power (New York: Free Press, 1960), and Robert M. Marsh, Comparative Sociology (New York: Harcourt, Brace & World, 1967), p. 179.

[10] Also interesting was the readiness of respondents of all classes to identify the nation's problems. Very few respondents had no opinion or felt they did not know. The average number of problems named by Peronists was 2.2, which was only slightly lower than the national average (2.4).

TABLE 8.4   ECONOMIC SITUATION: EVALUATION AND EXPECTATIONS
(In percent)

	All Argentines ($n =$ 2,014)	Core Peronists ($n =$ 365)	UCRP Voters ($n =$ 413)	Upper ($n =$ 157)	Class Middle ($n =$ 960)	Lower ($n =$ 721)
Economic situation compared with one year ago						
Better	24.0	15.9	31.2	31.8	26.7	17.8
Worse	34.5	49.9	28.8	26.1	28.6	45.5
Same	40.9	34.0	39.5	42.0	43.8	36.1
Don't know	0.7	0.3	0.5	—	0.9	0.7
Expectation of economic situation one year later						
Better	47.9	38.6	54.5	51.6	52.2	41.6
Worse	18.2	27.4	13.8	19.7	15.2	22.7
Same	18.0	15.1	23.7	18.5	17.3	17.1
Don't know	15.8	18.9	8.0	10.2	15.3	18.6

Source: Responses to Questions 1 and 2 (Appendix B).

were marked. Even more marked was the contrast between Peronists and UCRP supporters.[11]

The level of agreement among Peronists about several demands concerning economic betterment of the lower classes is both distinctive and unique. Their solidarity on these issues contrasts with their division on other subjects and defines the demands that gave birth and continued existence to the movement. A sense of the priority and urgency of the demands for economic justice (since the treatment of wage earners was considered unfair, amelioration would constitute justice) is provided by the fact that Peronists themselves did not define Argentina's principal problems in terms of the restoration of Perón. They might have. The question concerning Argentina's most important problems permitted such responses. That these responses were not forthcoming indicates that

[11] Two surveys done by Encuestas Gallup de la Argentina in March and April 1966 in greater Buenos Aires showed even more marked general pessimism about the economic situation. In the March survey ($n = 1,004$) 48 percent said they expected it to deteriorate; in April, in Buenos Aires (excluding the suburbs) ($n = 850$), 39 percent said they expected the situation to get worse. Unfortunately, breakdowns by class were not published. See EGA, "Argentina," pp. 22, 26.

the Peronists conceived the economic needs of the lower classes as more pressing than the restoration of their leader. It would appear that Perón, like Peronism, was viewed as an instrument for achieving the special, ignored interests of the lower classes.

The survey included two fixed-alternative questions to elicit respondents' views on specific issues. Responses to these questions tell us nothing about the salience of issues for Peronists or others but provide interesting data on the distribution of opinions on a number of problems. They also confirm the existence and priorities among demands established previously, identify other demands of less salience, and indicate differences in the patterns of policy preference of different population categories.

A fixed-alternative question on domestic policy inquired, "Let's look at some problems of domestic policy. For example, would you be for or against a candidate for president who . . .," then listed one by one possible positions on a range of economic and political issues.[12] Responses to these questions are particularly useful in identifying subjects on which there was greatest consensus among Argentines and among Peronists, as well as those on which there was the sharpest disagreement among Peronists and between Peronists and others.

More than 90 percent of all Peronists agreed on five of nine items in the fixed-alternative question: this high level of agreement existed about the desirability of (1) imposing strong price controls on items of daily use, (2) using the government's resources to create employment, (3) raising wages to match the cost of living, (4) ending the use of force and violence in political activity, and (5) ending governmental corruption and inefficiency. On three of these issues more than 90 percent of all Argentines agreed, but on wage and price controls the overall agreement dropped significantly. The graph in Figure 8.1 depicts the levels of agreement among Argentines and among Peronists on the tested issues.

An analysis of the distribution of demands in Argentina is complicated and hampered by the lack of reliable comparative information on the range and level of consensus found in different countries and in different types of countries. Although there is a large accumulation of survey data concerning mass opinion on social and political problems, no studies have been done to establish normal levels of agreement in various types of societies about the appro-

[12] Questions 17a–17j.

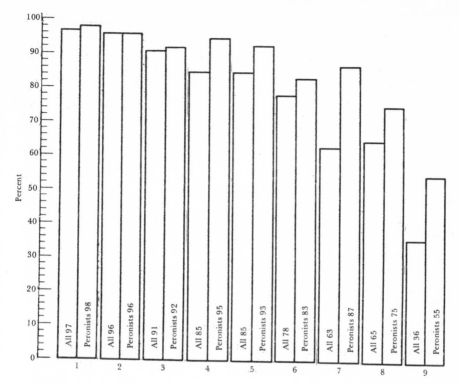

Figure 8.1   Levels of Consensus: All Argentines and Peronists

Source: Compiled from responses to Questions 17a–17j (Appendix B)
    1. Will use the government's resources to create new jobs.
    2. Promises to stamp out corruption and inefficiency in the government.
    3. Condemns the use of force and violence in political activity.
    4. Supports strong price controls on basic items that affect most people's cost of living.
    5. Believes wages should be raised to match increases in the cost of living.
    6. Believes the military should not intervene in government policies.
    7. Believes in the expropriation of private lands for redistribution to landless farmers.
    8. Favors reforming the tax system to provide for higher taxes on large incomes and business profits.
    9. Wants to eliminate private enterprise from key sectors of the economy.

priate uses of power, purposes of authority, or means of resolving outstanding problems.

Available survey data on Latin America indicate widespread agreement about the desirability of using the government to resolve economic problems and to accomplish such welfare-state objectives as eliminating unemployment, controlling prices and wages, and guaranteeing a minimum living standard. Certainly there was a high level of agreement in Argentina on these questions, and there was a correlative scarcity of laissez-faire orientations. Not only was the agreement widespread among all Argentines on a number of problems of public policy, but the most salient problems were also those on which there was greatest consensus: cost of living, unemployment, low wages, and maladministration in government (see Table 8.5). It is surely significant that almost everyone agreed that government should act to end unemployment and that more than 80 percent of all Argentines agreed on public action to establish price and wage controls (see Figure 8.2). Conversely, the issues on which there was greatest disagreement have low salience (see Figure 8.3). These more divisive issues were also those about which the highest percentage of Argentines did not have opinions. The average of those without opinions on the four most controversial issues was 15 percent, compared with 3 percent on the high-consensus issues.

Analysis of distinctive political responses indicates that the issues on which there was most disagreement between Peronist and UCRP rank and file were those involving policies punitive of some economic sector, that is, issues of class struggle. They are also the demands on which there was the lowest level of agreement among Peronists themselves.

On the issues of greatest disagreement between Peronists and UCRP supporters, the Radical position was closest to that of the average Argentine, a finding consistent with the broadly aggregative

TABLE 8.5   SALIENCE AND CONSENSUS COMPARED AMONG ALL ARGENTINES

Rank Order Salience	Rank Order Consensus [a]
High cost of living	Use of government to solve unemployment
Poor economy	End corruption and inefficiency in government
Unemployment	End force and violence in politics
Maladministration in government	Strong price controls
Inadequate housing	Raise wages
Low wages	Oppose military intervention in politics

[a] The six items that rank highest in salience and consensus do not coincide exactly because salience reflects spontaneous mentions by respondents of problems of greatest concern (Question 16); consensus was measured on items mentioned in the fixed-alternative question (Question 17).

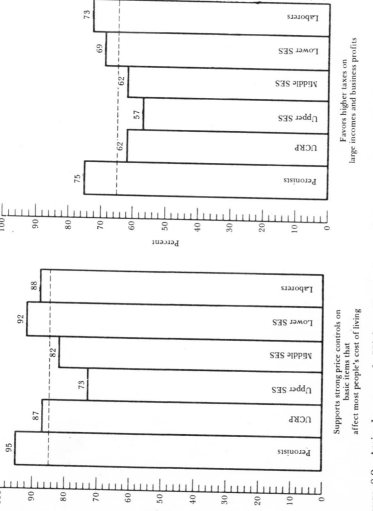

Figure 8.2 Attitudes toward Higher Taxes for Business and Price Controls
Source: Compiled from responses to Questions 17e and 17a (Appendix B)

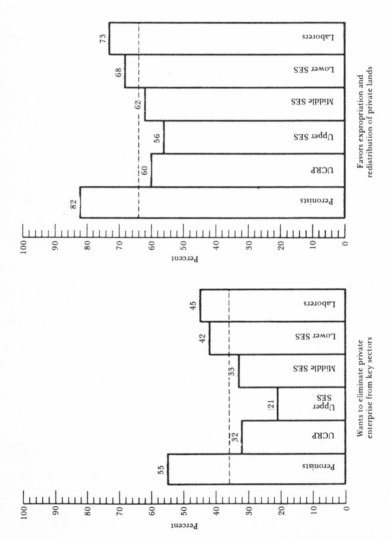

Figure 8.3 Attitudes toward Private Ownership, Key Industries, and Large Landholdings
Source: Compiled from responses to Questions 17g and 17f (Appendix B)

character of that party. On these same issues, UCRP positions most closely coincided with those of middle-class respondents, and Peronist distributions most closely approximated those of the lower classes and of labor (see Table 8.6). However, on each of the most controversial demands, more Peronists than laborers and more Peronists than lower-class respondents supported the controversial demand. This finding confirms earlier ones that show Peronists as more united in pressing class-oriented demands than the whole of the relevant class. There are clichés concerning monarchists more royal than the king, Catholics more papist than the Pope, and modern radical movements have provided many examples of parties more proletarian than the working classes. The Peronists barely qualify as the vanguard of Argentina's proletariat. But Peronists' controversial demands were not qualitatively different from those of the lower classes and laborers. Peronists were merely the most advanced portion of the laboring class; that is, they most often supported the use of political power to achieve economic goals.

The fact that Peronists agreed with most Argentines about most demands, did not deviate far from majority positions on any issue, and deviated even less from felt demands of the lower classes confirms the general view that Peronists were not genuinely radical. They did not desire profound or comprehensive changes in society, personality, and culture. Their interests were reformist rather than structural. However, it should also be noted that Peronists, more frequently than others, support limited structural changes.

Orientations to Foreign Policy

The nationalist note was forcefully sounded by Perón in 1943 when he was still a member of the GOU (Grupo de Oficiales

TABLE 8.6 UCRP AND PERONIST DEVIANCE FROM NATIONAL AVERAGES
(In percent)

	UCRP Voters	Core Peronists
Eliminate private enterprise from key sectors	— 4.6	+ 19.0
Favors expropriation of private lands for redistribution	— 3.0	+ 18.6
Favors raising taxes on large incomes and business profits	— 3.3	+ 9.8
Supports strong price controls on basic items	+ 1.7	+ 9.9
Favors raising wages to match cost of living	— 4.5	+ 8.0

Unidos). Political and economic nationalism was one of the ideological pillars on which he rested his claim to power. "Peronism," asserted Perón again, and again, and again, "is exclusively Argentine." Peronist nationalism had the universal characteristics associated with nationalism plus some distinctively Latin American additions. It not only stressed the importance of national power, political autonomy, and international respect but also of economic independence. Perón promised that under Peronism Argentina would be controlled by no one except Perón and the people. Perón's doctrine of popular sovereignty affirmed national independence at the same time that it asserted popular sovereignty:

> We have not been dominated by imperialism; we have not been dominated by the forces of all kinds set in motion by the oligarchy; nothing is going to dominate us, in any way—nothing except the people; all those who have not understood should now be convinced: the Peronist government cannot be dominated except by one single force: the people.[13]

A long-time student of Latin nationalism and of Argentina, Arthur P. Whitaker, comments on Perón, "Nationalism was one of his major themes from the start, and he linked it to social reform." [14] The link was simple and strong. Perón proposed to glorify the nation by elevating the people, and to glorify the people by making them members of a powerful integral nation.

His famous "third position" in world affairs justified neutrality first in World War II and then in the cold war. As Whitaker comments, he departed from this aloof neutrality "only to denounce Yankee imperialism." [15]

Economic nationalism, like economic imperialism, is of special importance in Latin American politics. The combination of political independence with strong foreign control in the economic sphere is a familiar one on the South American continent, and it has charged the concept of economic independence with the same emotion that nationalists elsewhere have attached to political sovereignty. Even before he came to full power, Perón emphasized the importance of eliminating foreign control in the Argentine

[13] Speech of November 25, 1954, quoted in Pierre Lux-Wurm, *Le Péronisme* (Paris: R. Pichon et R. Durand-Auzias, 1965), pp. 225–226. The simultaneous assertion of indomitable force and willing submission is psychologically interesting.

[14] Arthur P. Whitaker, *Argentina* (Englewood Cliffs, N.J.: Prentice-Hall, 1964), p. 116.

[15] Ibid., p. 124.

economy. In his suggestive volume, *Nationalism in Latin America: Past and Present,* Whitaker asserts:

> Juan Perón made two outstanding contributions to the development of economic nationalism during his twelve years in power. . . . Together, these crowned the work begun by Irigoyen a generation earlier. The first was Perón's formal "Declaration of Economic Independence" in 1947. Made on the anniversary of Argentina's declaration of political independence in 1816, and at the same place, this dramatized the issue as perhaps nothing else could have done, and fired the achievement of economic independence irrevocably (at least in the minds of most Argentines) as a major objective of public policy. Second, and even more important, Perón revolutionized the social implications by identifying it with social revolution for the benefit of the Argentine underdogs, the descamisados.[16]

In 1946 Perón turned the hostility of then Ambassador Spruille Braden and the U.S. State Department's Blue Book to his own uses. The slogan "Perón o Braden" was believed by many observers to have won votes for Perón by identifying Perón and the nation as partners in a struggle against Yankee imperialism.[17]

For these and other reasons, Peronism has been identified with nationalism, anti-Americanism, and autarky. Nationalism is said to be associated with the famous nativist strain in Peronism. Its well-known glorification of *Argentinidad* against foreign and cosmopolitan influences contributed a quasi-racial strain. Clearly, Perón's policies justified the characterization of his movement as nationalist and as anti-Yankee. But whether and to what extent his followers shared these sentiments and policy preferences is not known. Peronism, like many another ism, was and is a multifaceted phenomenon with multiple appeals. Followers need not share all or even most aspects of an ideology to follow the leader. This section attempts to determine the extent to which Peronists shared with distinctive frequency or intensity orientations and demands associated with nationalism.

First, however, *the low salience of foreign policy must be noted.* Under 4 percent of Peronist respondents (and of all Argentines) alluded to any aspect of foreign relations when mentioning Argentina's principal problems (of those, almost all, 2.5 percent, mentioned then current problems with Chile). Further, international or foreign-

---

[16] Arthur P. Whitaker, *Nationalism in Latin America: Past and Present* (Gainesville: University of Florida Press, 1962), p. 50.

[17] We have no direct evidence that this was a factor in the mass electoral choice.

oriented references were entirely missing in respondents' characterizations of Peronism and justicialism. There were no references to
national power, nor international prestige, nor national independence in these Peronist self-portraits. The international arena
clearly had very low visibility for rank-and-file Peronists. Nationalism was quite obviously not a principal preoccupation or the subject
of salient demands. The only aspect of international affairs mentioned without prompting by a substantial number of Peronists
(and Argentines) related to pride in the nation's record of peace.
This, plus the absence of demands for deference and power, provides
strong evidence that, among Peronist rank and file, nationalist demands had very low priority. It is also clear that national power
and prestige were no more salient for Peronists than for persons of
other political persuasions (see Table 8.7).

But opinions and actions are not limited to the most important
areas of life. The fact that a subject has low salience does not mean
it lacks importance, first, because the salience of problems changes
and, second, because action is continually required on problems of
low salience. Furthermore, there is no necessary or reliable relationship between salience and intensity. Views of high intensity may be
held on subjects of low general salience. Therefore, it is often desirable to ascertain the structure of opinion on issues of relatively
low salience. For this reason, questionnaires often include questions
soliciting opinions on specific issues. The low salience of foreign
affairs among Peronists effectively proves that nationalist demands
were not controlling in the movement; it does not necessarily signify
rank-and-file indifference to foreign policies. And, as the following
tables indicate, most rank-and-file Peronists did have views about
what was and was not desirable in the international arena. Predictably, the percentages of Peronists (and Argentines generally) with-

TABLE 8.7   SALIENCE: FOREIGN AFFAIRS
(In percent)

	All Argentines (n = 2,014)	Core Peronists (n = 365)	UCRP Voters (n = 413)
Problems with Chile [a]	2.5	2.5	2.2
Communist infiltration [a]	1.1	1.1	1.5
Pride in nation's record of peace [b]	9.2	10.1	9.4

[a] Responses to the open-ended issue question, previously cited (Question 16).
[b] Responses to Question 5 (Appendix B); taken from *The Civic Culture*.

out opinions on questions of foreign affairs were significantly higher than those without opinions on domestic affairs. The average "don't know" responses on foreign affairs was 19.7 percent compared with 9.7 percent for domestic affairs.

Orientations to the United States

Several dimensions of the international scene were inquired about. Questions were included to elicit attitudes toward international issues on which Perón had taken public positions, especially on subjects about which he had made repeated pronouncements. A few additional questions were included concerning events that had occurred after the fall of Perón. Attitudes toward the United States, toward Latin neighbors, toward foreign ownership of economic enterprises, toward the cold war were all inquired about, and rank-and-file Peronists were found to share in distinctively large numbers orientations and demands associated with the name of their leader.

On questions concerning Argentine relations with the United States, anti-American attitudes occurred with predictably greater frequency among Peronists than among other Argentines (see Table 8.8 and Figure 8.4). Peronists less frequently expressed friendly feelings and more frequently expressed hostile attitudes. The difference between Peronist and UCRP attitudes was especially marked (see Table 8.9).

On cold war–oriented questions, Argentines generally favored a policy of neutrality, but Peronists were the most neutral of all. Finally, on questions involving attitudes toward communist nations, a majority of Argentines of all categories was clearly anticommunist and anti-Castro, but fewer Peronists were anticommunist than others (see Table 8.10).

TABLE 8.8   ATTITUDES TOWARD THE UNITED STATES
(In percent)

	All Argentines ($n = 2,014$)	Core Peronists ($n = 365$)
Argentina should strengthen ties with U.S.	64.3	50.4
Argentina should be more independent from U.S.	62.0	74.2
U.S. most often tries to help Argentina	31.5	16.4
U.S. most often creates problems for Argentina	19.1	29.0
Argentina should have few or no relations with U.S.	22.8	33.2

Sources: The first two items were derived from responses to Questions 18, 18i, and 18j. The others are from responses to Questions 19, 20, and 21 (Appendix B).

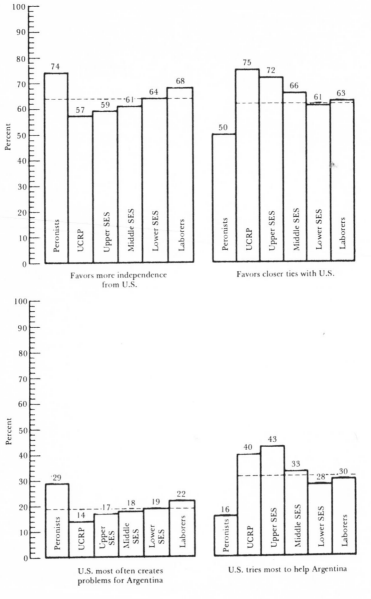

Figure 8.4 Orientations toward the United States

Source: Compiled from responses to Questions 18j, 18i, 20, and 19 (Appendix B)

TABLE 8.9   PERONIST AND UCRP ATTITUDES TOWARD THE
UNITED STATES
(In percent)

	UCRP Voters
Argentina should strengthen ties with U.S.	+ 15.0
Argentina should be more independent from U.S.	− 24.2
U.S. most often tries to help Argentina	+ 24.0
U.S. most often creates problems for Argentina	− 15.2
Argentina should have few or no relations with U.S.	− 14.1

Source: Same as Table 8.8.
Note: Each cell reflects the difference between Peronist and UCRP responses.

Demands: Core Peronist and Pro-Peronist

In the electoral arena Peronists' votes regularly exceeded the approximately one-fifth of the electorate that we have characterized as core Peronists. Peronist parties, when allowed to name candidates and participate, polled nearly one-third of the national vote. The additional votes were normally drawn from the less reliable Peronist supporters we have termed pro-Peronists. We have already seen that there were certain social differences between core Peronists and those with generally sympathetic orientations to the movement. The lower classes, the most poorly educated, and laborers were less heavily represented among sympathizers; that is, the class and social com-

TABLE 8.10   PERONIST ATTITUDES RELATING TO
COMMUNISM
(In percent)

	All Argentines (n = 2,014)	Core Peronists (n = 365)	UCRP Voters (n = 413)
Supports admission of private foreign capital	71.2	63.6	77.0
Supports a neutral position in cold war	65.7	70.4	65.4
Favors friendly relations with Castro, Cuba	18.5	25.5	15.3
Favors U.S. coming out on top in cold war	55.0	42.2	69.5
Blames U.S. for Dominican crisis	14.5	20.0	12.3
Favors seeking technical assistance from communist countries	17.7	20.3	15.3

Source: Responses to Questions 18 and 18e, 22, 21, 22b, 68, and 18 and 18a (Appendix B).

TABLE 8.11   SHARED DEMANDS: PERONISTS AND PRO-
PERONISTS
(In percent)

	Core Peronists	Pro- Peronists	Not Favor- able to Peronists	UCRP Voters
Domestic				
Favors higher taxes on large incomes and business profits	74.8	77.9	57.9	61.7
Favors expropriation and redistribution of private lands	81.6	74.0	55.3	60.0
Wants to eliminate private enterprise from key sectors	55.1	44.3	27.9	31.5
Supports strong price controls	95.1	88.3	81.3	86.9
Foreign				
Favors seeking aid from communist countries	20.3	28.2	13.4	15.3
Favors friendly relations with Castro's Cuba	25.5	30.4	12.5	15.3
Supports neutral cold war position	70.4	72.3	62.1	65.4
Advocates more control of foreign corporations	77.3	82.7	70.5	78.7
Supports strengthening ties with U.S.	50.4	59.4	70.0	74.6
Supports more independence from U.S.	74.2	72.3	54.9	57.1

Sources: Responses to Questions 17e, 17f, 17g, 17a, 18a, 18b, 18c, 18h, 18i, and
18j (Appendix B).

position of sympathizers was less distinctive. So were their orientations to major social groups and to the structure of political authority. *It appears that demands rather than social composition related these persons to the Peronist movement.* Table 8.11 demonstrates that sympathizers shared many demands with core Peronists and that on controversial issues their opinions more closely approximated those of the core Peronists than those of UCRP voters or of other Argentines.

9

The Peronist Movement in Perspective

This chapter is devoted to discussing several broad, rather complex questions about the Peronist movement, specifically, the relation of Peronist orientations to Argentine political culture, the relation of Peronists' expectations, identifications, and demands [1] to formal Peronist doctrine, the extent to which the movement conforms to the model of working-class authoritarianism, and the potential durability of the movement. Most of the data discussed here are drawn from earlier chapters; however, some data not previously discussed will be introduced. Here, too, I try to make explicit theoretical assumptions, to specify relevant indicators of complex political phenomena, and to relate these explicitly to the data. This sometimes involves me in questions within questions, explanations within explanations, but it seemed to be the only approach appropriate to my purposes.

Do Peronists Constitute a Political Subculture?

Several conceptions of political culture are current today in the social sciences, and, while there are marginal differences among them, all have a core concern with the subjective orientations of individuals toward political objects and take account of both cognitive and affective aspects of those orientations. Emphasis on the symbolic aspects of political systems is at least as old as Plato, who was especially sensitive to the necessary congruity of personality, culture, society, and government. But despite the antiquity of the concern, there has been little systematic investigation of the sym-

[1] The web of expectations, identifications, and demands that positions an individual in a given political arena and defines his purposes there may be termed his ideology. This definition sidesteps questions of what political purposes ideology serves: to buttress the status quo, map a revolution, or delineate a utopia. It bypasses questions of the relation of ideology to reality—does it merely reflect wishful fulfillment fantasies or serve economic interests? But it includes the relevant cognitive and affective dimensions. For a discussion of the various definitions of ideology see David W. Minar, "Ideology and Political Behavior," *Midwest Journal of Political Science*, vol. 5, no. 4 (November 1961), pp. 317–331.

bolic and affective dimensions of political life at the mass level. One consequence is that we know little about the levels of consensus that are characteristic of different types of political regimes. No standards exist by which to discriminate between the levels of consensus and dissensus that are significant for governmental stability. Little is known about the extent of a shared culture in polities noted for their unity and cohesion.[2] Is the totalitarian goal of complete agreement on political life ever achieved? Political observers agree that working democracies require a rather high degree of consensus on a range of matters, but how much consensus? And on which matters? How much prior agreement underlies "the agreement to disagree"?[3] How much disagreement and about what matters is compatible with maintaining the agreement to disagree? There are no certain answers to these questions; existing speculation lacks an empirical base.

Available evidence suggests that monolithic cultural unity is lacking even in quite small, simple societies as well as in modern, urban, industrial nations. It appears that complete cultural unity is either a dream or a nightmare, and that the Kluckhohn and Strodtbeck description of value orientations is more relevant to existential social systems. They assert, "value systems of cultures are not systems of single dominant values but are, instead, interlocking networks of dominant and variant value positions which differ only in that there is a variable ordering of the same value-orientation alternatives."[4] If this is so, then we should expect variety within unity.[5]

[2] *The Civic Culture* reveals that in the United States and Britain there is no general agreement about such basic questions as a citizen's obligation to participate in public affairs at the local level. Agreement is higher in Italy, where only 10 percent of the respondents agreed that they have an obligation to participate. See Almond and Verba, *The Civic Culture*, p. 169.

[3] Herbert McClosky, "Consensus and Ideology in American Politics," *American Political Science Review*, vol. 58, no. 2 (June 1964), pp. 361–382, and James W. Prothro and Charles M. Grigg, "Fundamental Principles of Democracy: Bases of Agreement and Disagreement," *Journal of Politics*, vol. 22, no. 2 (May 1960), pp. 276–294. See also Juan Linz, "Cleavage and Consensus in West German Politics: The Early Fifties," in Seymour M. Lipset and Stein Rokkan, eds., *Party Systems and Voter Alignment: Cross-National Perspectives* (New York: Free Press, 1967), pp. 283–321, and Linz's citations of relevant literature in fn. 45, p. 320.

[4] Florence R. Kluckhohn and Fred L. Strodtbeck, *Variation in Value Orientations* (Evanston, Ill.: Rowe, Peterson, 1961), p. 366. Another economical statement of this view of a society's value orientations is found in Florence R. Kluckhohn, "Dominant and Variant Value Orientations," in Clyde Kluckhohn, Henry A. Murray, and David M. Schneider, eds., *Personality in Nature, Society, and Culture*, 2nd ed., rev. and enl. (New York: Alfred A. Knopf, 1955).

[5] Many political scientists assume or postulate coexistence within any polity of dominant and variant views about the purposes and modes of political authority.

Perhaps, then, it is reasonable to define an integrated political culture as one in which populations united by certain broad, pervasive understandings about the world share a limited range of differing values and cognitive orientations, so distributed that no type of deviance is concentrated within a single sector of the population. Basic and pervasive understandings may be defined as those that comprehend and condition a range of specific issues, as views about the purposes of authority condition positions on a large number of policy questions, or as a common religion conditions attitudes toward many special ethical issues. Posture vis-à-vis political events, whether manipulative or contemplative, is another example of a broad orientation that affects orientations to many specific questions. Near-universal sharing of a few such basic and limiting orientations is a sine qua non of a unified political culture. Disagreement on other issues is not inconsistent with a unified political culture, providing that the distribution of disagreements does not reinforce other differences. If the distribution of perspectives follows social divisions—racial, economic, linguistic, religious, or regional—it may signal the existence of separate political cultures.[6] But when the same range of perspectives occurs in all major social categories, not necessarily with equal frequency, we are dealing with a unified political culture.[7]

By this standard, Argentina possesses an integrated political culture. The data on Argentina reveal marginal variations in frequency,

---

See, for example, Samuel H. Beer's discussion of this point in *British Politics in the Collectivist Age* (New York: Alfred A. Knopf, 1965), especially pp. x–xii, and A. H. Birch, *Representative and Responsible Government* (Toronto: University of Toronto Press, 1964), especially pp. 20–22. Walter Bagehot's doubts about the impact of a mass franchise on British political life also rested on assumptions about working-class variations of the dominant political culture, in *The English Constitution and Other Essays* (New York: D. Appleton and Company, 1889), especially pp. 1–35. Hegel and Marx were, of course, also preoccupied with the existence of variations within a culture.

[6] Presumably, political units comprising diverse and often previously autonomous social units—for example, tribes and linguistic or ethnic groups—lack unifying belief systems, values, and standards.

[7] My position here is similar, though not identical, to that of Lipset, who also emphasized that political cohesiveness and stability require that "all segments of the population . . . react in the same direction to major stimuli: that is, if conditions facilitate the growth of leftist opinion, the socialists will gain votes among both the well-to-do and the workers, although they will remain relatively weaker in the upper strata . . . an indicator of low consensus would be a situation in which a political tendency grows only among the groups to whom it primarily appeals." See Seymour Martin Lipset, *Political Man: The Social Bases of Politics* (New York: Doubleday & Company, 1960), p. 33.

intensity, and ordering of a rather limited range of perspectives. *One of the most striking findings of the December 1965 survey is the absence of major, socially based cultural discontinuities in Argentina.* There were no wide gaps between generations, between regions,[8] or between political groups. The distinction between *porteño* and *campesino,* a stereotype that may have always been more descriptive of elites than masses, has apparently been eroded by migrations, urbanization, and mass communications.

There are, to be sure, evidences of the continued existence of aspects of traditional culture alongside the modern, as Germani and others have suggested.[9] But we have learned to expect as normal the persistence of preindustrial cultural patterns in modern political cultures.[10] The absence of major discontinuities does not imply monolithic cultural unity but indicates the broad sharing of some basic and pervasive value and cognitive orientations.

The elements of this politically relevant cultural unity are several. Religion is one. Anthropologists, psychiatrists, sociologists, and poets alike have stressed the functionality of religion for maintaining authority as well as cultural unity. It not only provides meaning, defines ultimate aims, and prescribes paths for achieving them, but it also provides a common symbolism, a common institutional loyalty, and typically reinforces and legitimizes the political order. In Argentina the Catholic religion is widely shared throughout the population. Rich, poor, and middle class alike identify with Catholicism. This identification extended across generations, regions, occupations, sexes, and political lines, defining Argentina as a Catholic culture. Like religious identification, laxity in the fulfillment of religious demands is distributed through the whole population. Argentina does not have a Catholic upper class and a de-Christian-

---

[8] The absence of truly rural respondents (peasants or inhabitants of towns of less than 2,000) gives us no adequate basis for estimating urban and rural discontinuities.

[9] The persistence of aspects of traditional culture is emphasized by Germani in his article, "Hacia una democracia de masas," in Torcuato S. di Tella, Gino Germani, Jorge Graciarena y colaboradores, *Argentina, sociedad de masas* (Buenos Aires: Editorial Universitaria de Buenos Aires, 1965), pp. 206–209.

[10] Almond and Verba, *The Civic Culture,* stress the persistence of premodern cultural elements: "This political system with predominantly participant cultures will . . . include both subjects and parochials" (p. 20). The persistence of traditional orientations and their positive functions for a modern system are also discussed in Gabriel A. Almond and G. Bingham Powell, Jr., *Comparative Politics: A Developmental Approach* (Boston: Little, Brown and Company, 1966), and in much of the literature on development.

ized proletariat as France is said to have. Religious differences do not coincide with economic, regional, racial, or political divisions. They do not emphasize and exacerbate other distinctions among Argentines. It is widely believed that politicized religious differences give to political struggles an ultimate messianic flavor. Argentine parties and politicians may disagree on questions about the role of the Church in the civil sphere, but their disagreement takes place within a context of shared religious convictions. Catholicism is almost equally widespread among Peronists, UCRP supporters, and other segments of the population. Religious ties do not reinforce political divisions.[11]

A manipulative orientation to economic problems was also broadly shared by all major segments of the population. Low wages, unemployment, and poor housing were not seen as fate, or the will of God, to be endured in patience and fortitude. They were viewed by almost everyone as problems to be dealt with. The transition from a contemplative to a problem-oriented posture vis-à-vis one's situation is a basic one—separating civilizations, distinguishing modern scientific from traditional societies, static from mobile ones. The transition was long since made in Argentina and has been assimilated by all classes of this mobile society in which people move up the economic ladder and across professional lines as well as from place to place.[12] Perhaps it was Perón who translated personal misery into a problem of public policy for Argentina's *descamisados* and in this fashion simultaneously created demands and politicized them. Certainly, Argentina's lower classes, like her higher ones, believe the economy is amenable to human influence and that economic wants are economic problems.

There was also near-universal consensus in Argentina that it is the business of government to solve these economic problems. Laissez faire orientations were nearly absent. No numerically significant segment of the population advocated that government not involve itself with employment. The number opposing the regulation of prices and wages was similarly small. These statements did not imply absence of disagreement on economic questions. Socioeconomic classes split according to conventional right-left stereotypes on a

[11] Lipset emphasizes the importance of the coincidence of religious and political affiliations to the development and stability of democratic institutions in Lipset, *Political Man*, p. 84.

[12] Less than half (47 percent) of the respondents lived in the towns of their birth. The other half had moved at least once.

number of economic and welfare issues. Increased government regulation of the economy was most frequently opposed by upper-class
respondents and supported by lower-class respondents, with middle-
class frequencies falling in between. So were higher taxes, redistribution of land, and nationalization of basic industries. But the differences occurred within a limited range. The virtual absence of laissez
faire orientations among Argentines means that the "right," as
measured by economic issues, began approximately at the welfare-
state position and extended "left" to a semisocialist economy with
national ownership of key industries.[13]

There was far less agreement about several quite basic aspects of
political life. Consensus was lacking about a citizen's obligations to
participate in public life. No more than half of all Argentines shared
the activist model of citizenship; conversely, fewer than a third
shared the subject model of citizenship. But these different models
of citizenship were widely diffused throughout the population, not
concentrated in a single sector.[14] Similar dissensus existed concerning
the justice, integrity, and purposes of government. Confidence in
government coexisted with doubts about who controls and who
profits. Whether from cynicism or realism, only about one-fourth of
Argentines believed that government was not the property of special
interests who ran it for their own benefit.[15] But doubts about whether
government was really regulated by the invisible hand of special
interests were found in all sectors of the population.

The form as well as the function of the political system was a
subject for disagreement. Elite disagreements about political forms
appeared to be reflected or shared at the base. A large sector of the
community thought a strong man could provide better government
than could "laws and talk." But another sector had had its fill of
strong men, and still another either did not know or did not care.
A more recently published poll revealed similar disagreement about

---

[13] "Left" and "right" coincide more nearly with Continental, for example,
French or German, than with North American models. Peronists definitely fall
on the "left" end of this spectrum.

[14] The ideal of participation was somewhat more widely shared among upper-
socioeconomic groups. If these classes have the superior influence and access to
communication media often attributed to them, it is reasonable to expect that
the activist model may become more widely disseminated. And it is interesting to
note that the level of agreement about the obligation to participate is approximately as high in Argentina as in the United States.

[15] The remainder either *did* believe the government was controlled by special
interests (42.5 percent) or felt they did not know (28.8 percent).

the utility of a legislative chamber. In late 1967 approximately 39 percent believed the nation was better off without a Chamber of Deputies, while 24.7 percent believed the nation would profit by its restoration.[16]

The single procedural aspect of political life on which there was general consensus was the undesirability of using force and violence to resolve political questions. There was also widespread agreement about the undesirability of military participation in politics. But the extent of agreement on military participation was less than that about economic issues affecting day-to-day living. For Argentines generally, political issues, both substantive and procedural, had lower priority than economic issues. And while there were differences among Argentines on a wide range of political subjects, the differences were not coterminous with other social divisions.

If Argentina had a class-bound politics, as some observers have asserted and others imply, it did not have a class-bound political culture. Cleavages existed, but they were not chasms separating persons of greatly differing identifications, expectations, and demands. Classes did not comprise subgroups with profoundly different comprehensive ideologies. Economic roles, social backgrounds, and regional differences had not produced very different modes of perceiving or organizing reality, nor of orienting oneself in it. The discontinuities of traditional societies with scientifically oriented, modernizing elites were lacking; so, too, were the wide generational gaps characteristic of nations in the process of rapid change,[17] and the deep cleavages characteristic of a nation rent by the mutual hostilities of large sectors who perceive one another as enemies. But if Argentina was not a society divided by deep cleavages, neither was it a frictionless machine characterized by mutual trust, common understanding, and community. It was an integrated culture in which coexisted a number of shared and divisive purposes, understandings, and demands. Among the subgroups within this single political culture are Peronists, whose perspectives identified them as political competitors united by more than the demand for power.

[16] These findings of a survey by Dr. José Enrique Miguens, a distinguished Argentine sociologist, were reported in the *New York Times,* August 27, 1967. The same source reported that 39.7 percent of the population believed the nation would suffer if political parties were reestablished.

[17] The existence of "sharp differences in the political orientations of generations" is identified by Pye as one of the characteristics of transitional politics. See Lucian W. Pye, *Politics, Personality, and Nation Building: Burma's Search for Identity* (New Haven: Yale University Press, 1962), pp. 22–24.

Peronist Distinctiveness

As with other subgroups, orientations shared by Peronists were of two types: those that occurred evenly throughout the society, and those that occurred with distinctive frequency among Peronists. Whether Peronists constituted a subculture would depend on the content, extent, and intensity of their distinctive orientations and, derivately, on the extent to which they were socially insulated.

Since the various elements of Peronists' orientations have been described in earlier chapters, a brief summary should suffice here to delineate the Peronist universe. The centrality of social class is perhaps the clearest characteristic of the Peronist demands and expectations.[18]

Class divisions were not equally important in the perspectives of all Peronists. But the importance of class for many Peronists is one of the most distinctive characteristics of the movement. Peronists' lower-class identifications and demands were stronger than those of the lower classes generally. Despite the presence in their ranks of persons of diverse occupations, Peronists were more concerned with the interests and demands of laborers than was the whole group of laborers. It is therefore clear that Peronists' perspectives and demands did not simply mirror those of the lower or working classes. In fact, only about half of the lower-class respondents identified with the Peronists or shared their demands. *Peronists comprised part of the working class, identified with the whole of it, and made demands in the name of the whole that exceeded the demands of the whole class.* They not only reflected but magnified the perspectives and demands of the laboring classes, and they justified them by the distinctively Peronist belief in the oppression of the laboring class. They both emphasized and disapproved of the differential class shares in the distribution of values.[19]

Peronists were not only uniquely sensitive to the hardships of

[18] This fact, it should be emphasized, was not assumed but emerged from the analysis.

[19] In this regard, as in others, the contemporary orientations of the movement were apparently unchanged since the fall of Perón. Kalman Silvert commented that "Peronism did succeed in setting class against class more sharply than in any other period of Argentine history," and added, "There is no contradiction in the fact that the more equitable income distribution and greater feeling of participation on the part of lower elements was accomplished in part through the fomenting of overt class antagonisms." See Silvert, "The Costs of Anti-Nationalism: Argentina," in Kalman H. Silvert, ed., *Expectant Peoples: Nationalism and Development* (New York: Vintage Books, 1967), p. 367.

lower-class Argentines but were convinced that this hardship resulted from inequity. Wage earners, both laborers and white-collar workers, did not receive a just share of available goods. More frequently than others, Peronists supported policies looking to the redistribution of wealth, policies that would penalize the "have" sectors—entrepreneurs, landowners—to reward the "have not" sectors. The lower classes, they believed, could not count on fair treatment from the courts. Nor could they hope for much from government, for government, more Peronists than others believed, was the property of special interests and was run for their own profit. Peronists believed their principal economic organizations (trade unions) did not receive fair treatment from government. Neither did they believe their political organizations were justly treated. More than others, Peronists doubted the influence of average citizens on public policy, but they also tended more frequently than others to believe good government resulted from having strong men in power.

Of all sectors of Argentine society, Peronists most frequently saw their situation as deteriorating. They were not always so badly off, but, things being as they were, they were likely to get still worse. A sense of loss and pessimism about the future heightened felt deprivations with consequences that are not yet clear.

Peronists' preoccupation with the concrete problems of daily life left little room for attention to political problems or foreign affairs. But when their attention was directed to international events, their dreams were not of glory but of economic independence and neutrality; and both were flavored with anti-Yankee feelings.

The foregoing portrait is not an accurate description of all rank-and-file Peronists. It is a description of attitudes more often held by Peronists than by others; that is, it is a portrait of distinctive Peronist attitudes. It was the frequency, not the presence, of these attitudes that distinguished Peronists from UCRP supporters and from non-Peronists generally. The same attitudes were found throughout the population, but their distinctive frequency among Peronists gave the movement distinguishing style and content. The presence of these attitudes among non-Peronists, and of different orientations among rank-and-file Peronists, in short, *the broad overlapping of Peronist and non-Peronist orientations to political objects, suggests that Peronists' orientations fell well within the national political culture.*

This summary also makes clear the strong ideological affinity between Peronist masses and Peronist leadership. To an impressive extent rank-and-file Peronists shared the stated orientations and goals of Juan Perón, his principal lieutenants, and neo-Peronist leaders. They were all relatively antilandowner, anticapitalist, and anticommunist, anti-American and anti-Cuban, and anti-Chinese and anti-Soviet. They were also Catholic. They favored a redistribution of goods that would give Argentine rural and urban workers and the Argentine poor a bigger slice of the economic pie. They were not much concerned with how this redistribution would be achieved, but the radical impulse for the destruction of the traditional order was missing. Although economic and social structure had more importance for them than political structure, neither structures nor procedures occupied their attention. The reason for this ideological affinity of leaders and followers probably lay in the relationship of both to Argentine political traditions. While radical movements aim at restructuring politics, society, and personality and reject wholesale traditional organization and goals, Peronism was, and is, a type of traditional politics, not a rejection of it. It fits Silvert's characterization of Peronism as a continuation of syndicalist politics.

The social relations of rank-and-file Peronists to non-Peronists and to society confirms this view (see Table 9.1). The social world of rank-and-file Peronists was neither homogeneous nor insulated from the remainder of society. But Peronists were more likely than UCRP supporters or Argentines in general to live in a social world characterized by Peronist allegiances, more likely to have friends and wives who were also Peronists.

While Peronists were integrated into national communication networks, they also had distinctive media preferences that in part reflected their economic and cultural characteristics, in part reflected their political views (see Table 9.2). They were more likely than

TABLE 9.1 POLITICAL HOMOGENEITY OF SOCIAL WORLD: PERCENTAGE SHARING POLITICAL PARTY PREFERENCES
(In percent)

	Core Peronists ($n = 365$)	Pro- Peronists ($n = 411$)	Others ($n = 1,238$)	UCRP Voters ($n = 413$)
Friends and acquaintances	41.4	20.0	10.6	24.0
Spouses	32.9	20.0	14.3	28.1

Source: Responses to Questions 31 and 31a (Appendix B).

TABLE 9.2 PRINCIPAL SOURCES OF INFORMATION
(In percent)

	All Argen-tines (n = 2,014)	Core Pero-nists (n = 365)	UCRP Voters (n = 413)	Upper (n = 197)	Class Middle (n = 960)	Lower (n = 721)
Television	28.3	25.8	31.0	26.1	26.6	28.0
Radio	28.9	33.7	27.1	22.3	26.1	32.3
Daily papers	50.0	43.3	50.8	56.1	56.1	53.2
Political newspapers	5.8	5.8	5.6	8.3	6.1	4.3
Political leaders	4.4	4.1	5.3	7.0	5.0	3.2
Friends	8.2	8.3	10.4	7.0	8.0	8.5
Others	1.0	0.5	0.7	1.3	1.5	0.4
Don't know	0.5	0.3	0.7	1.9	0.6	—

Source: Responses to Question 49 (Appendix B).

other political aggregates to rely on radio as a principal source of news, a preference that is consistent with lower-class communication habits.[20]

Their newspaper preferences were also distinctive, but politics rather than class was the determining factor.[21] About one-fourth of the Peronists said they most frequently read *La Crónica*, which was especially popular in the Buenos Aires suburbs. *El Claren, La Razón,* and *La Prensa,* which ranked first, second, and third, respectively, among Argentines generally, were substantially less widely read among Peronists than among UCRP supporters. Peronists' newspaper preferences were *La Crónica* (24.4 percent), *El Claren* (11 percent), *La Razón* (10.4 percent), and *La Prensa* (4.7 percent).[22]

Certainly, Peronists did not constitute a nation within a nation in the sense that relatively closed linguistic or religious minorities can be so described. They were geographically dispersed, they had family ties that related them to non-Peronists, and they were integrated into national media networks.

The hierarchical organization and social insulation characteristic

[20] For a discussion relating communication to affective orientations see Karl W. Deutsch, *Nationalism and Social Communication* (New York: published jointly by the Technology Press of the Massachusetts Institute of Technology and John Wiley & Sons, 1953).

[21] Editor and Publisher Co., Inc., *International Year Book, 1966,* lists newspaper circulation by newspaper, by province.

[22] *La Prensa*'s share of the newspaper market had declined rather drastically in the last two decades. In 1948, 31 percent of all newspaper readers said they preferred it, compared to only about 13 percent in 1965. See ibid.

of totalitarian movements were not achieved by Peronist organizations even during Perón's presidency. Since his downfall, the Peronist movement has not been characterized by centralized organization, effective discipline, or social insulation. Some regional parties were virtually autonomous and only loosely related by loyalty to a leader whose political reality had dimmed. Many rank-and-file Peronists were not even members of a Peronist political organization. Although the "Bloc 62" trade unions served as an organizational infrastructure, the movement did not develop a mass membership party such as developed around the European labor movement. Still, social organization and object orientation identified the Peronist movement as a political aggregate based on some broad affinities, dissatisfactions, and social characteristics. Whether or not we term Peronists a subculture depends on how we conceive a subculture. The designation is essentially arbitrary. My understanding of the term suggests a greater distinctiveness and isolation than is exhibited by rank-and-file Peronists. However, even marginal differentiation is compatible with alienation, since alienation as well as isolation can serve as the basis of a subculture. This dimension of Peronists' relations to the remainder of their society deserves consideration.

Are Peronists Alienated from the Remainder of Argentine Society?

Obviously, whether Peronists are considered to be an alienated group within the society depends on the controlling definition of alienation. Several conceptions of alienation are current in the social sciences, which have as their common core the notion of a breakdown of shared values, of community. Marx conceived alienation as a consequence of capitalism's destruction of community, of its replacement of the "organic" relations of an integral community with functional, instrumental relations determined by profit. When only a cash nexus bound capitalist to worker, that is, when relations were totally depersonalized, man, viewed by others as object, viewed himself as object. The result was depersonalization, dehumanization. Alienation from fellowmen led ultimately and inevitably to alienation from one's self.

Many non-Marxist conceptions of alienation agree with the Marxist emphasis on capitalism as a cause of social atomization and alienation as a function of social disintegration. The aristocratic critique of capitalism also ascribes to it the replacement of "organic" relations among men in natural social units by rational, functional relations among individuals. If men were formerly members of larger political units by virtue of prior membership in smaller, more "natural" social units, under rational, functional, capitalist modes of social integration individuals are abstracted from natural group memberships. The result is a breakdown of community, an end to shared values, and the disappearance of the restraints of decency and law. Barbarism is said to result when the principles of natural order are not observed.

Both the Marxist and the aristocratic criticism emphasize emancipation from moral restraints as an aspect of alienation and suggest that the alienated man may be a fearsome creature, inhuman as well as dehumanized, incivil, intemperate, a desperado outside natural and written law.

Recent literature on development identifies alienation as one result of rapid social change. The transition from traditional to modern societies is said to produce profound personal dislocations. The displacement of face-to-face groups by larger social units, of particularistic by impersonal norms, of ascriptive by skill-based roles is said by many students of development to result in serious personal disorientation and alienation. Pye's outstanding work on the personal consequences of social and political change describes transitional man in terms identical with those used to describe alienated man.[23] Alienated man is mass man. He is Marx's "cripple," "monster"; [24] he is Ortega's barbarian who suffers "hermitism of the soul" and "has a deadly hatred of all that is not itself." [25] Undisciplined, unrestrained, unprotected, mass man has time on his hands, money in his pocket, and destruction in mind. William Kornhauser, whose *Politics of Mass Society* attempts to translate the theory of mass society into a series of verifiable propositions, has defined mass behavior, which is the behavior of an alienated mass, as

collective behavior exhibiting the following characteristics.

(a) *The focus of attention is remote from personal experience and daily life.* . . .

(b) *The mode of response to remote objects is direct.* . . . Violence in

[23] Pye, *Politics, Personality*, pp. 52–56. Alexis de Tocqueville made the same point in *Democracy in America* (New York: Alfred A. Knopf, 1945), vol. 1, p. 251: "epochs sometimes occur in the life of a nation when the old customs of a people are changed, public morality is destroyed, religious belief shaken, and the spell of tradition broken. . . ."

[24] *Capital*, vol. 1, Eng. trans. by E. and C. Paul, p. 381.

[25] José Ortega y Gasset, *The Revolt of the Masses* (New York: W. W. Norton, 1932), pp. 81, 84.

word and deed is the hallmark of the mass movement uncommitted to institutional means. . . .

(c) Mass behavior also tends to be highly unstable, readily shifting its focus of attention and intensity of response. Activist responses are likely to alternate with apathetic responses. . . .

(d) When mass behavior becomes organized around a program and acquires a certain continuity in purpose and effort, it takes on the character of a *mass movement*. . . . Mass movements generally have the following characteristics: their objectives are remote and extreme; they favor activist modes of intervention in the social order; they mobilize uprooted and atomized sections of the population; they lack an internal structure of independent groups (such as regional or functional units with some freedom of action).[26]

It is easy enough to measure Peronist rank-and-file ideology against Kornhauser's explicit criteria. The evidence is available. The results are clear.

The focus of attention of rank-and-file Peronists was not "remote from personal experience and daily life. . . ." To the contrary, the salience of the concrete problems of daily life, of bread-and-butter issues in the Peronist attention frames is an outstanding characteristic of Peronist orientations. The absence of abstract, long-range, even political concerns from the focus of attention of rank-and-file Peronists identifies them as people for whom personal concerns had not been displaced by symbols remote from daily life. Peronists' characteristic modes were personal rather than general, concrete rather than abstract, economic rather than political, and partial, scattered, and diffuse rather than comprehensive.

It is somewhat more difficult, but not impossible, to evaluate Peronist behavior against Kornhauser's second characteristic, which emphasizes the predilection to direct action. The Argentine political system is one in which direct action is a normal mode of interaction and competition. It is a political system with a tradition of direct action. Political parties and pressure groups alike press their claims to influence over policy and personnel through direct action. It is true that the two major Radical parties, the Conservatives, and the Christian Democrats appear to have eschewed direct action, though the evidence is not conclusive. In the early decades of the century, Radicals repeatedly resorted to coups in an effort to achieve power, and individual Radical leaders have been involved in plotting the overthrow of subsequent governments. Violence breeds vio-

[26] William Kornhauser, *The Politics of Mass Society* (New York: Free Press, 1965), pp. 43–47; Kornhauser's emphasis.

lence; direct action breeds direct action. Indubitably, the Peronist movement pursued its political goals by direct action as well as other means. There is no evidence that either Peronist rank and file or leaders were committed to achieving their goals through democratic means (which might be defined as including propaganda, political organization, electioneering, and adjudication). But can direct action reasonably be described as indicative of alienation in a context in which direct action is a traditional form of political competition in the community? I think not.

Measured by voting habits, rank-and-file Peronist behavior was stable. The attachment to Perón was remarkable for its durability in an environment in which political loyalties are notably volatile.

Certainly, Peronism had a mass following, but it is less clear whether it is a mass movement demonstrating characteristics associated with mass movements of the alienated. (1) Its objectives were not remote and extreme, it was not dedicated to chiliastic ends, it did not postulate distant utopias. (2) There is no evidence that Peronists "favor activist modes of intervention in the social order." They did not eschew them. But rank-and-file support was greatest and most reliable when the means of competition were legal. (3) It is difficult to determine whether the Peronist movement mobilized "uprooted and atomized sections of the population." There is general consensus among students of the movement that internal immigrations supplied the mass base of the original Peronist following. The 1965 data also show slightly higher rates of mobility for Peronists than others.

But "uprooted" and "atomized" are concepts normally used to imply psychological and social displacement, not simply changed residence, though changed residence is usually interpreted as one of several precipitating factors (see Table 9.3). The notion of being uprooted normally refers to social and moral disorientation or alienation. Persons who have never internalized prescriptions, standards, and perspectives characteristic of their cultures are spoken of as without roots; those who have lost once internalized cultural perspectives, values, and so forth are spoken of as uprooted. The test of uprootedness would seem then to be whether a given individual or group shares the dominant culture. Atomization, on the other hand, typically refers to the disintegration of independent social groups—based on common kinship, economic role, geographic position, religious conviction, shared interests, and so forth. An atomized society is one in which natural social groups have broken down, in

TABLE 9.3   RESIDENTIAL MOBILITY: PERONISTS AND OTHERS
(In percent)

	All Argentines (n = 2,014)	Core Peronists (n = 365)	UCRP Voters (n = 411)
Lived in city less than 10 years [a]	19.7	23.1	17.9
Lived in city 10 to 20 years	15.9	16.2	14.0
Lived in city more than 20 years	15.8	14.8	20.3
Lived whole lifetime in city	47.5	45.2	46.7

Source: Responses to Questions 72 and 72a (Appendix B).
[a] More Peronists than UCRP supporters had lived in the city less than a year (3.3 and 1.7 percent, respectively), one to three years (4.4 and 3.9 percent), three to five years (4.7 and 3.6 percent), and five to ten years (10.7 and 8.7 percent).

which the social structure has become unglued at the base, and "individuals are not directly related to one another in a variety of independent groups" but are "an aggregate of individuals . . . related to one another only by way of their relation to a common authority, especially the state." [27] Atomized individuals are isolated from one another by lack of a common culture, by the absence of interlocking roles. They are the products of social distintegration, which has wrested them from meaningful family, occupational, and religious groups and left them alone, unintegrated into meaningful social units. According to most theories, portions—especially classes —of a society can be atomized without the society suffering total social disintegration. One test of atomization in a society is said to be the extent of membership in voluntary independent groups.

If a lack of shared culture and a lack of group memberships are acceptable specifications of uprootedness and atomization, respectively, then it is clear that the Peronist movement did not qualify as a mass movement of the alienated. Peronists' expectations and demands fell within the dominant Argentine political culture; their distinctive orientations constituted variations compatible with a membership in a single culture. Divisions found elsewhere in the society were found also among Peronists; consensus broadly shared elsewhere in the society existed among Peronists. Peronists were not socially isolated. They identified with the Church and fulfilled religious obligations in approximately the same proportions as did UCRP supporters and others. They joined labor unions and identified with them. Peronists then quite clearly did not constitute an alienated mass movement, in Kornhauser's sense of the term.

[27] Ibid., p. 32.

A different conception of alienation would produce a different conclusion. There is a common, almost slang, meaning of alienation that equates alienation with dissatisfaction. A dissatisfied group is termed an alienated group. Dissatisfied or disapproving individuals are described as alienated. In this loose sense, implying dissatisfaction, disapproval, or demand for change, Peronists were alienated. They were the most dissatisfied major group in Argentina's political system. Their dissatisfaction was not vague, pervasive, or undefined malaise. It had specific content related to concrete experience with problems. Their demands were explicit, stable; the same stability characterized their attachments. Neither the blandishments of Frondizi nor the punitive legislation of other governments had persuaded rank-and-file Peronists to abandon their attachment to Perón and the movement. Peronists' demands were also limited. Rank-and-file ideology had no flavor of either radicalism or nihilism. But it did contain criticisms of the system and demands for change. Peronist rank-and-file ideology reflected alienation in the conventional, but not the rigorous, sense of that word. Perhaps the *descamisados* who flocked to Perón's banner in the 1940s were alienated and disoriented by the transition from a traditional rural to a modern urban society. But twenty-five years had passed, and these internal migrants appeared to have been assimilated. It is often said that Perón himself integrated them into the polity. Perhaps in the process they changed and the polity changed, with today's political culture as the result.

Peronists' Antidemocratic Orientations

One purpose of this study was to determine the extent to which Peronists shared antidemocratic political orientations and the extent to which such orientations were unique to Peronists or more widely shared within Argentine society. Were the authoritarian proclivities of rank-and-file Peronists a major obstacle to Peronist integration into a democratic society?

In considering political orientations unfavorable to democratic institutions, it is important to distinguish between orientations that are explicitly hostile to democratic practices or explicitly favorable to nondemocratic institutions and those nonpolitical psychological orientations and predispositions that are sometimes said to be linked to nondemocratic or antidemocratic preferences. A belief that elected representatives make less-good governors than one strong man is an example of the former; a high level of distrust in other people is an example of the latter. Support for Juan Perón constitutes prima facie evidence of relative indifference to some democratic political procedures, or at least suggests a deviant understanding of those procedures. This support also constitutes definitive proof that Peronists will accept an autocratic leader providing he has the other qualities exhibited by Juan Perón. It does not prove that they prefer an autocrat.

There is no direct evidence that Perón's authoritarian style or behavior was or is a factor in the attachment of Peronists to his leadership. Far more important, the evidence suggests, were the actual and apparent economic benefits he bestowed on workers. Fillol asserts that Argentine workers have long enjoyed a standard of living well above the subsistence level and so concludes that their attachment to Perón was based on twin psychological drives: need dependence and need aggression.[28] But we have seen that concrete personal economic concerns occupied the foreground of Peronists' attention and, further, that the Peronist movement was overwhelmingly perceived as an instrument for the accomplishment of economic aims. Perón's mass following might be explained by the absence of other political leaders who combined a high level of personal political skill and political salience [29] with a stated concern for the status, income, and power of the lower classes. It is entirely possible to account for Perón's original mass following without recourse to hypotheses concerning the authoritarian proclivities of his followers. In any case, an explanation of Perón's mass following during his rise and reign tells us little about the mass base of the post-Perón movement. Unfortunately, the available data are ambiguous about whether the later movement can be explained by objective factors such as the continued absence of alternative leaders to express the economic interests of Peronists, or whether the political proclivities of the followers are needed to explain the movement's continued strength. However, the priority of economic demands among rank-and-file Peronists and their identification of the movement with these demands suggest that their attachment to Perón was derivative.

Rank-and-file Peronists' support for authoritarian leadership may

---

[28] Tomás Roberto Fillol, *Social Factors in Economic Development: The Argentine Case* (Cambridge, Mass.: The M.I.T. Press, 1961), p. 77.

[29] This salience was originally achieved by way of his place in the military establishment and participation in their 1941 coup.

have been fortuitous and not an expression of positive political proclivities. Regrettably, there is little information on explicit preferences concerning political regimes.[30] Views were elicited on military participation in politics, and, like other respondents, Peronists were in large majority opposed to military intervention in political life. Questions were included on force and violence in politics, and Peronists, like others, opposed it. Open-ended questions inquired about Argentine problems, but these were almost always identified as economic. Responses to only one question revealed a majority of Peronists to be explicitly and distinctively inclined to support autocratic government. Approximately 58 percent of the core Peronists agreed that "a few strong leaders would do more for this country than all the laws and talk." [31] Another 13 percent had no opinion, and fewer than one-third opposed this statement. Peronist responses to this question indicate that support for Perón may have reflected a general orientation to politics. Furthermore, not only did a clear majority of Peronists affirm their preference for autocratic government in the only question that specifically elicited their views about it, but they expressed other attitudes and preferences widely believed to be associated with authoritarian proclivities. Many of the characteristics associated with "working-class authoritarianism" were found with distinctive frequency among the Peronists.[32]

[30] In retrospect, I think other questions could have been included in the survey concerning political style, procedures, and institutions. However, valid questions of this sort are exceedingly difficult to frame. They require a degree of political information and sophistication surpassing that of most informants. Surveys in Buenos Aires done by Encuestas Gallup de la Argentina (EGA) indicate relatively low levels of political information among the Argentine population. For example, fewer than half could name three members of Congress; approximately three-fourths could not name the minister of labor, minister of defense, or governor of Tucumán; and one-half to two-thirds did not know who was the commander-in-chief of the armed forces, the minister of the interior, or the leader of the lower house. This information level can be compared with the 86 percent who were able to name Horacio Acavallo as a recently installed world boxing champion. See EGA, "Argentina," Polls, vol. 2, no. 3 (Spring 1967).

[31] Compared with 41 percent of the pro-Peronists and 35 percent of the UCRP voters (Question 15c, Appendix B).

[32] Examples of studies that illuminate either (a) lower-class (urban or rural) support for authoritarian movements or (b) lower-class intolerance or opposition to personal liberties are, among others, Stanley Hoffmann, Le mouvement poujade (Paris: Libraire Armand Colin, 1956); Gabriel A. Almond, The Appeals of Communism (Princeton: Princeton University Press, 1954); H. J. Eysenck, The Psychology of Politics (London: Routledge & Kegan Paul, 1954); Hadley Cantril, The Psychology of Social Movements (New York: John Wiley & Sons, 1941); Samuel A. Stouffer, Communism, Conformity, and Civil Liberties: A Cross-section

A well-known version of working-class authoritarianism was first stated by Lipset, who cites Peronism as a prime example of this type of movement.[33] Lipset calls the Peronist movement an example of left-fascism. It is, he says, a type

largely found in poorer, underdeveloped countries and appeals to the lower strata against the middle and upper classes. It differs from Communism in being nationalistic, and has usually been the creation of nationalist army officers seeking to create a more vital society by destroying the corrupt privileged strata which they believe have kept the masses in poverty, the economy underdeveloped, and the army demoralized and underpaid.[34]

He asserts that the mass base of left-fascism is drawn from the lower classes, some of whose attitudes and life styles predispose them to support authoritarian goals. Distinctive attitudes are

1. a tendency to seek immediate gratifications, reinforced by the absence of any sense of past and future and of means-ends relations;
2. focus on concrete, immediately perceivable phenomena;
3. "a desire for immediate action," and preference for "activist" politics;
4. "a tendency to view politics and personal relations in black-and-white terms";
5. "impatience with talk and discussion";
6. "a readiness to follow leaders who offer a demonological interpretation of the evil forces . . . which are conspiring against him." [35]

The widespread distribution of these attitudes in the lower classes is said to account for their support of Peronism, which Lipset de-

---

of the Nation Speaks Its Mind (Garden City, N.Y.: Doubleday & Company, 1955); Angus Campbell, Philip E. Converse, Warren E. Miller, and Donald E. Stokes, The American Voter (New York: John Wiley & Sons, 1960); Lipset, Political Man; and Wilhelm Reich, The Mass Psychology of Fascism (New York: Orgone Institute Press, 1946; published first in German in 1933). Mass movements that illustrate these characteristics include the mass communist parties of France and Italy, the British Union of Fascists, Poujadism, McCarthyism, Getulio Varga's movement in Brazil, and Peronism in Argentina, all of which are examples of authoritarian movements with substantial lower-class support.

[33] Lipset, Political Man, pp. 97–176 passim.

[34] Ibid., pp. 133–134.

[35] Ibid., p. 120. See also Trevor-Roper's extremely interesting discussion of witchcraft and social movement in H. R. Trevor-Roper, "Witches and Witchcraft," Encounter, June 1967, pp. 13–34.

scribed as a movement with a "strong-state" ideology, strong anti-parliamentary content, stress on the direct relationship between leader and people, a marked nationalist bent, and a glorification of the armed forces.[36] These attitudes are said to result from

1. Child-rearing patterns that stress immediate gratification. Whereas middle-class parents are said to stress deferrence of gratification for the achievement of long-range ends, lower classes are said to be oriented to immediate pleasure.

2. Low education, which limits experience and limits the frame of reference, produces a present-minded orientation and psychological and social insulation.

3. Lack of economic security and a concomitant lack of psychological security that leads to high tensions, which in turn predispose individuals to explosive, cathartic, direct action.

4. Harsh discipline in child rearing, which predisposes recipients to aggressive behavior.

5. High levels of hostility and aggressiveness plus low intellectual sophistication, which make scapegoat theories especially satisfying.

The survey data are adequate for testing some but not all of these propositions.

Orientation in time is illuminated by responses to questions dealing either with the past or with the future. Presumably, declining to project one's self forward or backward and make comparisons based on a time dimension would indicate a preemptive focus on the present. The data indicate no unwillingness or inability of Peronists to make comparisons with the past but an interesting reluctance to make projections regarding the future. Peronists, lower-class respondents, and laborers were distinctively reluctant to imagine what their situations might be a year in the future.[37]

---

[36] Lipset, *Political Man*, p. 173. In fact, this is not an adequate description of the elements of Peronism in power, since it stresses some relatively unimportant qualities, for example, glorification of the military—and omits some important ones—for example, glorification of workers and the concept of the "third position." See Pierre Lux-Wurm, *Le Péronisme* (Paris: R. Pichon et R. Durand-Auzias, 1965), pp. 223–243 passim, for a more adequate description, or George I. Blanksten, *Perón's Argentina* (Chicago: University of Chicago Press, 1953), pp. 161–298 passim.

[37] Fillol emphasizes the future's lack of reality for Argentines in general. Our data, however, indicate distinctive reactions of different population categories. See Fillol, *Social Factors in Economic Development*, p. 13.

TABLE 9.4 PROJECTIONS CONCERNING THE FUTURE: PER-
CENTAGE DECLINING TO COMPARE CURRENT WITH PAST
AND FUTURE SITUATIONS
(In percent)

	Future	Past
Political preference		
Core Peronist ($n = 365$)	18.9	0.3
UCRP voter ($n = 413$)	8.0	0.5
Class		
Upper ($n = 157$)	10.2	—
Middle ($n = 960$)	15.3	0.9
Lower ($n = 721$)	18.6	0.7
Profession		
Laborer ($n = 410$)	20.0	0.7
Business, professional ($n = 248$)	17.3	0.4
Clerical ($n = 301$)	10.0	—

Source: Responses to Questions 1 and 2 (Appendix B).

Peronists focused sharply on concrete, day-to-day problems, but
so did Argentines in general. However, upper-class and upper-
educational-level respondents demonstrated a greater tendency to
generalize problems and a superior awareness of relationships and
phenomena removed from daily life. But this difference is most
probably a function of education. No data are relevant to the ability
to defer gratification.[38]

*Peronists' predilection for direct action and activist politics is
problematic.* It has been pointed out that the Argentine tradition
sanctions direct action in the political sphere. Peronists' views about
how to influence policy were almost identical with those of UCRP
supporters. Also, the regularity and reliability with which Peronists
supported electoral objectives of the movement indicate a capacity
for sustained indirect action in support of political objectives;
second, the fact that a greater number turned out to vote than to
demonstrate does not support the notion that there are masses of
Peronists longing for the opportunity for direct action.

*Peronists exhibited a distinctive impatience with political discus-
sion* and a preference for government by a strong man. (See Table
9.5.) They were, after all, a demand aggregate united around the

---

[38] Daniel Goldrich describes the inability to defer gratification as a characteristic of the Latin poor. See "Toward the Comparative Study of Politicization in
Latin America," in Peter G. Snow, ed., *Government and Politics in Latin America: A Reader* (New York: Holt, Rinehart & Winston, 1967), p. 255. It should
perhaps be noted, however, that he does not cite evidence to support this
assertion.

TABLE 9.5   "A FEW STRONG LEADERS WOULD DO MORE FOR
THIS COUNTRY THAN ALL THE LAWS AND TALK": AGREE
(In percent)

Political preference	
Core Peronist ($n = 365$)	57.8
UCRP voter ($n = 413$)	35.1
Class	
Upper ($n = 197$)	38.9
Middle ($n = 960$)	38.8
Lower ($n = 721$)	44.5
Profession	
Laborer ($n = 410$)	44.9
Business, professional ($n = 248$)	44.4
Clerical ($n = 301$)	35.9

Source: Responses to Question 15c (Appendix B).

demand for the return of a strong man to power. The appeal of the
strong man is thus definitively, behaviorally established. And the
same proclivity was revealed by survey responses.[39]

Peronists also showed a distinctive tendency to *"demon" explanations.* More than any other category of persons, they blamed their
lack of information about public affairs on government officials.
They also most frequently saw government as controlled by special
interests for special interests. This too indicates a tendency to
explain events in terms of the machinations of "bad guys." (See
Table 9.6.)

A related tendency to view themselves as victims was especially
widespread among Peronists. Demonological explanations not only
postulate demons but also require victims. Persecutor and persecuted
interact symbiotically. Worlds ruled by demons are peopled with

TABLE 9.6   TENDENCY TO EXPLANATION BY HOSTILE GROUP
(In percent)

	Core Peronist ($n = 365$)	UCRP Voter ($n = 413$)	Lower Class ($n = 721$)	Laborer ($n = 410$)
Government controlled by special interests	53.4	37.3	39.7	45.1
Government to blame for lack of information	56.2	31.2	40.5	42.0

Source: Responses to Questions 23 and 47c (Appendix B).

[39] Residents of small towns also showed marked preference for the strong-man
solution to problems. Among residents of towns of 2,000 to 25,000, 58 percent
agreed with this proposition.

victims. I have already commented on Peronists' propinquity for perceiving as victims the groups with which they identify. That wage earners, trade unions, lower classes, Peronists—in short, they themselves—are victims of unjust discriminatory treatment was believed by almost all Peronists. Their orientations in foreign affairs, especially their anti-American attitudes, may also reflect a tendency to seek scapegoats or at least to explain problems in terms of enemies. The tendency to view politics in black-and-white terms has an obvious relation to demonological explanations.

No data directly relevant to child-rearing practices are available. We therefore cannot say whether Peronists were subjected to particularly harsh discipline. Di Tella and Fillol both describe child-rearing practices of the lower classes as erratic and periodically harshly punitive, but neither offers evidence to support the assertions.[40]

Hostility and aggressiveness are obviously related to feeling victimized. Feeling oneself the object of unfair treatment, discrimination, or neglect breeds hostility toward the perceived perpetrators and justifies aggression; it is characteristic of a paranoid orientation.[41] More than any group in Argentine society, Peronists perceived themselves as victims, and more than any group they supported policies that, however justified, were psychologically aggressive (punitive). Expropriation of large estates may represent social justice for the landless. It nonetheless constitutes a significant deprivation for landowners. Its advocates subscribe to that deprivation. Higher taxes on business profits and nationalization of key industries also constitute deprivations. Their advocacy involves a willingness to inflict punishment.

Both psychological and economic insecurity were widely felt among Peronists; they are also psychologically related to hostility and aggressiveness (see Table 9.7). Economic insecurity relates not to level of income but to expectations. Security is associated with stability; insecurity, with flux. More than others, Peronists, laborers, and lower-class respondents felt their economic situations had gotten worse and believed deterioration was likely to continue. Feelings of

[40] Torcuato S. di Tella, *El sistema político argentino y la clase obrera* (Buenos Aires: Editorial Universitaria de Buenos Aires, 1964), pp. 13–16, and Fillol, *Social Factors in Economic Development*, p. 25.

[41] No implication is intended concerning the realism of the feeling of being victimized. Psychiatrists have often observed that paranoid feelings of persecution are not necessarily objectively unjustified, though they may be displaced.

TABLE 9.7   INSECURITY, POLITICAL POSITION, AND CLASS
(In percent)

	Core Peronist (n= 365)	UCRP Voter (n= 413)	Upper (n= 157)	Class Middle (n= 960)	Lower (n= 721)	Laborer (n= 410)
Believe economic situation *worse* than last year	49.9	28.8	26.1	28.6	45.5	41.5
Believe economic situation will be *worse* next year	27.4	13.8	19.7	15.2	22.7	22.7
Believe people will take advantage of you whenever they can	89.9	77.2	83.4	82.6	85.0	87.8
No one much cares what happens to you	75.3	61.7	58.0	68.5	71.6	70.7

Source: Responses to Questions 1, 2, 15b, and 15h (Appendix B).

loss, threat, and pessimism are associated with apathy, and also with radical politics. That radical protest movements are more likely to be precipitated by loss or decreasing hope of gain than simply by deprivation is now widely accepted.[42] Assuming that distrust reflects interpersonal insecurity, then it too was more prevalent among Peronists than others. Psychological insecurity is believed by many to be especially widespread among transitional people en route from rural to urban life, from agricultural to industrial roles and life styles.[43]

Fortunately, survey data are available that demonstrate that Peronists' felt economic insecurity and pessimism were not simply functions of an Argentine lower-class tendency to make dismal projections about the future. Lower-class pessimism in 1965 did not reflect a permanent orientation but was a response to topical events. In 1947, in the heyday of the Peronist era, lower-class respondents had a much more optimistic view of their situation. More believed their situation had improved; fewer believed it had deteriorated. Further-

[42] See, among others, Crane Brinton, *The Anatomy of Revolution* (New York: Prentice-Hall, 1952).

[43] Gino Germani emphasizes the large number of transitional types among Peronists and characterizes the movement as a political by-product of transition to a modern society. See his "Hacia una democracia de masas" and the essay he coauthored with Kalman H. Silvert, "Estructura social e intervención militar en América Latina," in di Tella, *Argentina, sociedad de masas*, pp. 206–248 passim.

TABLE 9.8   COMPARISON OF ECONOMIC SITUATION FROM
1946 TO 1947 AND 1964 TO 1965
(In percent)

| | Situation | | | | | | | |
| | Better | | Same | | Worse | | Don't Know | |
	46–47	64–65	46–47	64–65	46–47	64–65	46–47	64–65
Class								
Upper	36.7	31.8	45.4	42.0	14.6	26.1	3.8	—
Middle	38.9	26.7	40.1	43.8	19.2	28.6	1.8	0.9
Lower	37.0	17.8	43.1	36.1	16.7	45.5	2.5	0.7
Profession								
Housewife	31.6	21.7	46.6	43.5	20.1	33.7	1.7	1.1
Business and professional	39.7	25.0	42.6	45.2	16.4	29.4	1.3	0.4
Laborer	44.8	18.5	39.9	39.3	14.0	41.5	1.3	0.4
Clerical	49.1	33.9	35.5	37.5	14.6	28.6	0.8	—

Sources: 1946–1947 data from International Research Associates; 1964–1965, from responses to Question 1 (Appendix B).

more, all classes had approximately the same perspective on their economic situations from 1946 to 1947, whereas, comparing 1964 and 1965, lower-class respondents reported with unique frequency greater deterioration and less improvement than others (see Table 9.8).[44]

Economic insecurity (as reflected by perception of declining fortunes) was greater at the end of 1965 than in the post–World War II Peronist period, and it was less evenly distributed among classes. Perhaps the prosperity of 1947 was more evenly shared than the problems of 1965. Perhaps class-based patterns of perception had become more marked. In any case, in 1965, laborers and lower classes much more often than middle- or upper-class respondents saw their situations as deteriorating. Unfortunately, we have no information on how each class viewed the other's situation. But the widespread Peronist belief in 1965 that laborers and white-collar workers did not receive a fair wage and had needs ignored by government implies that deprivations were being unevenly distributed.

At the end of 1965 the Peronist movement did display many of the characteristics associated by Lipset with working-class authoritarian-

[44] See Hadley Cantril, *The Pattern of Human Concerns* (New Brunswick, N.J.: Rutgers University Press, 1965), for a discussion of development and past, future orientations, pp. 184–193 passim. Data on 1946–1947 are from a national public opinion survey conducted by International Research Associates in late 1946 and made available to me by that organization.

ism. However, the data provide less support for Lipset's broader hypothesis "that the lower strata are relatively more authoritarian." [45] Lower-class respondents were more likely than others to agree with the statements that "A few strong leaders would do more for this country than all the laws and talk" (45 percent of the lower-class respondents agreed, compared with 39 percent of the middle class), "People like you and me don't have any say about what the government does" (58 percent of the lower class agreed compared with 52 percent of the middle class), and "If you don't watch yourself, people will take advantage of you" (85 percent lower class and 82 percent middle class). But somewhat more middle-class than lower-class respondents agreed with all three statements (45 percent middle class and 41 percent lower class). Education turned out to be more significant than economic class in determining responses to all three items. Seventy percent of the respondents with no more than a primary education agreed with all three statements.[46] This finding is consistent with the low educational level of rank-and-file Peronists.[47] *Obviously, the Peronist movement has attracted the most authoritarian sectors of the lower class.*

Peronists were not the only Argentines who found autocratic institutions acceptable. There were others who favored military participation in political life. There were others who preferred unidentified strong men to parliamentary government, and there were others who believed the country to be better off without a representative legislature. Peronists were the largest political group with a predisposition to support autocratic institutions. But such predispositions were found elsewhere in Argentine society, a fact that helps to account for the multiple types of support available to autocratic

[45] Lipset, *Political Man*, p. 101.

[46] The exact questions asked are given in Appendix B (Questions 15c, 15f, and 15b). Education is also revealed as very significant in determining response to military intervention. Approximately 62 percent of all respondents favorable to the military had no more than a primary education. Of the respondents favorable to the military, 64 percent were middle class and 46 percent were lower class. The finding that educational level may be more important than class in determining authoritarian proclivities is consistent with the findings of Zeitlin concerning Cuban workers; see Maurice Zeitlin, *Revolutionary Politics and the Cuban Working Class* (Princeton: Princeton University Press, 1967), pp. 242–276. On the same subject see Lewis Lipsitz, "Working-Class Authoritarianism: A Re-evaluation," *American Sociological Review*, vol. 30, no. 1 (February 1965), pp. 103–109.

[47] Though by no means all persons of little education supported the Peronist movement. Some 61 percent of the population had no more than primary school education.

leaders. These predispositions are perhaps the subjective counterpart of the objective fluctuation of regimes described in Chapter 3. This is not to say that autocratic predispositions have brought to power the various autocratic governments of the recent period; more than the autocratic predispositions of Perón's supporters caused Perón's regime. Political behavior cannot be inferred from attitudes.[48] Still, there existed a satisfying psychocerebral "fit" between Perón and his followers. But the future consequences of the relative authoritarianism of rank-and-file Peronists depends on factors other than attitudes. The quality, style, and commitments of available leaders are obviously important. So is the total political context. After Perón's fall, most Peronists conformed to the rules of successive governments while supporting the return of their leader.

In any case, Peronists are, it must be emphasized, only *relatively* authoritarian. Compared to other sectors of the Argentine population, preferences and perceptions believed to be associated with authoritarian character were more frequent. But we do not know how authoritarian these character biases must be before their possessors find democratic political modes intolerable. *Certainly there is no evidence that the distribution of authoritarian perspectives at the base has had any determinative influence over events in Argentina since 1955.* After that date and until the seizure of power by General Onganía, Argentine masses, including rank-and-file Peronists, generally observed democratic procedures. They voted; they did not engage in massive illegality. Elites, most specifically military officers and leading members of the political class, controlled events surrounding the successive displacement of governments (Lonardi, Frondizi, Illía). It could be argued that the staunch attachment of rank-and-file Peronists to their leader precipitated military intervention and so contributed to the establishment of authoritarian governments. But even if true, it would demonstrate only an indirect, contingent relationship between the authoritarian trends of rank-and-file Peronists and authoritarian political institutions. Political events are too complex, and the influence of attitudes in nondemocratic regimes too indirect, to warrant inferring a causal relationship between the existence of authoritarian personality trends and the existence of autocratic gov-

[48] The pitfalls of psychologism have been repeatedly exposed in recent literature. See, among others, Edward A. Shils, "Authoritarianism: 'Right' and 'Left,' " in Richard Christie and Marie Jahoda, *Studies in the Scope and Method of "The Authoritarian Personality"* (New York: Free Press, 1954), pp. 24–29. See also Lipset, *Political Man*, p. 100.

ernments. Most autocratic rulers in Latin America and elsewhere have come to power through other than democratic procedures. In such societies the principal importance of widespread authoritarian orientations would seem to be that they facilitate the mobilization of mass support for and acquiescence in tyranny.[49]

How Durable Is the Peronist Movement?

If it is to be systematic, concern for the future involves the stipulation of the relevant context, the description of relevant trends, and the projection of alternative development probabilities. The future of the Peronist movement depends as much on other political developments in Argentina as on the development of Peronist organizations and their relations with followers. And organizational development depends as much on the skills and unity of leaders as on the orientation of rank-and-file followers.

The projection of predispositions is easier than the projection of contextual conditions. The impressive durability of rank-and-file attachment to Perón and Peronist organizations has been referred to repeatedly in this study.

By the end of 1965 Perón had been defeated and banished; his character and record had been attacked by the Church and a succession of governments; Peronist organizations had been intermittently banned, purged, and "intervened"; non-Peronist leaders had attempted seduction of the Peronist masses. But Perón and various labor and political organizations acting in his name remained strong.

By late 1965 the movement had demonstrated a capacity to persevere out of power and to persist in the absence of its leader. However, this perseverance was demonstrated during a period when the restoration of Perón could be regarded as a realistic if remote possibility. There remains the question: What will happen to the movement (1) as the memory of Perón's regime dims and (2) after his restoration becomes impossible either because of his disability or death? Juan Perón is an old man in his seventies. Obviously, it will not be long until the Peronist movement entirely loses its unifying symbol. What happens then will depend on the skills and goals of Peronist leaders and on the political context at the time.

The survey data indicate the existence of a sizable number of

[49] For a highly suggestive discussion of Latin orientations relevant to autocracy, see Francisco José Moreno, *Legitimacy and Stability in Latin America* (New York: New York University Press, 1969).

Peronists who share distinctive social characteristics, demands, and expectations. These constitute a demand aggregate that will survive Perón's death as it has survived his exile. In it are represented young as well as old Argentines. But to be an effective political force, a demand aggregate requires leadership and an organization through which it can compete in a political arena. There are many examples in the contemporary world of the impotence of unorganized demand aggregates. Almost surely Republicans still exist in Spain, and Social Democrats in Yugoslavia.

If organizational unity can be established and maintained, then Peronists can be expected to exert significant influence on Argentine political life. But organizational unity assumes that some individual or group can establish preeminence and rally middle-echelon and rank-and-file Peronists. This may not prove possible.

The multiple schisms and convoluted rivalries that have afflicted the movement in recent years testify to the problems of establishing leadership in the movement. The survey data confirm that no leader had established his preeminence by the end of 1965. To an open-ended question inquiring "Are there any Peronist leaders you particularly admire?" (and if so) "Could you tell me their names?" almost a third of the core Peronists mentioned Matera, who was ousted from leadership in 1963, compared with 13 percent who named Framini, also ousted from the leadership, and 7 percent who named then current leaders, Vandor and Niembro. The relative standing of these Peronists was the same among pro-Peronists and among other Argentines, though few persons not favorable to Peronists found any of the leaders admirable (see Table 9.9).

TABLE 9.9   PERONIST LEADERS MENTIONED AS ADMIRED
(In percent)

	Core Peronists ($n = 365$)	Pro-Peronists ($n = 411$)	Not Favorable to Peronists ($n = 1,238$)	All Argentines ($n = 2,014$)
Raúl Matera	31.8	20.2	5.1	13.3
Andrés Framini	12.6	2.4	0.2	2.9
Paulino Niembro	6.8	2.9	0.2	2.0
Augusto Vandor	6.8	1.0	0.2	1.5
Tecera del Franco	4.7	1.9	0.2	1.3
Alberto Iturbe	3.0	0.7	0.1	0.1
Admire no one	49.0	73.0	93.8	81.4

Source: Responses to Questions 40 and 41 (Appendix B). Only persons are listed who were named by more than 3 percent of the core Peronists.

TABLE 9.10   OPINIONS OF PERONIST LEADERS
(In percent)

	Framini	Vandor	Tecera del Franco	Niembro	Matera
Favorable					
Core Peronists	35.9	26.6	29.4	28.5	60.5
Pro-Peronists	14.6	10.5	13.6	14.4	45.3
Unfavorable					
Core Peronists	13.4	11.8	7.7	4.7	3.3
Pro-Peronists	33.6	30.2	16.3	18.5	11.2
Neutral					
Core Peronists	20.3	22.5	18.1	17.0	11.2
Pro-Peronists	20.4	18.5	20.9	19.5	14.6
Don't know					
Core Peronists	30.4	39.2	49.9	49.9	24.9
Pro-Peronists	31.4	40.9	49.1	47.7	29.0

Source: Responses to Question 41 (Appendix B).

The most significant aspect of responses to this question is that approximately half of the core Peronists and three-fourths of the pro-Peronists regarded no Peronist leader as admirable. There was no heir apparent to Juan Perón. By the latter part of 1965 the objective struggle for organizational leadership was polarized between Augusto Vandor, neo-Peronist secretary general of the CGT and leader of the powerful Metallurgical Workers' Union, and José Alonso, Perón loyalist and former CGT secretary. Neither enjoyed significant strength among rank-and-file Peronists. The two principal leaders of Unión Popular also lacked popular support: Rodolfo Tecera del Franco and Carlos Bramuglia.

Survey questions designed to explore the popular image of major Peronist leaders yielded similar results (see Table 9.10). Two ex-Peronists were more favorably regarded than any of the current leaders.[50] Matera was favorably regarded by almost twice as many respondents as any other person identified as a Peronist leader. He was better known, and he inspired the least hostility. The more radical Framini ranked a weak second. He elicited fewer favorable and

[50] A poll conducted by Encuestas Gallup de la Argentina in greater Buenos Aires in March 1966 ($n = 891$) inquired whether Alonso or Vandor would be better able to promote Peronism. Twelve percent indicated Alonso; 10 percent Vandor; the remainder of all respondents declined to choose. The same poll inquired whether the rivalry between Alonso and Vandor would produce a split. Twenty-five percent expected a split; 24 percent expected no split; 51 percent said they did not know. See EGA, "Argentina," pp. 25–26.

more unfavorable responses. Respondents seemed unaware that at the time of the survey both men had been purged from the Peronist leadership.

What can be the future of a political movement that ousts its most popular leaders and still continues to be rent by rivalries?

Perón himself has been a major source of factionalism. His retirement will remove the friction deriving from controversies over personal loyalty, but it will also remove the single symbol of unity around which the movement has rallied. The disappearance in the foreseeable future of the demand aggregate described in this study seems unlikely. The persistence in younger Argentines of orientations associated with Peronism constitutes persuasive evidence that these orientations represent responses to conditions in Argentine life that are unrelated to the personal appeals of Juan Perón. But the influence of the individuals who share these orientations is problematic, as is the future of Argentine politics itself. If Argentina continues to be ruled by authoritarian leaders of the present type, then one can anticipate that there will continue to be some degree of relatively autonomous organization.

In this type of political context a demand aggregate such as the Peronist can influence policy and personnel in several ways. Its existence itself exerts a negative influence on the calculations and decisions of government officials who desire peaceful acquiescence in their policies. In addition, as long as significant organizational autonomy and a governmental policy of limited repression exist, there is the possibility of influencing the movement's decisions through mass actions such as strikes and demonstrations. Under traditional authoritarian regimes, as under conditions of democratic political organization, the extent of organizational unity affects the influence of the Peronist movement on national political life. Splintered, the movement is a less important factor in the calculations of authoritarian decision makers, just as it would be a less important factor in electoral politics.

Under conditions of democratic competition, core Peronists alone would constitute an important electoral bloc—if they were united. If a united movement could, in addition, retain the support of sympathizers, then in a democratic arena it could, together with a Radical party, provide the basis of a two-party system in which two large parties were flanked by numerous small splinter parties. The retention of broad support would probably entail relatively moderate leadership and a program that aggregated interests of various population groups.

If, however, under conditions of democratic competition, the movement split into two or more competing factions of relatively equal strength, the influence of the demand aggregate on Argentine political life could easily be dissipated in factional quarrels. Tradition provides precedent for such destructive splintering.

Epilogue

The military coup of September 1955 ended Juan Perón's rule. The coup of June 1966 ended all prospects of his restoration. Many Argentines, especially Peronist leaders and supporters, believe the true victim of the 1966 coup was the Peronist movement, whose 1965 electoral victories had dismayed non-Peronist civilian and military leaders alike. When General Juan Onganía replaced President Illía in the Casa Rosada, formal democracy came to an end in Argentina, and the possibility of a Peronist restoration by way of the ballot box was effectively eliminated.

General Onganía's elevation to the highest office was announced with the usual rhetoric of revolution. It was followed by the usual limited changes. There was *one* important change in the Argentine political system: majority opinion was eliminated as a determinant of the decision process. A corollary consequence was that political party leaders whose influence had rested on popular support were eliminated as major competitors for power. Otherwise, the system has not been significantly altered. Unions have remained an important power base, and labor leaders have continued to compete for influence over personnel and policy. So have industrialists, landowners, and clergymen. Terrorist groups such as the Tacuara have continued their quest for influence as have military leaders, both in and out of the Onganía government. But the one arena in which the Argentine people could regularly, peaceably, and legally participate in the competition was eliminated. To be sure it is still possible for ordinary Argentines to influence events through strikes and demonstrations. Masses may act, but there is no arena in which majorities may speak. Not only was popular sovereignty eliminated as the principle of legitimacy, public opinion was eliminated as a power base.[1] Under conditions of nondemocratic competition, the

---

[1] I have been told that the government of General Onganía has repeatedly commissioned public opinion polls to test popular opinion on various issues. If this is true, it is the first example known to me of a nondemocratic government using polls to inform itself privately of public opinion.

preferences of Argentine masses are no longer a counter in the contest for political power.

Otherwise, General Onganía's rule has to date been a period of politics as usual. The government has attempted, so far successfully, to divide and conquer but not to vanquish opponents. Political parties were disbanded, but no determined effort has been made to eliminate their infrastructures, and in fact the party organizations continue to exist and to engage in quasi-clandestine activities. A campaign was mounted against the CGT, but the attack was superficial and largely ineffective. Party leaders, labor leaders, dissident military leaders, and others continue their efforts to influence government decisions.

I do not desire to understate the government's efforts to control the activities of other actors in the various arenas. Repeated attempts have been made to inhibit political activity. But these efforts have been limited. Major strikes are possible, as the Ensenada oil workers proved in the fall of 1968. Demonstrations are possible, as Raimundo Ongaro and his followers proved about the same time.[2] Opposition to the government is possible, as the Alsogaraes and others have repeatedly demonstrated. Every example of overt opposition to the government demonstrates that competitive politics still exists in Argentina. And the responses of the government have shown that the Onganía administration is a continuation of the polycratic tradition.

The regime has remained in power because it has so far prevented the coalescence of civilian and military opposition to the government. That is, it has remained in power because of the divisions among the actual and potential opponents. There have been some repeated efforts at cooperation among representatives of the various opposition groups, but so far they have been limited in scope and duration.

Efforts to achieve unity have not been able to offset the splintering schismatic tendencies that affect opposition groups. The CGT has split into "official" and "rebel" factions. Peronist unions were afflicted with continuing internal quarrels between Vandor's "moderate" opposition to the government and Ongaro's intransigent hostility. And Vandor's assassination intensified internal labor struggles. Chronic rivalries, both personal and ideological, have infected Peronist political councils. The Radical leadership has been

[2] Ongaro is the leader of extreme Peronist or left-wing persuasion. He led several unions out of the CGT and formed an "opposition CGT."

similarly rent, and Rome has intervened in an effort to harmonize politically relevant splits within the Church hierarchy.

The government has stimulated these divisions whenever possible. But its policies have not caused the divisions from which it profits. The tendencies to factionalism antedated the rise of General Onganía and will almost surely outlast him. His government, too, has been afflicted by organizational disunity. Conflict between the nationalist *desarrollistas* and the laissez faire–oriented liberals has conditioned both economic and foreign policy. Disagreements about the organization of political power have compounded disagreements about its use. Disagreements within the military establishment and between the president and some of his military chiefs have heightened the political drama. In a sudden "presidential coup d'etat," General Onganía replaced all three commanders in chief of his armed services in the summer of 1969. This impressive demonstration of strength revealed the extent of disunity within as well as without the government. So, of course, have other sudden resignations and departures from the government.

These undoubted facts bring us to the most striking conclusion of this study: that the chronic (that is, institutionalized) instability of Argentine governments rests on rivalries within the elite rather than on mass conflicts. More accurately, the study reveals that institutional instability derives from interpersonal conflicts rather than from deep cleavages at the base. This study of political attitudes has established several characteristics of Argentine political life that may be usefully summarized here:

First, it demonstrates that there is a quite high degree of consensus on political demands among the whole population, that agreement is highest on the demands with the greatest salience, and vice versa.

Second, it reveals that political orientations have been much more stable than political organizations; both Peronist and Radical orientations have been more enduring than any organization embodying them.[3]

Third, it demonstrates that there are no sizable groups who are deeply alienated from dominant values, goals, and beliefs.

[3] Perhaps the same configuration characterizes other political systems beleaguered by factionalism and fragmentation. The stability of left-right orientations in France and the relative instability of pre-Gaullist party organizations and cabinet coalitions suggest that the French pattern may be similar to that of the Argentines.

Finally, it confirms the existence of high levels of mutual distrust, of cynicism about government, and of lack of agreement about the desirable form of political organization.

One clear and significant implication of these findings is that the divisions that split parties, legislatures, cabinets, armed forces, unions, and related groups largely reflect elite rivalries and interpersonal conflict rather than mass opinion. A second implication is that there is a poor fit between mass demands and institutional performance. The agreement on goals that exists at the base is not reflected at the top. It appears that Argentine political institutions more often fracture political interests than aggregate them, that elite recruitment practices elevate men who are more preoccupied with articulating personal and intellectual disagreements and stating positions than with articulating the demands broadly shared by Argentines. (The reason these types are so often raised into leadership positions is probably that they are so numerous in Argentine society.)

This study suggests that Argentina's most important political problems are problems of political organization, problems deriving from the failure of institutions (parties, unions, legislatures, cabinets, and so on) to reflect and implement the agreement on goals that exists at the base of the society.

What accounts for these problems? Why should a people have such difficulty devising institutions that will effectively translate widely shared understandings and demands into social policies? There is, of course, the old theory according to which the ineffectiveness of institutions is seen as a result of the Machiavellian machinations of the "oligarchy." In fact, those who have most of what there is to get in Argentina probably profit from the disagreements that beset their actual and potential antagonists. Major landowners in Argentina would suffer if the widespread antilandowner sentiments revealed in this survey were translated into public policy. But to suppose that, because they profit from the endemic factionalism, they cause it, is to fall into multiple logical and existential fallacies. It attributes to the landowning class a unity, skill, and influence unwarranted by the evidence. The relatively high levels of mutual distrust are probably relevant but do not constitute an adequate explanation.

This study of political culture has eliminated one possible explanation for the fragility of Argentina's institutions. The divisions at the top do not reflect deep, irreconcilable divisions among the population concerning the purposes and goals of government.[4]

An examination of Argentina's history over the past century eliminates certain other hypotheses. We are left with a puzzle, the key to which is crucial to understanding the politics of the Latin-Mediterranean type. In approaching this puzzle, two alternative but mutually consistent hypotheses seem to merit exploration.

First, it may be that expectations are acquired in the process of political socialization that strongly predispose males (and perhaps females) in the society to believe that integrity can be maintained only by defending all positions adopted and by terminating relations with antagonists. A corollary would be a generalized expectation that disagreements naturally and normally lead to ruptures. This pattern of expectations could be contrasted to one that predisposed persons to believe that in situations where actors share general purposes disagreements are, and should be, resolved by compromise, majority rule, and good sportsmanship; that maturity is demonstrated by such compromises; and that integrity is maintained by giving priority to shared broad purposes rather than to a personal vision about how that purpose might best be achieved.

Second, in considering political systems such as that of Argentina, I think it is worth reopening the question about the functions of government. This pattern of politics reminds us that for many political actors half a loaf is not better than none. Radical party leaders, among others, have repeatedly demonstrated that they would rather lose an election than maintain party unity once some dispute has arisen within the leadership.

American politics and the whole Anglo-Saxon tradition predispose us to think of compromise as the heart of the political process and conflict resolution as the core political skill. In recent years we have even seen "interest aggregation" identified as a necessary and eternal function of all political systems.

Anglo-Saxon politics is interest-based politics, with interests most often defined in economic terms. In this century the principal values distributed through Anglo-Saxon political processes have been income, skill, safety, and well-being values. Where these are the stakes,

---

[4] The assumption that elite rivalries reflect mass cleavages is often encountered and is guilty of what might be termed the "democratic fallacy." It assumes that mass attitudes can be inferred from elite behavior. This assumption of the necessary congruence of mass and elite orientations is almost entirely unwarranted for most types of political systems.

it is better to get something than nothing. Furthermore, one person's share does not necessarily diminish that of another. Distribution of wealth, for example, is not necessarily a zero-sum game. Likewise with education, health care, and police protection. Making these available to you need not decrease my share. In any case, it is crucial that compromise is possible in the distribution of these values, because even smaller shares retain value.

Such is not the case for certain other values. Rectitude and deference alike have an exclusive quality that makes it exceedingly difficult to compromise conflicts in which they are involved. Conflicts involving rectitude have a unique intensity that explains the unparalleled destructiveness of religious wars. Moral struggles cannot be compromised by moral men. When morality is compromised, immorality is the only result. There is, of course, a suggestive and fascinating correlation in political systems between the rhetoric of intransigence and the level of institutional fragility. Similarly, deference may be so interpreted as to make interests mutually exclusive. If each of two conflicting parties requires that the other occupy a social position inferior to his own, their conflict cannot be compromised. Neither is satisfied by merely being equal.

It seems likely that not all values are involved to the same extent in all political systems. Therefore, empirical investigation of the involvement of different values in different political systems could yield important results. If it were established, for example, that deference values had unexpected importance in Argentina, the relationship between Perón and Argentina's lower classes (and deference-starved men of the interior) would be more fully comprehended. If it were determined that questions of economic interest or personal preference were habitually perceived as moral questions, the ubiquity of organizational schisms would be illuminated.

The tendency of Argentina to gravitate repeatedly toward and acquiesce in autocracy might be explained by the relatively low requirements of autocracy for compromise, conciliation, and cooperation.

This study has not explained the apparent paradoxes of Argentine politics. It has limited the number of available explanations and suggested next steps in the search for understanding of the relations among masses and elites, between culture and organization.

Appendix A

Description of Sampling Procedures

The data presented in the preceding pages are based upon personal interviews conducted among a representative sample of adult Argentines during October, November, and December 1965. The fieldwork was carried out by International Research Associates.

In total, 2,014 interviews were conducted. A description of the methods employed in the selection of the sample is set forth below.

The Universe of Study

The universe of study was defined as all persons of voting age in Argentina (18 or over) residing in towns of 2,000 or more inhabitants.

Certain states were eliminated from the study because of their sparse population and their remoteness. These were Chubut, Neuquén, Río Negro, Santa Cruz, and Tierra del Fuego, all of which are located in the southern portion of Argentina and together accounted for only approximately 3 percent of the Argentine population in 1960.

These departures from a pure random sample were designed to keep interviewing costs at a practical level.

The Selection of the Sample

Probability sampling techniques were used in the selection of the sample. In all, 3,122 homes were designated for interviews, and in 2,014 of these the assigned interview was successfully completed— a mortality of 35 percent.

Stratification On the basis of 1960 census data, the Argentine population was stratified into five groups according to the size of their cities or towns of residence and then further stratified into five geographic regions. The five strata that were developed to reflect the differing degrees of urbanization were the following (distribution shown in Table A.1):

1. Cities of more than 500,000 inhabitants
2. Cities of between 250,000 and 499,999 inhabitants
3. Cities of between 50,000 and 249,999 inhabitants
4. Cities of between 10,000 and 49,999 inhabitants
5. Towns of between 2,000 and 9,999 inhabitants

The five geographic regions were drawn to include the following states (distribution shown in Table A.2):

1. Federal Capital
2. Greater Buenos Aires (referring to suburbs of the capital)
3. Santa Fe, Córdoba, and the province of Buenos Aires
4. Entre Ríos, Corrientes, Misiones, Chaco, Formosa, San Luis, La Rioja, Santiago del Estero, and Catamarca
5. San Juan, Mendoza, Tucumán, Salta, and Jujuy

Selection of Sampling Points

1. Primary Sampling Points

Cities or towns were designated as the primary sampling units. These were selected with a probability proportionate to their populations within each stratum.

Individual populations were listed and accumulated. Work loads were distributed among these cities within the cumulative lists by the use of systematic random procedures, with a random-start–fixed-interval mode of selection. A random number was chosen between one and the total population of each combined geographic–city-size stratum to designate the first work load in the first city; a skipping interval, calculated by dividing the total population by the number of work loads desired for the sample in that stratum, was added to this number to indicate the location of the second; this procedure was continued in circular fashion, first city succeeding the last, until the desired number had been drawn.

2. Selection in Subsequent States

Within each city or town selected, samples of city blocks were chosen through equally random procedures. On the best block maps available, all blocks were numbered in serpentine fashion and the desired number chosen in each case by a random-start–fixed-interval method.

Complete lists of all households on these sample blocks were then compiled by field personnel. Specific households were designated for interviews from the lists thus compiled, again through the use of systematically random procedures. The number of homes drawn into the sample in each block was therefore determined by the ratio that the population of that block bore to the population of all sample blocks for that city.

A single respondent was selected for interview within each household chosen in this manner. A list of all eligible family members residing at that address was compiled and a specific individual chosen through the use of a table of random numbers that appeared in the questionnaire itself. In no stage of the sampling process did the fieldworker have any option in the selection of the individual designated for interview.

A minimum of four attempts was made, if necessary, to locate the individuals designated for interview.

Assignment of Interviews The number of work loads per geographic–city-size stratum was determined on the basis of the proportional distribution of the Argentine population as projected from the 1960 census. Table A.1 indicates the distribution of work loads and the number of municipal units that were drawn into the sample on this basis. The number of interviews designated was designed to yield approximately 20 interviews per work load, and 2,000 in total, after allowance for anticipated sampling mortality.

Administration

All interviewing was carried out by Argentine nationals, trained and controlled by professional field supervisors. Overall direction of the project in the field was under the control of a leading Argentine survey research firm.

More than 20 percent of the interviews carried out by each fieldworker was verified by supervisory personnel, who returned to a sample of the homes visited by each interviewer and repeated all or part of the interview to make sure not only that the interview had been conducted but also that it was conducted precisely according to instructions.

Field materials were coded for computer tabulation in New York; tabulation of the data was accomplished and the final tables produced there.

Some Comments on the Sample

Socioeconomic Status The survey provided two measures of socioeconomic status. One was based on the respondents' self-classification. The other was determined independently through the following procedures. The interviewer carried a table that identified a number of specific criteria for classifying dwellings. These criteria related to the size, condition, and surroundings of the dwelling. On the basis of these criteria the interviewer scored each dwelling. He also noted the occupation and occupational rank of the respondent. The fieldworker supervisor then scored the respondent's occupation and rank according to criteria relevant to local practices. These two numbers were added and averaged. The resulting score served as the basis for classifying the informants' socioeconomic status.

Sample Characteristics The unavailability of census data prevented full comparison of the structure of the sample with the structure of the population. At the time of writing, the results of the 1960 census were still largely unpublished. Only one volume of tabulations on the entire nation has been issued, and it does not deal with many categories of data. The figures in Table A.3 reflect the relationship of the sample composition to the available census data.

TABLE A.1   SAMPLE DISTRIBUTION BY SIZE OF LOCALITY

Locality	Total Population	Number of Interviews
2,000–9,999	1,353,952	200
10,000–49,999	1,765,458	260
50,000–249,999	2,732,589	420
250,000–499,999	3,447,314	500
500,000 and over	4,158,406	620

Note: Places of various population levels were distributed among the different geographic regions (Table A.2).

TABLE A.2   SAMPLE DISTRIBUTION BY REGION

	Total Population in Each Region	Interviews per Region
Federal Capital	2,966,816	440
Greater Buenos Aires	3,795,813	560
Santa Fe, Córdoba, province of Buenos Aires	4,208,548	620
Entre Ríos, Corrientes, Misiones, Chaco, Formosa, San Luis, La Rioja, Santiago del Estero, Catamarca	1,221,866	180
San Juan, Mendoza, Tucumán, Salta, Jujuy	1,204,506	200

TABLE A.3   SAMPLE DISTRIBUTION BY SEX AND AGE
(In percent)

	1960 Census	Sample
Sex		
Male	47.7	46.0
Female	52.3	54.0
Age		
18–24	15.7	12.4
25–29	11.9	10.1
30–39	23.8	26.4
40–49	19.1	22.4
50–59	15.2	16.3
60 and over	14.3	11.8
Not ascertained		0.6

Appendix B

Questionnaire

1. With reference to yourself personally, would you say that your economic situation is better, worse, or about the same as it was a year ago?
2. And what about the future: Do you think that your economic situation will be better, worse, or about the same a year from now?
3. (SHOW CARD) As you know, every person has different characteristics. Could you tell me which of these qualities you admire most in a person?
3a. Does his job well.
3b. Active in public and social affairs.
3c. Ambitious, wants to get ahead.
3d. Generous, considerate of others.
3e. Thrifty, saving.
3f. Lets no one take advantage of him.
3g. Keeps to himself.
3h. Respectful, doesn't overstep his place.
3i. Don't know.
4. Among the great figures of the world, is there anyone you admire in particular? (Who?)
5. Here is a different type of question. Speaking generally, what are the things about this country that we, as Argentines, can be proud of?
6. We know that the ordinary person has many problems that take his time. In view of this, do you think the ordinary person ought to play a part in the local affairs of his town or district, or not?
6a. (IF "YES") What specifically ought he to do?
7. People speak of obligations that they owe to their country. In your opinion, what are the obligations that every man owes to his country?

8. How much influence would you say the average citizen has on what the government does—a lot of influence, some influence, or no influence?

9. Suppose a law were being considered by the national legislature that you considered to be very unjust or harmful. What do you think you could do? Anything else?

10. Suppose there were some question that you had to take to a government office, for example, a tax question or housing regulation. Do you think you would be given fair treatment, or not? I mean, would you be treated as everyone else is treated, or not?

11. If you tried to explain your point of view to the officials, what effect would it have? Would they give you proper consideration, would they pay only a little attention, or would they ignore what you had to say?

12. If you had some trouble with the law and the authorities, do you think it would be probable, or not very probable, that you would receive fair treatment from the police and the courts?

13. If you explained your point of view to the officials, what effect would it have? Would they give you proper consideration, would they pay only a little attention, or would they ignore what you had to say?

14. Thinking about what the national government does—the laws it makes, etc.—about how much effect do you think it has on you in your personal life? Would you say that what they do affects you personally a lot, some, a little, or not at all?

15. I'd like to ask you another kind of question. Here are things that people say, and we want to find out how other people feel on these things. I'll read them one at a time, and you just tell me whether you agree or disagree with each one of them.

15a. The way people vote is the main thing that decides how things are run in this country.

15b. If you don't watch yourself, people will take advantage of you.

15c. A few strong leaders would do more for this country than all the laws and talk.

15d. All candidates sound good in their speeches, but you can never tell what they will do after they are elected.

15e. People generally are helpful to one another.

15f. People like you and me don't have any say about what the government does.

15g. The individual owes his first duty to the state; his personal welfare is something secondary.

15h. No one much cares what happens to you, when you get right down to it.

16. What are the principal problems that Argentina faces these days?

17. Let's look at some problems of domestic policy. For example, would you be for or against a candidate for president who

17a. Supports strong price controls on basic items that affect most people's cost of living?

17b. Condemns the use of force and violence in political activity?

17c. Promises to stamp out corruption and inefficiency in the government?

17d. Will use the government's resources to create new jobs?

17e. Favors reforming the tax system to provide for higher taxes on large incomes and business profits?

17f. Believes in the expropriation of private lands for redistribution to landless farmers?

17g. Wants to eliminate private enterprise from key sectors of the economy?

17h. Believes wages should be raised to match increases in the cost of living?

17i. Believes the military should intervene in government policies?

17j. Believes Perón should return to power?

18. Let's look further at problems of foreign policy. Would you be for or against a candidate who

18a. Wants Argentina to seek financial aid and technical assistance from communist countries?

18b. Favors maintaining friendly relations with Castro's Cuba?

18c. Supports a neutral position for Argentina in the cold war?

18d. Favors Argentine collaboration with the United States within the Alliance for Progress?

18e. Favors the admission of private foreign capital to aid Argentine development?

18f. Supports the formation of an exclusively Latin American regional organization without the United States?

18g. Would refuse Argentine recognition to any dictatorial or military regime?

18h. Advocates more control over large foreign corporations in Argentina?

18i. Seeks to strengthen Argentina's ties with the United States?

18j. Favors more independence from the United States?

19. What country do you think most tries to help Argentina—or would you say that no other country helps us, in truth?

20. What country do you think most tries to create problems for Argentina and to impede our development?

21. Argentina maintains relations with many foreign countries. With which of them do you think we should have relations that are closer and more friendly than normal?

21a. And with which of them do you think we should have no relations at all, or just have minimal relations?

22. In the present conflict between Russia and the United States, do you think that Argentina should support Russia, support the United States, or, rather, remain completely neutral?

22a. With reference to this conflict between Russia and the United States, do you think that in the long run this will benefit us, that it will harm us, or that it will not affect us at all?

22b. Even if we have nothing to do with the matter, which of the two countries would you rather see come out on top in this conflict—Russia or the United States?

23. One sometimes hears that some people have so much influence over the way the government is run that the interests of the people are ignored and only the needs of the influential people receive attention. Do you think this is true?

23a. (IF "YES") Which are the groups that have that influence?

24. (SHOW CARD) How would you rate the following groups as most powerful, second most powerful, third most powerful: (ON THE CARD: BIG LANDOWNERS, AGRICULTURAL WORKERS, LABOR UNIONS, ARGENTINE ENTREPRENEURS, ARGENTINE COMMUNISTS, MILITARY SERVICES, INTELLECTUALS, PERONISTS, CHURCH HIERARCHY, MIDDLE-CLASS ARGENTINES, BUREAUCRATS, JUSTICIALISTS, FOREIGNERS, BLOC 62)

24a. Which of these groups has the least power in Argentine life? (SHOW SAME CARD)

25. Now let's think about the different groups that might support a candidate. Would you be for or against a candidate who was supported by

25a. Big landowners

25b. Agricultural workers

25c. Labor unions

25d. Argentine entrepreneurs

25e. Argentine communists

25f. Military services

25g. Intellectuals

25h. Peronists

25i. Church hierarchy

25j. Middle-class Argentines

25k. Bureaucrats

25l. Justicialists

25m. Foreigners

25n. Bloc 62

26. Several people have told us that if it were not for the intervention and help of the military, the country would find itself in a chaotic situation. Do you think that this is true or not?

27. Is there any military figure in Argentina that you particularly admire, or not?

27a. (IF "YES") Who?

28. Are you currently a member of any political party or organization, or not? (IF MEMBER, SKIP TO QUESTION 30)

28a. Were you ever a member? Which one?

29. Do you consider yourself a supporter of any particular political party? Which one?

29a. (IF "NO") Toward which political party do you lean?

30. Have you ever been active in a political campaign? That is, have you ever participated in any political activity, such as contributing money, demonstrating, and so on?

31. You say you are a (member of, support, lean toward—select appropriate one) the _____ party. What about your friends and acquaintances? Would you say that most of them do, that some of them do, or that almost none support the same party?

31a. What about your wife (or husband)? Does she (he) support or oppose or just not care about that party?

32. In your judgment, which are Argentina's two or three most important political parties?

33. What kind of party is the _____ party? (ASK QUESTIONS 33a THROUGH 33d FOR EACH PARTY MENTIONED)

33a. Is it the kind of party you would ever vote for, or not?

33b. Does it have good leaders, or not?

33c. Does it have a good program, or not?

33d. Does it stand for any particular group of people, or not? (Who?)

34. Would you like to see a new and different kind of political party organized in Argentina, or don't you think this would be necessary?

34a. (IF "YES") What kind?

35. If there were a presidential election tomorrow and you had a choice among the following men, for which one would you vote? (SHOW CARD WITH LIST OF NAMES)

35a. Tecera del Franco

35b. Illía

35c. Frondizi

35d. Hardoy

35e. Perón

35f. Thedy

35g. Aramburu

35h. Carreira

35i. Busacca

35j. Chioldi

35k. Onganía

35l. Matera

35m. (IF UNDECIDED) Even though you have no definite choice at this time, for which of these men would you be most likely to vote?

35n. (IF STILL UNCOMMITTED) Which of the following statements best describes your reason for not picking any of the men mentioned?

I'm not interested in politics.

I haven't thought about it sufficiently.

None of these men is good.

I like someone else better. (If so, whom?)

36. Which of these presidents do you think did the most to harm Argentina? (PERÓN, ARAMBURU, FRONDIZI, ILLÍA)

37. Do you think it would help or hurt Argentina if Juan Perón were allowed to return to the country?

37a. (IF "HELP") Do you think he should be allowed to become a candidate in a presidential election, or not?

37b. (IF "YES") If he became a candidate in a presidential election, would you vote for him, or not?

38. In spite of the fact that Perón went into exile, the Peronist

movement has continued to play an important role in the politics of the country. In general, do you approve or disapprove of what the Peronist movement has done since Perón left?

39. Do you think the treatment of the Peronist movement by the government and the military has been fair or unfair?

40. Are there any Peronist leaders you particularly admire? Could you tell me their names?

41. Here is a group of Peronist leaders. Could you tell me toward which of these men you have a favorable attitude and toward which an unfavorable attitude?

41a. Andrés Framini

41b. Augusto Vandor

41c. Rodolfo Tecera del Franco

41d. Juan A. Luco

41e. Alberto Seru García

41f. Alberto Iturbe

41g. Carlos Lascano

41h. Paulino Niembro

41i. Raúl Matera

42. In what respects does the Peronist movement deserve support?

42a. In what respects do you think the people should oppose Peronism? That is, in what respects are the Peronists wrong?

43. Have you heard of the "Sixty-two Organizations," or not?

43a. (IF "YES") As far as you know, what ends do they pursue?

43b. (If "YES") In general terms, are you in favor of or opposed to what the Sixty-two Organizations seek?

44. Have you ever heard of the term justicialism, or not?

44a. What does this term stand for, as far as you know?

45. Some people say that politics and government are so complicated that the average man cannot really understand what is going on. In general, do you agree or disagree with that?

46. Thinking of the important national and international issues facing the country, how well do you think you understand these issues? Very well, fairly well, or not very well?

47. Many people we've interviewed have said that they have trouble understanding political and governmental affairs. Which of the reasons on this list best explains why this happens? (IF NEEDED) Which is the major reason?

47a. The problems are too complex.

47b. People don't care and don't try.

47c. Those in power don't help people to understand.

48. (SHOW CARD) If you were looking for guidance in trying to make up your mind about a political question, to which of these sources of opinion would you be most likely to turn? (CARD WITH: UNIVERSITY PROFESSORS, RELIGIOUS LEADERS, LABOR LEADERS, EDITORIAL WRITERS, LOCAL POLITICAL LEADERS, NATIONAL POLITICAL LEADERS, OR MILITARY LEADERS)

49. (SHOW CARD) In getting information itself, where would you obtain more information about important events in Argentina? (CARD WITH: TELEVISION, RADIO, COMMERCIAL NEWSPAPERS, POLITICAL NEWSPAPERS, LISTENING TO POLITICAL LEADERS, SPEAKING WITH FRIENDS, OTHER MEANS)

50. What television stations do you watch most often?

50a. During what hours do you most watch television, as a general rule?

51. What radio stations do you listen to most, as a general rule?

52. What newspapers do you read most?

53. Do you think that, in Argentina, working people get a fair wage for the work they do, or not?

54. What about the white-collar workers? Would you say the white-collar workers receive a fair salary for the work they do, or not?

55. Do you think that most of the Argentine labor movement is controlled by any particular political party or group, or not?

55a. (IF "YES") Which party controls it?

55b. (IF "YES") On the whole, do you think this is a good thing or a bad thing?

56. Do you think the present government has treated labor and labor unions fairly, or not?

56a. (IF "NO") Why not?

57. Would you say that in recent years the labor unions have played a constructive or a destructive role in Argentine life?

58. Would you personally prefer the labor union movement to take an important part in politics, a limited part, or no part at all?

59. Do you (or your husband) belong to a labor union, or not?

59a. (IF "YES") Which union? (GET EXACT NAME OF UNION)

60. Speaking of the most recent elections, on the 14th of March of this year, did you vote in these elections or were you unable to vote this time?

60a.   (IF VOTED) For what party did you vote on that occasion or did you vote *en blanco?*

61.   Now let's think about the presidential elections of July 1963. Did you have the opportunity to vote on that occasion, or not?

61a.   (IF VOTED) For what party did you vote on that occasion or did you vote *en blanco?*

62.   And now the elections of March 1962 to elect congressmen and governors. Did you vote in those elections or not?

62a.   (IF VOTED) For what party did you vote on that occasion or did you vote a blank ballot?

63.   By the way, are you a Catholic?

63a.   (IF "YES") How many times have you been able to go to Mass during the last four weeks—or haven't you had a chance to go?

63b.   How would you classify yourself as far as religion is concerned? Would you say that you discharge almost all of your obligations as a Catholic, that you discharge part of your obligations, or that you rarely discharge your obligations?

63c.   As far as politics is concerned, how important do you think your Catholicism is as a guide to your opinions of politics and of the men who direct politics in Argentina? Would you say that it is very important, fairly important, not very important, or not important at all?

64.   With respect to politics in Argentina, would you say the role of the Catholic Church has been good or bad?

64a.   (UNLESS "DON'T KNOW") Why?

65.   Which groups in Argentine life do you think have received the least help from the Church?

66.   To what social and economic class would you say that you belong? To the upper class, the upper-middle class, the lower-middle class, or the lower class?

67.   You may have heard recently about the disturbances in the Dominican Republic, or Santo Domingo. Could you tell me who, in your opinion, is to blame for these troubles?

68.   When the United States sent North American troops to the Dominican Republic, did you think it was a good thing for them to do, or a bad thing?

68a.   (UNLESS "DON'T KNOW") What is the reason you thought this?

69.   Do you think that Castro and the communists had a great deal to do with the Dominican troubles, something to do with them, or nothing to do with them?

70.   Now here is a different kind of question. If the communists

were about to take over the government of Uruguay and it appeared that they could not be stopped from inside the country, would you be in favor of some foreign nation, including the United States, intervening to prevent a communist take-over, or not? Would you not be in favor of this?

71. Now suppose the communists were about to take over the Argentine government. Would you be in favor of some other country, including the United States, intervening to stop them, or not?

72. How long have you lived in this city (town)?

72a. (IF LESS THAN THEIR LIFETIME) Where did you live previously? And before that?

73. BACKGROUND INFORMATION:
Sex: Male_____ Female_____
Age: _____
Education: _____
Occupation: _____
(OCCUPATION OF THE HEAD OF HOUSEHOLD):____
_____
SES: _____
Nationality of Parents: _____

Index